The POWER of LICENSING

LICENSING

HARNESSING BRAND EQUITY

Michael Stone

Cover design by Elmarie C. Jara/ABA Design

The materials contained herein represent the opinions of the authors and/or the editors, and should not be construed to be the views or opinions of the law firms or companies with whom such persons are in partnership with, associated with, or employed by, nor of the American Bar Association unless adopted pursuant to the bylaws of the Association.

Nothing contained in this book is to be considered as the rendering of legal advice for specific cases, and readers are responsible for obtaining such advice from their own legal counsel. This book is intended for educational and informational purposes only.

From "somewhere i have never travelled,gladly beyond." Copyright 1931, (c) 1959, 1991 by the Trustees for the E. E. Cummings Trust. Copyright (c) 1979 by George James Firmage, from COMPLETE POEMS: 1904-1962 by E. E. Cummings, edited by George J. Firmage. Used by permission of Liveright Publishing Corporation.

Printed in the United States of America.

22 21 20   5 4 3 2

ISBN: 978-1-64105-164-4

Discounts are available for books ordered in bulk. Special consideration is given to state bars, CLE programs, and other bar-related organizations. Inquire at Book Publishing, ABA Publishing, American Bar Association, 321 N. Clark Street, Chicago, Illinois 60654-7598.

www.shopABA.org

This book is dedicated to
Patricia Hillary Grodd.
My wife, my poet, my best friend, my muse, my inspiration,
and my love, always.

(i do not know what it is about you that closes
and opens;only something in me understands
the voice of your eyes is deeper than all roses)
nobody,not even the rain, has such small hands

—From "somewhere I have never travelled,gladly beyond"
by E. E. Cummings

Contents

Introduction

When you purchase a Black & Decker toaster oven, a Westinghouse air conditioner, a quart of Hershey's chocolate milk, a can of Sunkist orange soda, a P.F. Chang's frozen meal, a Mr. Clean broom, or an AT&T landline phone, you are purchasing a licensed product. Sure, we all know that we are buying licensed products when we purchase a New York Yankees T-shirt or a Star Wars toy light saber or a John Deere toy truck or a U.S. Army wallet, but a true licensed brand extension is seamless in the eyes of consumers. From consumers' perspectives, the origin of the product is the brand itself; without looking closely at the labeling or packaging, consumers generally don't realize that the product actually comes from another source authorized by the brand to manufacture, market, and distribute the product, all subject to the brand owner's approval. Walk down the aisle of a Kroger, Target, Macy's, Lowe's, CVS, or Costco or scroll through Amazon or other brick-and-mortar or online retailers and see if you can discern which branded products are licensed and which are the core products coming from the brand owner itself. If brand licensing has been done correctly (and you will know what that means when you finish reading this book), you will not be able to separate the core products from the licensed products. And, importantly, as you will also learn, those licensed products are delivering a brand message and motivating the consumer to further participate with the brand. Licensing contributes, supports, and strengthens the "sticky" relationship that brands seek with consumers.

With regard to corporate brands using licensing, many marketers think of licensing as logo decoration on products, what is not surprisingly called "decorative licensing." You may have a Caterpillar baseball style hat in your closet or a McDonald's ceramic mug in your kitchen cabinet or a sweatshirt in your dresser drawer emblazoned with the blue oval logo of the Ford Motor Company. Sometimes the decoration goes a bit further with creative designs incorporating the brand trademark. Perhaps that Ford sweatshirt also features images of vintage automobiles or a Pepsi Cola notebook includes fun pop art images from past advertising campaigns (or even newly created artwork). Decorative licensing with corporate trademarks has been around a long time and is increasingly common. And there's nothing wrong with that kind of licensing. It helps promote the brand. It helps consumers identify with brands they enjoy. It creates a consumer connection to the brand.

But "brand extension licensing" represents a different approach to this marketing discipline, and that is the focus of this book. It's about that Black & Decker toaster oven. It's about products that are so closely aligned with the core product that consumers perceive the connection between the licensed product and core product as seamless.

Companies with famous (and some not-so-famous) brands use licensing for many purposes:

- Achieve overall brand and corporate goals and objectives
- Build brand awareness, affection, loyalty, and penetration
- Create new consumer touchpoints, engagement, and brand experiences
- Reach a new demographic or, simply, more consumers
- Reinforce or redefine, and communicate a brand message
- Drive incremental revenue through royalties
- Motivate and inspire consumers to purchase more of the core product

That last point is critical. It is at the heart of what marketing is ultimately all about—creating sales; driving consumers to a purchase, the last step in the shopping journey. Licensing has all of the attributes and objectives of any marketing/communications tool. In fact, that's what licensing is, a marketing and communications tool focused on recruiting, retaining, and further bonding consumers to a brand.

Why and how companies use that tool—and how you can capitalize on their experiences—is what this book is about. Indeed, for many sophisticated consumer product companies, brand licensing is now an important part of an integrated marketing strategy that can include disciplines such as advertising, public relations, product placement, packaging, point of purchase, social media, direct mail, experiential marketing, co-marketing and collaborations, and sponsorships, as well as other marketing tools. And licensing is also part of the consumer shopping journey (a journey that is getting increasingly complex in our connected world), which makes it integral to a brand's marketing and retail strategy, both online and offline retail.

Corporations, entertainment properties, food companies, sports leagues, artists, fashion designers, celebrities, and personalities all participate in licensing. Although licensing is actually a legal act—it is the contractual permission to use a name, a slogan, a logo, a likeness, a character (i.e., an intellectual property) in conjunction with a product or service for a prescribed period of time, in exchange for a payment in the form of royalties or fees—the reasons for its use are much broader than simply granting rights to use intellectual property. Specifically, for brands, it's about connecting and engaging with the consumer. It's about touching and communicating with the consumer along the way in the shopping journey (something that will be discussed in greater detail in Chapters 11 and 12). Brand licensing as a tool to solidify consumer brand engagement and connectivity. In a world where consumers, particularly younger consumers, have short attention spans and jump very quickly from one connection to the next, brand licensing can play a very effective role.

This is not a book about entertainment licensing (e.g., motion pictures, television programs, and characters). It's not a book about sports licensing programs (e.g., MLB, the NFL, and the NBA) or fashion licensing programs. But that's not to say that sports, entertainment, and other types of properties cannot become brands. Certainly, the New York Yankees, the New England Patriots, Disney's *Frozen*, and the Teenage Mutant Ninja Turtles, among many others, are all brands and are very successful in their licensing activities. And many of these organizations are extremely professional and creative, utilizing the very best practices and commiting significant resources with regard to licensing (e.g., NBA Properties and Disney Consumer Products). But their licensing objectives are different from those of corporate brands. It's less about marketing and more about ubiquity, serving fan identity, and revenue. The chapter on celebrity licensing (Chapter 8) has been included as a vehicle to discuss how some celebrities become brands through licensing. Most important, this book is not a step-by-step manual for creating or negotiating a license agreement or a licensing program, although several chapters will explain what brand owners must do to plan, develop, and manage a licensing program as well as mitigate the risks (Chapters 4, 5, and 6). Many good technical books exist on these subjects and can provide brand owners with negotiation strategies and license and other related agreement templates.[1] But by reading the case studies and examples and understanding why and how others have used licensing effectively, you will grasp the licensing path for any brand, including sports and entertainment brands.

Trademark licensing has been around for more than 100 years (see Chapter 2), but true brand extension licensing is a relative

---

1. Sample merchandise license agreements (as well as other sample agreements between brand owners and licensing agencies and for manufacturer representatives) are available to all members of LIMA (the licensing industry trade association) on the LIMA website, www.licensing.org.

newcomer to the marketing mix. In recent years, due to a variety of factors that you will learn about in subsequent chapters, it has taken on even more importance and has been embraced by an ever-growing list of iconic brands and brand owners. From Procter & Gamble (P&G) to Stanley Black & Decker, from The Coca-Cola Company to Energizer, from Caterpillar to Harley-Davidson to BMW, licensing has been used (and is being used) as a highly effective marketing/communications discipline. We live in a time of transformative and accelerating change in how consumers get information and access brands and products, as well as how, where, why, and when they do their purchasing (see Chapter 11). Given all of the paths to consumer engagement and to making a purchase, licensing has taken on an even greater importance today. You will learn the significant role that brand licensing can play in this new world order. And you will learn about the challenges and opportunities presented by licensing and what it takes to develop a world-class licensing program for your brand.

Just as organizational executives were once eager to read books about advertising, today's marketing leaders must understand the evolution of licensing as a brand-building and marketing endeavor and know how to adapt it to their purposes. The goal of this book is to facilitate this understanding, providing explanation, examples, and prescriptive elements to help companies unlock their brand equity, their most valuable asset. This book provides many case studies and examples because by examining how famous brands have used this tool effectively and, in some instances, not so effectively, we can understand a great deal about licensing.

I have learned a great amount about licensing over the years— more than 30 years, in fact. During that time as the head of Beanstalk, a company I cofounded in 1991 [and beginning in 2005 is majority owned by Omnicom Group, a multinational marketing/communications holding company (NYSE: OMC)], I have assisted hundreds of corporate brands develop licensing programs all over the world. I have observed the evolution of brand extension licensing during that time and our agency and others have played an instrumental role in that evolution and in advocating an awareness of licensing as an important tool to engage and further bond with consumers. I have found, however, that getting experienced marketing professionals to understand this concept isn't always easy. The old view of licensing (i.e., licensing used as decoration) is embedded in their perceptions. Unfortunately, this perception is widespread—at the biggest brand companies as well as at marketing services agencies. As a result, it has often been difficult for licensing to get a seat at the "marketing table," particularly when marketing executives have no experience with the licensing discipline and what it can offer. But that is changing. When lecturing about licensing to students and professionals, I have been very dissatisfied with the few books available on licensing; none of them explain brand extension licensing and why and how companies use or should use licensing as part of their marketing arsenal and retail strategy. Accordingly, this book is long overdue.

As you will discover, this is an examination that looks at licensing within a branding framework. To that end, case studies will often provide some history about the brand—how the brand began, the vision of its founder(s), and its early brand message. The history often offers a valuable context in which to view the brand today. It's remarkable how many iconic brands, many more than 100 years old, are still delivering the same brand message crafted by their entrepreneurial founders, albeit modernized. In order to use brand licensing effectively, we must understand that message, the essence of the brand, and the heart of the brand's equities. For it is those equities and that message that must be translated and represented effectively by licensed products. Unlike an advertising or a social media campaign that can be discontinued quickly and relatively easily if it proves ineffective, licensed products can take a year or more to launch (just like any new product launch), and if you get it wrong, taking the products off the shelves can be a nightmare. So quite an investment of time and resources are required for successful brand licensing. To make that investment pay off, a knowledge of brand history helps. That history can provide some important clues about the brand's DNA. The more we understand brands on this molecular level, the better able we are to engage in brand licensing in ways that feel organic and genuine to consumers and the marketplace.

Consider the Kellogg brothers, for example. Will Keith Kellogg and Dr. John Harvey Kellogg—basically invented cold cereal in the late 1800s as a healthier alternative to eating dinner leftovers for breakfast. And health and nutrition are key components of the brand today. John Pemberton, the inventor of Coca-Cola in 1886 (followed by Asa Candler who purchased the company in 1891), initially positioned Coca-Cola as a medicinal remedy but shortly thereafter also as a refreshing drink, a pause during a busy day, and a lifestyle product. Sound familiar? And early in the last century, two builders, S. Duncan Black and Alonzo Decker, found stationary electric drills cumbersome to use. So they invented the world's first portable drill that made construction work easier with a reliable and user-friendly product they marketed under their new corporate name, Black & Decker. "Easy to use, portable, and reliable" continue as equities of the Black & Decker brand today. Although the early brand messages of these founders have been modernized, the equities of the current brands are still rooted in their histories.

Just as we can learn a great deal from the history of a brand, we can also learn from the future-forward approaches of cutting-edge marketers. As you will discover, a number of companies are using licensing in ways that are as innovative and effective as anything in their toolbox. Licensing, nevertheless, remains underutilized by many brand marketers. Marketing professionals continue to scour the marketing landscape seeking ways to reach consumers with their brand messages while considering the plethora of options they now have to reach and engage with consumers. They are selling their brands short by not paying attention to how brand licensing can help them achieve these objectives. Some brands don't get it, but many sophisticated brands do.

CHAPTER 1

Why Now? The Rise of Licensing

Are Brands Dying?

Contrary to what you may have heard or read, the answer to that question is "no." But the marketing environment has changed so radically in recent years that it can create the illusion of brands in decline. To understand the new reality, let's start with another, more relevant question and find our way back to answering whether brands are really dying.

Why are corporate marketing leaders and others turning to licensing as never before? Or if they aren't, why should they? Well, anyone who doesn't live under a rock knows that in recent years, the Internet and everything associated with it has diminished the effectiveness of traditional advertising and complicated how brands (and retailers) engage with consumers and drive consumers to make a purchase. Technology has enabled the accelerating changes in marketing and retailing. Consumers now have multiple entertainment and information platforms with which to engage brands, learn about products, and comparison shop. They also

1

have multiple options with regard to purchasing. And brands possess multiple platforms to use in reaching consumers, frequently in genuine ways. Not so long ago, we received much of our product information from traditional advertising—television, print, and radio. The purpose of brands, after all, is to assure us of the quality of a product and to make our buying decisions easier. It's all about trust. Consumers are generally confused about what to purchase (in virtually every product category, particularly a first purchase before they develop brand loyalty), and they want their buying decisions to be made easier and faster. Moreover, they want to feel safe in making their purchases. Advertising was their source of information; it was what drove trust in brands, loyalty and, most importantly, buying decisions. And that's where brands, understandably, devoted the majority of their marketing and communications resources.

In many respects, advertisers had a monopoly on the information that consumers received about brands and products. If anyone wanted to take a deep dive into brand and product research, that person purchased the relevant edition of *Consumer Reports*. That wasn't so long ago. Now, however, that monopoly has been broken apart. The Internet and technology has turned everything on its head. Consumers have all of the information at their fingertips about products they could possibly want (actually, much more than they really want). With a click, they can obtain this information from experts, from "influencers," and from each other, sharing what they know in online reviews, posting and blogging, and from referring to all sorts of other available content. And it's all free (in the old days, we had to pay for an issue of *Consumer Reports*). They don't need to rely on advertising as they once did. Increasingly, they don't even need to see, touch, and feel the product, ordering online sight unseen. But the requirements, expectations, and needs of consumers have also become more robust, driven by all of this information, and brands (to be successful) must address those elements of the consumer's connected shopping journey.

Yet a cultural paradox has emerged. Yes, information that we used to rely on advertising to give us about brands and, importantly, about products, is now readily available on the Internet (so we need brands less). But also, yes, we want help making our buying decisions (brands give us that help), and we seem to have even less time to make those decisions than we used to. We still want speed and ease with our buying decisions (brands deliver decision-making ease and speed as does, of course, the Internet). We need brands less (maybe) because we can research little known or unknown "brands," and we need brands more (maybe) because we don't have time and want to be able to trust our purchase decisions.

This is the cultural paradox referred to earlier. We need brands less, but we also need them more. Ultimately, it depends on how brands choose to deliver their brand message to us.

One school of thought holds that brands have much less value in this new world of easily accessible product information. This thinking suggests that brands are dying. If brands were necessary to make consumers feel secure about product quality and their buying decisions, what role do they play now that all of this information is freely available to every consumer about every product on the market, famously branded or not? Isn't that why it's so much easier to introduce a new product with a new brand name today than it used to be? No need to have a huge advertising budget. Launch your new brand or product on the Internet, write a blog or post, use social media, advertise on Facebook. There's a proliferation of new brands coming at us every day now, and some become quite successful (see Chapter 12).

In a recent book, *Absolute Value: What Really Influences Customers in the Age of (Nearly) Perfect Information*, by Itamar Simonson and Emanual Rosen,[1] the authors argue that with the better sources of information available to consumers today, including user reviews, expert opinions, and social media,

---

1. *Absolute Value: What Really Influences Consumers in the Age of (Nearly) Perfect Information*, by Itamar Simonson and Emanual Rosen, Harper Business, 2014.

consumers can easily discover the quality profile of products in which they are interested and can more ably predict the experience they will have with those products (the "absolute value" of the product). This leads the authors to conclude that brands are needed less. They suggest that the value of brands, particularly as proxies for quality, will decline (and is declining) as consumers have more information on which to base their buying decisions. And, of course, that also means a decline in brand loyalty. Although the authors concede that brands have value for other reasons (particularly in certain product categories), they conclude that a brand's value in making it easier for consumers to make purchasing decisions will diminish. That is a pretty scary thought for brand marketers (and for licensing, by the way, which relies on a brand's fame and consumers' emotional attachment to the brand). But the premise relies on the assumption that consumers are using and relying on all of that available information about product quality and the predictablility of the product experience and the fact that the information will drive the purchasing decision.

There's another school of thought. In *Harvard Business Review*, authors Jens Martin Skibsted and Rasmus Bech Hansen make the following argument:

> The role of a brand is—and never was—just about solving an information problem. It's about providing meaning and satisfying emotional needs. These fundamental human needs have not changed. To the contrary as consumers experience information overload, there might be a tendency to gravitate toward what's known and comforting. . . . So instead of discussing "brand versus not brand" marketers and executives should ask themselves: How can we strengthen our brand when the traditional tools such as advertising, corporate identity programs and PR are becoming impotent? . . . Brand builders must embed themselves across the customer value chain. Products and services must be able to tell a story and

communicate value without an extra advertising layer on top. As information is more and more available and the importance of brands increases, the ability to tell a meaningful story through actions and products, not words, is the only way to win.[2]

That's more aligned with my way of thinking. It's why we drink Coca-Cola instead of a less familiar can of brown fizzy water. It's why, the authors argue, we prefer Google over Bing and Apple is among the most valuable companies in the world. Skibsted and Hansen warn us not to confuse the value of brands in today's world with how to build a brand, how to communicate the brand message. Certainly, quality matters. A great deal. And experience predictability matters as well. In our age of information access, consumers are less likely to be swayed by what a brand simply says about itself, as they were in the past. In that regard, I agree with Simonson and Rosen. To survive, brands must keep working at delivering their message of quality and product predictability. But there's much more to brand survival. I particularly embrace the thought expressed by the Skibsted and Hansen that brands need "to tell a meaningful story through actions and *products*, not words, (as) the only way to win" (emphasis added). And although the authors may not have been thinking of licensed products, their concepts dovetail with my approach to this marketing strategy: that licensed products are a way to tell the brand story, a way to communicate the brand message, a way to connect and engage with consumers, a way to burnish a brand's reputation for quality (and perhaps status), and a way to strengthen and build brand meaning. If you think about "marketing" as "persuasion," then in today's new digital world, the persuasion is more effective if it comes more from the product itself and less from just favorable words that the brand itself promotes. And although we now get "persuasive" communication from our

---

2. "Brands Aren't Dead, but Traditional Branding Tools Are Dying," by Jens Martin Skibsted and Rasmus Bech Hansen, *Harvard Business Review*, February 13, 2014.

peers, from experts, from bloggers, from influencers, and from reviewers online, increasingly, the product has (or certainly can) become the message. Simonson and Rosen might even agree with that premise. Brand survival depends on product quality, of course, but also story, emotion, history, and status. Licensed products that are aligned with the brand's marketing goals, quality promise, and overall brand promise, can communicate and deliver that brand message.

Brands have been dying and new ones have been born since the beginning of brand history. And that's no different today. Brands that don't understand the challenges they face due to the accessibility of information will decline, and some will disappear. New brands that understand these dynamics will enter the stage, and today, given social media, they can come along quite easily. But interestingly, all new brands endeavor to achieve "brand" status. That's because brands mean something to consumers. It's why some dormant brands can be brought back to life (see Chapter 9)— because brands matter to consumers. Smart brands use licensed brand extensions to deliver a brand message effectively, to bond with consumers, and to create loyalty and long-term connection. It's why trademark licensing has been growing for years—more brand owners are embracing licensing, and retail sales of trademark licensed products have consistently seen year-on-year growth. Brands still matter, but they need to adapt to this new information age with their core and licensed products and connect with consumers in fresh ways; many paths are available to them. Smart brands are doing just that and are becoming even stronger. Licensing is one of the marketing/communications tools in their toolbox.

We are at a tipping point in the history of marketing/communications. After 150 years or so of traditional advertising domination, marketers must adjust to the new, transformative era where the Internet, technology, and social media have gained the upper hand. In this digital age, traditional advertising (i.e., pushing out a message) has become less important as a branding tool (but certainly not unimportant). Consumers are able to obtain information about products and services from all sorts of digital sources. They can compare different brands; learn about new ones; and compare prices, ingredients, manufacturing, and product reviews in ways that diminish advertising's role. Advertising will always play a role, but that role is changing. So if marketers buy into the premise that brands can win by telling a story, that they can connect with consumers through actions and products (not just words), where can they turn to accomplish that goal?

Licensing as Content Marketing?

Among the various disciplines to which marketers can turn, licensing is one of them. It's all about telling a story and delivering a message through product. New product aligned with the core product, aligned with the brand promise. Today's consumers demand that marketers communicate authentically with them in a way that is relatable. Licensing provides that authenticity. And just like social media, public relations, sponsorships, and advertising, smart brands know that licensing can be used to accomplish the same goals as content marketing (whether they call it that).

Yes, content marketing. Marketing is all about content these days. That's what brand marketers are talking about. Content marketing can take the form of good, traditional advertising—the best ads frequently make their way to social media where they go viral and are often shared by millions of people. Consumers are attracted to an ad and become the distributors of that ad. That's the secret sauce of good advertising today—its "spreadability." Figuring out how to get the content out there is where the challenges arise. There are many paths to connect with the consumer. And if the content is informative or entertaining, it's acceptable even if it's also recognizable as advertising.

There are many examples of great brands utilizing what we commonly refer to as content marketing effectively to reach consumers. Two mentioned here have had a significant and positive impact on the brand. First, Dove's "Real Beauty Sketches: You're more beautiful than you think." It is one of the most successful marketing campaigns recently. Briefly, a sketch artist sits behind a curtain and sketches a woman based on her own verbal description of her appearance and again based on descriptions by strangers. The sketches based on the strangers' descriptions were generally more flattering than those based on the woman's own self-description. The campaign is all about how real women think about beauty; it's about a conversation about beauty. The campaign generated more than 114 million views in its first month and was available in 25 languages in 110 countries. There were 3.8 million shares on social media in the first month. Dove told a story, targeted its consumer, and engaged its target— all for a very low cost.

And who can forget the Old Spice man, played by Isaiah Amir Mustafo? The ad, released in 2010 titled "The Man Your Man Could Smell Like," was the original ad in a series of ads featuring the Old Spice man—in a shower, on a horse, at the beach, on a boat, at the lake, on a motorcycle—all narrated by Mustafo. The original ad alone has had more than 50 million views online—again, engaging the target consumer with great content about a brand. And no viewer could really doubt that these tools were designed to advertise Dove and Old Spice, to inspire purchasing. But that's okay. They connected with the consumer.

Although marketers are spending an increasing amount of time and resources on content marketing, they struggle with delivering or distributing the message effectively. BuzzFeed founder Jonah Peretti has said, "Content is king, but distribution is queen—and she wears the pants." In other words, how do you distribute the message? What's great about content marketing is that *it tells a story*, often provides information (such as how to fix your car), *targets the consumer*, and is very *cost-effective*. Content marketing engages new consumers as well as those who already exist. It's about mining for consumers; making connections; and, ultimately, driving sales. Tell a story. Provide information. Target the consumer. Cost-effective.

Can licensing be considered a form of content marketing? Is it characterized by those same descriptors? Smart marketing executives possess an intuitive sense that the answer is "yes," making licensing a much more significant part of their marketing mix. Licensing has many of the characteristics of content marketing as well as good advertising (as do other forms of marketing, such as influencer campaigns). It is targeted at a particular consumer. It has a clear objective, and it knows the context in which it is executed and the goal it wants to accomplish for the brand owner. Licensed products tell a brand story by extending the brand to logically associated categories that will resonate with the consumer, reinforcing the brand message or redefining the brand message. And it's cost-effective.

At its best, licensing builds brand awareness, inspires consumers to purchase a product, and drives them to the core product. Consumers who are satisfied with the quality and performance of their licensed Mr. Clean dishwashing gloves or sponges (i.e., their product experience) might be driven to switch from the liquid cleaner they have been using to Mr. Clean liquid cleaner. That's a big win for P&G and a great return on investment generated by the licensed product. Importantly, licensing engages consumers in new brand-aligned products. And unlike many other forms of marketing, with licensing, consumers make a voluntary decision to engage with the brand by purchasing the licensed product, bringing it into their homes and using it. For the brand owner licensing the logo and know-how to a licensee, this is a very cost-effective marketing technique and a great example of accomplishing the same goals as content marketing. Whether you agree that licensing is a form of content marketing, you can see the path licensing provides in an age where brands are looking for ways to connect with consumers.

How do companies that grasp the marketing value of licensing use it to further communicate their brand message and achieve marketing goals? Here's my first case study, the story of a brand that understood how licensing can be an incredibly powerful tool. It's an example of brand licensing at its best, an example of a brand that followed many of the best practices discussed in later chapters, and a good illustration for this first chapter.

The Stanley Brand

Stanley (a brand owned by Stanley Black & Decker) has been using licensing as an effective marketing and communications tool for 20 years. Virtually every household in America (and many around the world) has a Stanley product. Perhaps it's a hammer, a saw, or a screwdriver. And who doesn't have a Stanley FatMax tape measure stuffed in a kitchen drawer? (Stanley introduced the first steel tape rule in 1931.) It's the #1 brand of hand tools in the United States. Global sales are in the billions of dollars, with more than 40,000 different products offered every year, including hand tools, mechanics tools, fastening systems, air tools, hydraulic tools, door systems, access technologies, and pipeline equipment.

Stanley supports its products with a wide variety of marketing tactics. Of course, the brand engages in traditional advertising, primarily print advertising and public relations targeted at their consumer, but relies more on sponsorships and marketing partnerships. The brand actively sponsors events where their customers can be found, such as Major League Baseball, NASCAR, Professional Bull Riders, Chinese Basketball, and FC Barcelona. Digital marketing includes social and digital media as well as e-mail marketing and mobile landing pages; a comprehensive website; and in-store activation and partnerships with organizations such as Wounded Warriors, Disney, and the Super Bowl. And 20 years ago, Stanley identified licensing as having a full seat at the company's marketing table and a marketing tool that could be as powerful as any of the other disciplines just mentioned. In 1998, it was a bold decision for a leader in a category (i.e., the home improvement category) that featured practically no licensing activity.

Again, a bit of history goes a long way in understanding Stanley's brand equities and messaging and why they consider licensing so integral to their marketing efforts.

The history of The Stanley Works (the corporate name before it merged with Black & Decker in 2010) is actually the history of two tool companies of the mid to late 1800s. The company had its beginnings in 1843 when Frederick Stanley started a small shop in

New Britain, Connecticut (where the company is still headquartered today), to manufacture wrought iron bolts for sale to the residents of the area. The business did well, and Stanley expanded into forging other hardware products such as hooks and hinges. The company was named The Stanley Works in 1852. The Stanley Works took an important turn in 1854 when Stanley hired 19-year-old William Hart, a true visionary in the hardware business. Hart involved himself in all aspects of the business and, over the next 60 years, engineered new and innovative machinery for making tools, including the process for cold rolling steel and the invention of the telescoping cardboard box. By the early 1900s, The Stanley Works products were available in hardware stores all over the United States. By 1919, when William Hart died, The Stanley Works had grown from $7,000 in annual sales to $11.3 million.

At about the same time Frederick Stanley was building his bolt foundry, his cousin, Henry Stanley, was building the Stanley Rule & Level Co., manufacturer of rules, levels, and squares. In 1869, Stanley Rule & Level purchased Bailey, Chaney and Co., acquiring the right to manufacture the famous Bailey plane. Henry Stanley moved Leonard Bailey and his entire company to New Britain. And then in 1920, The Stanley Works purchased Stanley Rule & Level, which, by that time, had become the largest manufacturer of planes and related tools in the country.

But as was true of so many famous companies founded in the late 1800s and early 1900s (e.g., The Coca-Cola Company, Kleenex, and Harley-Davidson), the success of The Stanley Works was due not only because it produced a quality product but also because its executives believed in branding and marketing. In the early 1900s, The Stanley Works developed magazine advertising campaigns encouraging do-it-yourself projects on which fathers and sons could work together. And to this day, Stanley encourages do-it-yourselfers who aspire to perform tasks as well as professionals (i.e., those who use hand tools to earn a living). During the 1930s, The Stanley Works placed products in industrial and vocational schools, ensuring that future professionals would be loyal to the

Stanley brand. Today, the Stanley brand continues to target professionals with its marketing and its products.

Stanley continued to grow after the war, organically and through acquisitions, both domestically and overseas. And in 2010, Stanley merged with the leading power tool company Black & Decker to form Stanley Black & Decker. Today the Stanley brand is an industry leader, manufacturing and marketing tools and hardware for home improvement, consumer, industrial, and professional use. The company makes tools that build and repair homes and cars as well as tools that build and repair infrastructure.

Stanley's goal is to be the leadership brand of the hard goods industry: to inspire and motivate professionals and people who think like professionals to fully realize their skills, vision, and creativity. Because Stanley knows that consumers rely on their tools to get a job done, the company is focused on delivering the toughest, strongest, most innovative hand tools and power tools on the market—from the hammer in a toolbox to sawhorses for the construction site and even to the automatic doors people walk through every day at the supermarket. This is a category of products where quality matters a great deal.

Let's break down the company's brand message to its essentials. What are the key elements?

1. Motivate professionals and people who think like professionals.
2. Make tools to help realize skills, vision, and creativity.
3. Make tools that are tough, strong, and innovative.

In short, the Stanley brand delivers tools to professionals and those who think like professionals to get the job done. Stanley stands for the following equities:

- Smart
- Empowering
- Experienced

- Reliable
- Innovative
- Tough

Any licensed product that Stanley allows into the marketplace must satisfy the three stated objectives, and the products must represent the equities of the Stanley brand.

How has Stanley been inspired by its history, its goals and objectives, and its equities to develop a brand extension licensing program? In 2016, retail sales of Stanley Black & Decker licensed products exceeded $1.5 billion,[3] with more than 60 licensees worldwide selling product in more than 90,000 retail doors. Think about how all of those products help the Stanley Black & Decker brands bond and connect with their already loyal consumers as well as attract new consumers to the brands. Think about the number of added brand impressions not only in the same aisles of a store where Stanley's core products are sold but also in different aisles of the store as well as entirely different retailers. And if Stanley's licensed products are remaining consistent with and further supporting the brand's goals, objectives, and equities, its brand promise, this has become a highly effective way for the company to market and communicate its brand message and engage with consumers. And Stanley gets paid by its licensees! Each of those Stanley licensees is paying Stanley a royalty equal to a percentage of its wholesale sales (as is generally true of any licensing model). That percentage is generally between 5 and 10 percent. As a collateral benefit, licensing generates profit-rich revenues for the brand

---

3. "Top 150 Global Licensors," *License Global*, April 2017, Volume 20, Number 2. Stanley Black & Decker is listed as #41. This data about Stanley Black & Decker combines the licensing activity of all brands licensed by the company, including Stanley, Black & Decker, and DeWalt. Each year *License Global* magazine publishes its list of "Top 150 Global Licensors." The rankings are based on retail sales of licensed products or services, with the data being provided voluntarily by licensors. Although not an audited report, it provides a solid indication of the size of individual licensing programs.

owner (i.e., no manufacturing costs, costs of goods, inventory costs, sales costs, etc. are associated with the licensed products).

Following is a list of some of the products that are licensed by the Stanley brand in the United States and Europe. As you read through the list, think about Stanley's history, its goals and objectives, and its equities. Are the licensed products true to the heritage of the brand? Do they support Stanley's goals and objectives? Are they consistent with the brand's equities? Are they helping the brand reach and communicate with consumers, further connecting them to the brand? Those are the questions that should be asked with respect to any licensing program.

- Wet/dry vacuums
- Piston pumps for industrial washing
- Welding equipment
- Work wear
- Work lights and spotlights
- Garden tools (see Figure 1 in the photo insert)
- Work gloves
- Job site tough mobile accessories
- Paint tools
- Personal protective equipment (eye, face, head, hearing, and respiratory protection) (see Figure 1 in the photo insert)
- Work boots
- Pool maintenance tools
- How-to books
- Generators
- Compressors
- Fans and heaters
- Safes
- Ladders
- Office products
- Electrical accessories
- TV mounts

Consider that Stanley went far beyond the old licensing norm of conjuring up a list of products that might be logically associated with the brand or slapping a logo on products simply as decoration or being opportunistic about companies eager to use Stanley's famous logo to promote their own line of products. This is an example of a company, of a brand, that focused in a very targeted way on the outcome it wanted licensing to achieve—an outcome that supported its goals, that reached the right consumer group, that fortified its brand message. Stanley used licensing as an authentic and genuine way to communicate with consumers and enter their lives with innovative licensed products, products that can barely be differentiated from Stanley's core products. In fact, if you were to fill a room with Stanley's own products as well as the company's licensed products, you would not be able to differentiate between the two. Licensing has been used by Stanley as a true marketing/communications tool, and the company makes a significant commitment of resources to support the program.

Stanley Black & Decker is a good example of what any company embarking on a brand licensing program must understand, answering the following critical set of questions:

- What is the history of the brand? Where did it come from? What was the vision of its founders? How did the brand represent itself in its early years? What were its brand equities at the beginning, and what are they now?
- What are the brand's goals and objectives? What is the brand trying to accomplish? Which consumer groups is the brand trying to target? How is the brand reaching those consumers? Who is the brand's competition?
- What are the equities of the brand that can be translated into licensed product?

These are questions we will be returning to as we explore how a wide range of brands have used licensing to achieve ambitious marketing goals. As you'll learn, Stanley and other brands have created their programs relatively recently. If you go a little farther into the past, you will find that it wasn't always this way. How did brand licensing evolve over the years and decades? Let's examine that evolution and, in so doing, discover how this marketing method responded to the needs of companies at given moments in time.

CHAPTER 2

The Evolution of Brand Licensing

As you have learned, corporate brand licensing has evolved from a largely transactional and promotional tactic to a strategic tool that is aligned with and supports a company's overall communications goals and objectives, engaging with consumers in an authentic way. This evolution is worth examining in detail. Besides being a highly entertaining history lesson, the story of The Coca-Cola Company's changing and brilliant use of licensing, which is worth studying in and of itself, provides insight into how and why brand licensing has become such an effective marketing tool.

The history of licensing is also the history of the relationship of consumers with media and with brands. To grasp the value of licensing in today's marketing and retail environment, you need to see how it evolved over time as the consumer/media relationship changed. As you'll discover, each time licensing evolved, it was the result of innovative thinking that took advantage of changes and cultural shifts that were occurring in a given era.

Consider the historical context. Simply, licensing and its precursor, merchandising, started as advertising vehicles. Traditional radio and television advertising then came along and ultimately became the marketing focus. And, more recently, as traditional advertising declines, licensing has been embraced again, but this time as a different kind of marketing tool.

That's the highly condensed elevator version of licensing's evolution. But to see why brand licensing is a discipline whose time has come, we need to delve a bit deeper into the history.

The Early Years

Although it's impossible to know who was the first person or company to use licensing, we do know that at the start, licensing involved the following very basic criteria: A person or an entity owns an intellectual property and grants permission to a third party to use that property on a specific product that will be sold to consumers at retail. Now let's break down that definition into its component parts: first, ownership of intellectual property; second, a grant by the owner to a third party to use that property; third, a description of the product to be sold at retail to consumers that can feature the property.

That's about as simple a "license" as one can have. Other criteria to consider are compensation by the third party (the licensee) to the property owner (the licensor) for the usage; a term of years during which the usage may continue; licensor approval rights with respect to the product; and a written document. Without the existence of a written document, however, it's difficult to determine the "contractual" terms of what might have been agreed to or appear to be a license. Indeed, many lawyers would argue that a written document is absolutely necessary unless the agreement was for less than a year. Moreover, in the United States today, under federal law, a license agreement without product approval provisions (or any exercise of control over the quality of the product) is deemed a "naked license" and can lead to the abandonment of the trademark.[1] For this particular historical exercise, be aware,

---

1. In *Eva's Bridal Ltd. v. Halanick Enterprises, Inc.*, 639 F.3d 788 (7th Cir. 2011), the court

however, that many of the early "grants of rights" were without a document or the document was lost (if it ever existed) and the terms of the arrangement unknown. We can consider these commercial enterprises "licenses" or the "ancestors of licensing" as we know licensing today.

Modern day licensing had its early beginnings in the late 1800s and early 1900s. Although references exist of much earlier instances of then-famous personalities granting permission to use their names on products, we need to focus on the end of the nineteenth century and the beginning of the twentieth century when licensing became a true commercial endeavor. We also need to look at the early licensing of characters, athletes, and other celebrities to fully understand how licensing as commerce came into existence.

Palmer Cox and the Brownies
Palmer Cox is perhaps the first true pioneer of licensing. Yes, Palmer Cox (1840–1924). With the exception of Palmer Cox enthusiasts (a relatively small group) and the occasional reference, Cox has been largely forgotten. Yet he holds a very important place in the early days of an industry that, in 2016, accounted for more than $262 billion in worldwide retail sales.[2] Cox's business practices influenced Beatrix Potter's early licensing of Peter Rabbit in 1903 and Walt Disney's early licensing of Mickey Mouse in 1929.

Palmer Cox created a group of illustrated characters that went by the name of the Brownies, first appearing in the February 1883 edition of *St. Nicholas*, a magazine for children. As has been true of many children's characters for more than 125 years, the Brownies engaged in adventures, mischief, curiosity, and fantasy,

---

ruled that the plaintiffs abandoned the "Eva's Bridal" Mark by engaging in naked licensing—that is, by allowing others to use the mark without exercising "reasonable control over the nature and quality of the goods, services, or business on which the [mark] is used by the licensee."

2. "LIMA Annual Global Licensing Industry Survey, 2017 Report," commissioned by LIMA and prepared by Brander Consulting LLC, page 16.

always with a lesson about being kind and doing good for others. The Brownies were a group of little men who had personalities, engaged in sports, faced problems to be solved, and helped others (this is starting to sound a bit like the Teenage Mutant Ninja Turtles!). The Brownies were all the rage among children and their parents for more than 30 years.

Not only was Palmer Cox responsible for creating a group of famous characters for children, he well might have been the first to license his creative work beginning in the mid-1880s. Cox was aggressive in trying to protect his work, and licensing was a tactic that he used fairly effectively, although many other individuals and groups simply outright copied or imitated his characters and used them without permission. In 1890, a Buffalo, New York–based company asked Cox for permission to manufacture Brownie dolls and Cox agreed. The dolls went on sale shortly thereafter at a store in Buffalo. In fact, on April 1, 1890, the Library of Congress awarded the first patent for a doll based on a fictional character (i.e., the Brownies) used with the author's permission.[3] This inspired Cox to develop a strategy to license his characters for a host of other products, including toys, games, bowling pins, books, carpets, wallpaper, dinnerware, glassware, flatware, picture frames, and photo albums. This was the beginning of toys and other products based on characters being marketed with the author's authorization. Clearly, some of these products were for adults as well. Many of these product categories remain important categories for character licensing today.

And the Brownies were also likely the first characters used by then-famous brands to help sell their core products. Of particular note was Brownie Log Cabin biscuits introduced by the National Biscuit Company, now Nabisco, just before the turn of the nineteenth century. This was perhaps the first time characters were used to promote a food product, a very active area of licens-

3. *When Canadian Literature Moved to New York,* by Nicholas James Mount, University of Toronto Press, 2005, page 63.

ing today. And then there's P&G. In 1882, Harley Procter, son of P&G cofounder William Procter, ran the company's first print ad, promoting the company's new product Ivory Soap. Harley Procter is considered the father of advertising at P&G. And in 1883, Harley Procter used the Brownies to advertise Ivory, possibly the first use, with permission, of an artist's characters in advertising and certainly the first use of characters by P&G (actually, Cox created original illustrations for the Ivory soap advertisement). Today P&G continues to use famous characters, through licensing, to help sell its products (e.g., Pampers with Sesame Street, Thomas & Friends, and Hello Kitty; Crest with Star Wars, Spiderman, and Disney characters; and Bounty with Disney characters and Universal's Minions), as do many other famous consumer products brands.

Consider P&G's rationale for licensing the use of the Brownies to help sell Ivory soap in 1883. In those days, advertising wasn't a particularly trusted source of information. And it was difficult for brands to break through the clutter, engage with consumers in a meaningful way, and motivate them to purchase a product (in many ways, no different than today). In fact, in 1883, when P&G used the Brownies, there were more than 300 soap brands in the United States. The Brownies helped Ivory stand out amid all of this competition. Moreover, the Brownies equities were aligned with those of Ivory soap—harmless, helpful, friendly. This particular intersection of art and commerce made sense. Perhaps this analysis, by a forward-thinking executive at P&G, was not very different from the analysis that was likely undertaken more recently when P&G obtained the licenses mentioned above (such as using the Sesame Street characters on P&G's #1 brand Pampers). You can draw a straight line from P&G's use of the Brownies with Ivory soap in 1883 to P&G's use of the Sesame Street characters with Pampers in 2017.

Finally, no story about Palmer Cox would be complete without mentioning Kodak. Have you ever heard of the famous and groundbreaking Brownie camera? Many assumed that the camera was named after its manufacturer, Frank Brownell, but Kodak was actually taking advantage of Palmer Cox' Brownies, both the name and the characters, and without permission. Although Cox was aggressive about protecting his creation, he simply couldn't stop all of the unauthorized uses. Perhaps seeing that others were effectively using affiliations with the Brownies, Kodak used the characters for several years (maybe not even realizing that others had asked for permission). Kodak dropped the use of the characters in 1905 and then used the Brownie Boy, inspired by Buster Brown.

Honus Wagner

At the turn of the nineteenth century, the great shortstop Honus Wagner started his professional baseball career playing with the Louisville Colonels. Louisville was also the home of Bud Hillerich who started manufacturing baseball bats in 1894, which he named Louisville Slugger. Ballplayers using Hillerich's bats would often engrave their name on their bat so that they would know which Louisville Slugger bat was theirs. And that's what Honus Wagner did. Wagner left Louisville in 1900 to play for Pittsburgh, where he was the National League Batting Champion in 1900, 1903, and 1904. Although he left Louisville, Wagner and Hillerich remained friends from their days in Louisville. And in 1905, Hillerich and Wagner signed a contract that permitted Louisville Slugger to imprint Wagner's name on baseball bats sold to consumers in retail stores. It thus appears that Wagner became the first professional athlete to license his name for use on a product for money.

Teddy Roosevelt

Let's look at perhaps the first celebrity to license his name. In 1902, Theodore Roosevelt, U.S. president and famous outdoorsman, was invited by the governor of Mississippi, Andrew Longino, to go bear hunting in Mississippi. When the president couldn't find a bear to shoot, some members of the hunting party found an old, sick bear that they tied to a tree and presented to Roosevelt to shoot. But the president couldn't kill a sick bear tied to a tree. That's not the sportsman he considered himself to be. The bear was released, and on Roosevelt's order, the bear was put down to end its suffering. The story (real or myth?) spread through the newspapers as political cartoonists began illustrating Roosevelt with various bears, often refusing to shoot the sick bear tied to a tree, and the connection was made.

All of this came to the attention of Morris Michtom, the owner of a candy shop in Brooklyn, New York. Michtom's wife stitched a couple of stuffed bear dolls and offered them for sale at the candy shop. Morris decided to ask President Roosevelt for permission to use his name to sell the bears. As told by Morris Michtom's descendants, the president granted permission, on White House stationary (now a lost document), but remarked that he didn't think the stuffed bears would sell very well.[4] Michtom, though, sold a lot of "Teddy's Bear" and ultimately formed the Ideal Toy and Novelty Company in 1903. With the granting of permission to use his name (likely, however, without any compensation or time restrictions), Teddy Roosevelt was responsible for the Teddy Bear, which remains a popular doll to this day worldwide, although the moniker became generic (if it was ever even protectable) a very long time ago.

Besides these examples of character, sport, and celebrity "licensing," instances of corporate brand licensing can also be found in those early days. Some believe that merchandising as we know it today actually began with a corporate brand license when, beginning in 1897, Adolphus Busch allowed manufacturers to produce and sell a wine key that included a blade, a foil cutter, and corkscrews with the name "Busch" on it (beer bottles had corks back in those days). Other early corporations using licensing as a tool in those early years include the Campbell Soup Company, which licensed the images of the Campbell Kids as early as 1903 and The Coca-Cola Company (more on that company later).

---

4. Information based on a conversation the author had with Susan Sarna, Chief of Cultural Resources, Sagamore Hill, National Historic Site, June 2016.

Licensing Through the Decades

Clearly, an entire book could be written about the history of licensing through the decades. And when examining the history of corporate brand licensing, one cannot ignore the historical context without a brief (in this case, very brief) examination of the history of licensing in other segments. Accordingly, after the discussion of Palmer Cox, Honus Wagner, Teddy Roosevelt, and Adolphus Busch, we'll now look briefly at some of those other segments of licensing—characters, fashion designers, celebrities, and sports (as well as corporate brands).

Following is a stroll through the first hundred years or so of character, fashion designer, celebrity, and sports licensing, with some extra commentary here and there for the particularly groundbreaking episodes. This is not even close to an exhaustive list, just a sampling, stopping with the 1980s. The subsequent decades are less about history and more about contemporary licensing programs. Those years, however, are also rich with great, not-so-great, and disappointing licensing programs and stories, some of which will be covered in subsequent chapters.[5]

Early 1900s

In 1903, Beatrix Potter is said to have authorized a soft toy based on the character she created, Peter Rabbit, in a book she published in 1901.

The Buster Brown characters appeared in a comic strip in the *New York Herald* in 1902, and by 1904, the characters had been licensed to more than 20 licensees, including a footwear company, the Brown Shoe Company.

Late 1920s/Early 1930s

Disney's Mickey Mouse was licensed for thousands of products, and the licensing program literally saved the near-bankrupt com-

---

5. For a more in-depth history of licensing, see "The New & Complete Guide to Licensing," by Greg Battersby and Danny Simon, Kent Press, 2018.

pany. In 1934, General Foods paid $1 million to put Mickey Mouse cutouts on the back of cereal boxes. One story has Macy's New York selling a record 11,000 Mickey Mouse watches in one day! The first licensing program generated by a motion picture was launched by Disney in 1937 following the release of *Snow White*.

1930s

The Looney Tunes characters, led by Bugs Bunny, entered licensing.

Shirley Temple licensed both her persona and motion picture characters for dolls, clothing, accessories, soap, school supplies, and more. By 1941, sales of Shirley Temple dolls exceeded $45 million.

Created in 1932, Superman soon became the first superhero to be licensed. And with the continuing publication of the comic books, other related superheroes soon followed (e.g., Superboy and Supergirl).

The first (of 66) Hopalong Cassidy motion pictures appeared in 1935. William Boyd, who played Hopalong, earned millions of dollars from licensed products. In 1950, Hopalong Cassidy appeared on the first lunch box to feature a character, and by that year, there were more than 100 licensees generating more than $70 million in sales of licensed products.

1940s

Marvel characters (1939), Batman (1939), Archie (1941), and Thomas the Tank Engine (1946) first appeared in the 1940s and would eventually inspire licensing programs, in some instances generating billions of dollars in retail sales today.

1950s

The Howdy Doody Show first appeared on live television in 1947 and for the next thirteen years was among the most popular children's television program. It was also actively licensed throughout the 1950s with products including toys, games, apparel, food, and books. Macy's, featuring Howdy Doody dolls in its Herald Square store in New York City, sold out in a matter of hours, at a time when no one even knew how many people were watching television! A 24-page catalog of licensed products was published in 1955. This was, perhaps, the first comprehensive licensing program based entirely on the new medium—television.

One of the most popular licensed product properties of all time, Peanuts, was launched, based on a newspaper comic strip created by Charles Schulz.

In 1952, jazz guitarist Les Paul licensed his name to Gibson Guitar to produce a Les Paul guitar. This was, perhaps, the first time a musician licensed his name, a practice that continues today with many musical artists (e.g., P. Diddy, Madonna, Adam Levine, Gwen Stefani, and Justin Bieber).

The first issue of *Playboy* magazine appeared in 1953. The first license was granted in 1955 for Playboy cuff links. The Playboy name and Rabbit Head logo are still actively licensed today in a host of product categories.

Elvis Presley started licensing his name and image from almost the beginning of his famous career in the 1950s and remains one of the top-grossing celebrity estates in the licensing business.

Smurfs licensing began in 1959 with figurines available in French- and Dutch-speaking countries, soon to be followed in the 1960s by PVC figurines that were more broadly distributed. In those early days, the characters were also licensed for advertising purposes in Europe, and the figurines were given away for free at gasoline stations.

The licensing of Barbie, The Honeymooners, and Davy Crockett (if you were a little boy in the 1950s, you likely had a Davy Crocket coonskin cap) all started during this decade, with great success.

1960s

The Flintstones, the first successful prime-time animated television series on network TV, debuted in 1960 and quickly inspired a licensing program. In addition to the traditional array of licensed products, The Flintstones entered new ground for licensing with products such as chewable multiple vitamins with Miles Labs (still on the market today) and Fruity Pebbles and Cocoa Pebbles ready-to-eat cereals by Post Foods (still on the market today). This successful licensing program followed Hanna-Barbera's first step into licensing in 1958 with Ruff & Reddy comics published by Dell.

And for those who were alive in the 1960s, who could forget Beatlemania? The Beatles were formed in 1960 and introduced to the American market in 1964 with their hit song "I Want to Hold Your Hand." Beatles merchandise followed quickly. T-shirts sold out in three days; Remco Toys produced 100,000 Beatles dolls and faced orders for 500,000; Beatles wigs were selling at the rate of 35,000 per day. In the 1960s, hundreds of products were licensed by their company Seltaeb (*Beatles* spelled backward) all over the world.

Licensing Corporation of America (LCA), the first agency devoted solely to licensing, was formed in 1960 to represent entertainment, sports, and celebrity properties. Years later LCA became part of Warner Bros. and eventually Warner Bros. Consumer Products, a major force in licensing today.

The sports leagues formed their licensing divisions in the 1960s—NFL Properties in 1963, Major League Baseball Properties in 1966, and NBA Properties in 1967.

The first comprehensive James Bond licensing program began with the third film (out of 24 at the time of publication), *Goldfinger.*

Daniel Boone, Sesame Street, and GI Joe all launched in the 1960s and gave rise to licensing programs. Both Sesame Street and GI Joe have inspired hundreds of licensed products that remain wildly popular today.

1970s
The decade began with the birth of the Ralph Lauren and Polo brands, which would become among the world's most recognized brands through the designer's own products as well as his licensed products.

The decade also witnessed the launch of Strawberry Shortcake by American Greetings, Mary Engelbreit who led the development of art as a licensing category, Garfield, and Cabbage Patch Kids.

The Coca-Cola Company launched its licensing program as a trademark protection exercise in the late 1970s. More on that to follow.

1980s

This decade marked the beginning of several groundbreaking and highly lucrative licensing programs: the Care Bears by American Greetings; Martha Stewart, who started with a book titled *Entertaining*; Teenage Mutant Ninja Turtles, which began as a comic book; The Simpsons; and designer Tommy Hilfiger.

It was also a time when several corporate brands commenced licensing programs: the Harley-Davidson Motor Company, which entered licensing as a trademark protection program; Pepsi-Cola; Coors beer; Hershey Foods; Dr. Scholl's; and John Deere. Several advertising campaigns inspired successful licensing programs: Wendy's *Where's the Beef?*; The California Raisins, developed by the California Raisin Advisory Board; the Taco Bell Chihuahua; and Mars M&M's characters.

Sears, Roebuck & Co., the leading U.S. retailer of the day, was extremely active in developing groundbreaking licensed programs beginning in the 1980s. First was the retail exclusive fashion program with supermodel Cheryl Tiegs in 1981, followed by top tennis player Evonne Goolagong's fashion program launched in 1983. But even more groundbreaking was the nation's #1 retailer's partnership with the nation's #1 fast food restaurant chain. Sears and McDonald's launched a line of licensed children's apparel, McKids, exclusively at Sears in 1987. This was followed in a partnership with Sears, in 1988, by the opening of seven McKids freestanding stores in malls across the United States. By 1991, there were 47 McKids stores. The program with Sears, ahead of its time, ended in 1991 when all of the McKids stores were closed.

And, finally, in what is likely the longest-running celebrity license of all time, Jaclyn Smith partnered with Kmart in 1985 on a women's apparel and accessories collection. At the time, Smith was an endorser for Max Factor, was a Breck Girl, was a star of the hit TV series *Charlie's Angels*, and was a star in other television shows and motion pictures. The Jaclyn Smith Collection at Kmart remains strong today. In many respects, Smith has transcended her career as an actor to one as a fashion brand—an important transition that many celebrities aspire to achieve (see Chapter 8).

This historical context would not be complete without a more comprehensive discussion of one of the world's most iconic brands, Coca-Cola. The Coca-Cola Company has consistently used the licensing and merchandising of its iconic brand since its early days to support its corporate marketing and communications goals and objectives, to connect with consumers, and to drive beverage consumption. How it has accomplished this and when provides insights into how licensing has evolved as well as why this evolution has naturally led to the emergence and importance of brand licensing today.

What examining the history of Coca-Cola as a beverage and as a marketing enterprise reveals in the case study below is as follows:

- First, the brand message has remained remarkably consistent since the company's earliest days in the late 1800s.
- Second, the company has always used innovative marketing and communication tools to connect with consumers in a manner aligned with that marketing message and, in many respects, has been a leader in marketing and advertising over the course of its history.
- Third, the company recognized very early (again, in the late 1800s) that non-beverage products, merchandising, and ultimately licensing could support its marketing initiatives and further connect the brand with consumers.

- Fourth, the evolution of the brand and the company's use of merchandising and licensing to engage with consumers is a lens through which we can understand the evolution of brand licensing in general.

The Coca-Cola Company and Licensing

History

Compared to other events of the 1880s, the origins of a soft drink on May 8, 1886, in Atlanta, Georgia, were modest. The Statue of Liberty was unveiled the same year, a dramatic symbol of America's welcome to the immigrant. In that decade the Canadian Pacific Railway and England's six-mile-long Severn Tunnel were completed, two engineering feats that opened important regions to trade and travel. Telephone service linked New York and Chicago; George Eastman invented the first push-button camera, and he and Thomas Edison developed the first movie film. Robert Louis Stevenson published *Dr. Jekyll and Mr. Hyde* and Arthur Conan Doyle introduced Sherlock Holmes. The world was growing closer, linked by wire, railroads and transatlantic steamers, and such pleasures as taking snapshots and reading whodunits. To those pleasures, Dr. John S. Pemberton added Coca-Cola.[6]

It was a beverage that would become the most popular drink in the world.

Pemberton was a pharmacist and inventor of proprietary medicines and beverages. His concoction, a caramel-colored syrup

---

6. *Coca-Cola: First Hundred Years*, text by Anne Hoy, published by The Coca-Cola Company in 1986 to celebrate the Company's Centennial, page 11. Much of the material in this section titled "History" for the period 1886 to 1986 was taken from this publication.

stirred in a brass kettle, contained ingredients from the coca leaf and the kola nut, thus the name of the beverage. Pemberton's first sales were at Jacobs' Pharmacy in Atlanta, Georgia (Atlanta still remains the headquarters of this global company). As was the custom of the time, Pemberton claimed that his carbonated beverage (five cents a glass at the soda fountain) cured a list of ailments.

Legend has it that at the soda fountain in Jacobs' Pharmacy, Pemberton ran a primitive focus group. He made one glass of the beverage by mixing the syrup with water and another by mixing the syrup with soda. The carbonated version was favored, and shortly thereafter, a sign appeared at Jacobs' reading "Drink Coca-Cola."

The famous Coca-Cola logo and distinctive Spencerian script was designed in the same year that Pemberton named the drink, 1886, by Frank Robinson, Pemberton's bookkeeper. Unlike logo development today, there was no design agency, no focus groups, no market testing. That very same script logo, slightly modified in 2007, is still in use today. It is one of the most iconic and recognized logos in the world and actively used in all of the company's marketing and communications, including its licensing program.

Following Pemberton's death, in 1888, local businessman Asa Candler became Coca-Cola's owner (purchasing the company for $2,300) and marketed the product aggressively. In many respects, Candler is the father of modern-day Coca-Cola. Candler recognized that to succeed with a low-cost beverage required high sales. He wanted to make the drink available everywhere and used then-popular forms of marketing to motivate purchase as often and in as many occasions as possible (all still goals of the company today). It's Asa Candler to whom we look for the early days of the company's marketing objectives and brand messaging. In an early example of merchandising, free Coca-Cola calendars were given away; Coca-Cola glasses, glass holders, serving and tip trays, clocks, wallets, pocket knives, paper fans, watch fobs, postcards, sampling coupons, matchbooks, and playing cards all proclaimed the qualities of Coca-Cola. Most of these products were given away for free at soda fountains where Coca-Cola was mixed by soda jerks. But it was all about using non-beverage products to promote the drink. There was even a Tiffany-style hanging lamp with the script "Coca-Cola" set into the stained glass. By 1895, Candler had made Coca-Cola a national beverage. The brand continued to rise to fame with catchy slogans (e.g., "Delicious and Refreshing") and newspapers, building signage, awnings, billboards, and lifestyle advertising, all featuring the iconic words "Drink Coca-Cola."

In 1919, The Coca-Cola Company was purchased by a group of investors for $25 million (not a bad return on investment for Mr. Candler) led by Ernest Woodruff of the Trust Company of Georgia. Ernest's son Robert ran the company beginning in 1923 for almost six decades. He is largely credited with transforming The Coca-Cola Company into the global enterprise it is today. From its very early days, the brand goals were Ubiquity and Lifestyle.

In the first quarter of the twentieth century as Coca-Cola became available in bottles (the iconic Coca-Cola contour bottle was created in 1915 as part of a competition run by the company), it could be purchased at many locations other than the soda fountain—at grocers, in a new six-pack carrying case, and from new coolers and vending machines. "The pause that refreshes" could be found "Around the Corner from Everywhere." And as the automobile caught on and Americans began to travel, Coca-Cola was wherever they found themselves. The brand was advertised on highway billboards; in illuminated signs (e.g., Manhattan's Times Square); at highway service stations in ice-cold coolers; and, beginning in 1935, in coin-operated vending machines. It was everywhere. Ubiquity.

With the advent of motion pictures, movie stars became even more important, and Coca-Cola advertising let consumers know that even stars enjoyed a refreshing pause—Cary Grant, Claudette Colbert, Loretta Young, Jean Harlow, Robert Montgomery, and even little Jackie Cooper were featured in Coca-Cola marketing.

The company used radio effectively as well—not just for advertising, but also as a sponsor of celebrated radio music programs featuring many of the big bands of the era: Benny Goodman, Tommy Dorsey, Sammy Kaye, and Gene Krupa. Some programs even used the name of the company as part of the name of the program, such as a music and talk show called "The Coke Club." Lifestyle. The use of stars and music has continued up to the present time. Coca-Cola has been promoted by artists such as The Beatles, David Bowie, George Michael, Elton John, Michael Jackson, Whitney Houston, and Taylor Swift.

And as television became popular in the 1950s, Coca-Cola moved quickly into the new medium. TV commercials took the jingles of radio and the imagery of print ads and gave them the live actors and drama of theater. The jingle "Things Go Better With Coke" was recorded by more than 50 popular artists, including Gladys Knight & the Pips, the 5th Dimension, the Bee Gees, Jay and the Americans, Petula Clark, Marvin Gaye, Neil Diamond, Ray Charles, Aretha Franklin, and the Supremes. Coca-Cola commercial themes changed regularly and became part of the country's cultural fabric—"Look Up America"; "It's the Real Thing"; "I'd Like to Teach the World to Sing," which was recorded in four versions over a period of 15 years from 1971–1985; "Have a Coke and a Smile"; and "Coke Is It!"

The Coca-Cola Company is one of the largest advertisers in the world today. The company was ranked #15 in global advertising by *Ad Age* with $4 billion spent globally in 2016.[7] Indeed, for decades, the history of Coca-Cola advertising has been woven into the culture of not only America but also many other countries around the world.

Sports have always been important to the image of Coca-Cola. The company was the first official sponsor of the Olympic games in 1928 in Amsterdam and has been an Olympic sponsor ever since. The company is and has been a sponsor of many other sporting

---

7. "World's Largest Advertisers 2017," *Ad Age*, December 4, 2017.

events and organizations, including the FIFA World Cup, NAS-CAR, Major League Baseball, the NFL, the NBA (the company signed a 100-year sponsorship agreement with the NBA in 1994), and the NHL. Coke is the official drink of many U.S. collegiate football teams as well as a sponsor of Little League. The list goes on and on.

The history of Coca-Cola reveals a brand that has relied on recognition and ubiquity—a brand that was always presented as more than just a drink, but a lifestyle, decade after decade. Those were goals of Asa Candler, and those goals continue today. Indeed, Coca-Cola is recognized and appreciated all over the world with the same trademarks, packaging, and quality. Whether on grocery shelves, in vending machines, on drugstore signs, in trucks, as sponsorships, as advertising, on social media, Coca-Cola is likely the most ubiquitous consumer products brand in the world. And those consistent goals were supported first by product merchandising at the soda fountain and later by licensing, and for a very long time. The licensing activated by The Coca-Cola Company has evolved over the decades and has become increasingly creative, innovative, and groundbreaking—and in that regard, the company's use of merchandising and then licensing traces the evolution of corporate brand licensing as a marketing and communications discipline and a path to the consumer.

Merchandising and Licensing Through the Decades

1880s and 1890s
The first nondrink products authorized by the company were those that could be used at the point of sale (first, at soda fountains) and had a practical purpose, such as tip trays for servers, serving trays, and syrup urns, all considered a form of free advertising (often featuring the famous artwork of "Coca-Cola Ladies" enjoying the beverage). But in his zeal to promote the brand more aggressively, in addition to promoting consumption of the beverage, Asa Candler came to view non-beverage products (e.g., pencils, pens, and

pocket mirrors) as tools he could also use to enable consumers to experience brand "Coca-Cola" at other times in their daily lives. The products were a strategy of sorts to drive the ubiquity of the brand. These items are collectible today and very rare. Coca-Cola calendars from the 1890s are often valued over $10,000. A 1903 metal sign recently sold at auction for $12,000.

Early 1900s
But these promotional and give-away items were just the precursors to Coca-Cola licensed products. In the early 1900s, the company licensed its name for chewing gum followed by cigars and candy. By the second decade of the twentieth century, the famous Coca-Cola script and logo could be found on outdoor thermometers, soda fountain trays, baseball cards, and all sorts of tin decorative signs. Many of these products are still part of the company's worldwide licensing program (albeit from different manufacturers).

1920s and 1930s
During these decades, children became a target demographic for the drink, and licensing was not far behind to help reach this consumer. Toy trucks, among the first of many products licensed for children, were sold in select cities in the 1930s (Metalcraft), 1940s (The Smitty Company), and 1950s (Matchbox). All of these trucks remain popular with collectors today.

1950s and 1960s
In the 1950s and 1960s, both Louis Marx and Buddy L, two leading toy companies of the time, produced Coca-Cola toy delivery vehicles. Buddy L also produced dolls; Milton Bradley produced games such as chess, checkers, darts, dominoes, and backgammon; and the Atlanta-based Rushton Company produced Santa Claus dolls. However, although the company did grant permission to use its trademarks, there is no record of manufacturers paying royalties for these rights to Coca-Cola, as the company viewed the prod-

ucts simply as part of its marketing strategy. Further, although many such products were authorized by the company, generally they were standard items that simply featured the Coca-Cola logo and red and white colors of the brand. It was all about advertising and promoting Ubiquity.

Slowly the company started to realize that the Lifestyle objective of the brand could also be supported by licensing. Perhaps one of the most interesting ventures into licensing at the time was a program Coca-Cola developed with Sears, Roebuck & Co. in the early 1960s. This was the era of *American Bandstand* and the emergence of pop music. Coca-Cola bottlers were sponsoring talent contests across the nation that were extremely popular (although on a much smaller scale, not dissimilar to *American Idol*). During this time, Sears became the exclusive retailer for T-shirts decorated with Coca-Cola bottles, logos, and designs featuring music artwork. Today virtually every major retailer that sells apparel has one or more retail exclusives (see Chapter 7), but the Sears program may have been the first.

1970s

Nevertheless, despite these early forays into licensing and with some exceptions, the products were generally promotionally driven novelty items. However, in the mid to late 1970s, licensing became an important strategy championed by The Coca-Cola Company's Legal Department. For the lawyers, licensing wasn't viewed as a marketing tool, but rather a legal tool to be used to further strengthen the most famous trademark in the world. By licensing the trademark in certain categories and using it as the brand identifier (and not just decoration), the company would be in a position to register the Mark in a wide range of product classifications outside of the beverage category. The Marketing Department was responsible for seeking licensees, negotiating business terms, and managing the program in product categories identified by the Legal Department.

1980s

The licensing program grew rapidly in the late 1970s and 1980s. Products such as glassware, beach towels, footwear, socks, toys, hats, jigsaw puzzles, T-shirts, housewares, and tin signs appeared at retail. Licensees began developing creative designs using Coca-Cola iconography. And with royalties now being paid, the program was generating significant revenues. Although other corporate brands had been engaged in licensing for decades, The Coca-Cola Company may have been the first to develop a comprehensive formal program and early on created some of the best licensing practices in the industry. For example, contracts were highly protective of the company's assets, the product approval process was rigorous, quality assurance was strict (including testing of products by independent testing labs), product descriptions were contractually focused as were distribution channels and countries where the products could be sold, and comprehensive financial obligations to the company were part of each license agreement. Senior executives were dedicated to developing and managing the licensing program. And, importantly, the company controlled the graphic designs featured on many of the products. Other companies were developing their licensing programs in a similar fashion, but none as comprehensively, strategically, and creatively as The Coca-Cola Company.

During the mid-1980s, marketing objectives became as important as legal objectives for the licensing program, and the Marketing Department began to play a role equal to that of the Legal Department. During these decades, other brands also developed formal licensing programs, including McDonald's, Hershey Foods, Campbell Soup Company, Harley-Davidson, Dr. Scholl's, Miller Beer, Coppertone, and General Motors. In general, famous logos and other available advertising artwork were used as decoration on products, but Coca-Cola was about to move in yet another new and innovative direction.

Early in this period, Coca-Cola realized that for licensed products to sell at retail, more than just the famous script logo and red and white colors were needed to make them attractive to consumers. This applied even more so outside the United States, where consumers viewed these kinds of products as a form of advertising. To meet this challenge, the company made artwork available from its vast archives. However, this artwork looked back on the company's past, and although it served a purpose for particular products, the company also wanted to look ahead. Accordingly, beautiful artwork inspired by Coca-Cola iconography (e.g., the contour bottle, cans, bottle caps, slogans, and advertising characters such as the Polar Bears) and brand-aligned themes (e.g., sports, music, food, and holidays), often inspired by the powerful visual images the company used to support its brand, was regularly commissioned to be used in the licensing program. This was groundbreaking at the time—a famous brand recognizing that more than just its iconic logo was necessary to attract large segments of consumers to purchase licensed product.

Coca-Cola licensed products were no longer just about using a red and white logo. The creative development of unique graphics, artwork, and designs has remained a strength of the company's licensing program to this day and has been imitated by other corporate brand licensors, but rarely with the same level of resources that have been dedicated by Coca-Cola. Today some of the most active corporate brand licensors are committed to providing their licensees with exciting and creative artwork to use on licensed products, including Harley-Davidson, the Ford Motor Company, Guinness, and PepsiCo.

Coca-Cola Clothes
Apparel and apparel accessories have always been a staple of The Coca-Cola Company's licensing program (as has been true of many corporate brand licensing programs), beginning with the Sears program in the early 1960s. In the mid-1980s, the company did something that had never been done by a corporate consumer products brand licensor. The brand was licensed for an upscale line of fashion apparel. In 1985, the Murjani Group (famous for the

Gloria Vanderbilt denim collection) launched a full collection of fashion Coca-Cola apparel and accessories, all bearing the famous logo and colors. The lead designer for Coca-Cola Clothes was a young designer at Murjani named Tommy Hilfiger. Although Coca-Cola Clothes included shirts, jeans, and sweaters, it was the hats, rugby shirts, and sweatshirts that were the top sellers. Shortly thereafter, when Hilfiger went out on his own, it was his rugby shirts, with his name instead of the brand Coca-Cola, that the hip-hop crowd drove to fame. Importantly, with this initiative, the company strategically focused licensing to support the "Lifestyle" message of the brand, having already used licensing for the past 80 or 90 years largely to support the "Ubiquity" brand message.

Coca-Cola Clothes was heavily advertised, at least in terms of fashion apparel advertising, with slogans such as "Coming to a body near you," "It's popping yellow," and "It's bubbling blue." The slogans were incorporated into ads illustrated by famous artist Peter Max (who had collaborated with Coca-Cola in the past).

The clothing was sold at upscale department stores, including Saks Fifth Avenue, Bloomingdale's, and Nordstrom. In addition, Murjani opened a flagship store named *Fizzazz* on Columbus Avenue at 73rd Street in New York City's fashionable Upper West Side. The company wouldn't let Murjani use the brand name in the name of the store, so the name was a take-off on the "fizz" of the beverage. *Fizzazz* followed on the heels of the Sears/McKids freestanding store initiative mentioned earlier. Mono-branded licensed stores have been a strategy of other brands in recent years, such as Jeep, Crayola, Guinness, and Jaguar. In addition to using this pioneering concept, the store incorporated new features as well. Buyers chose their clothes on a monitor from videodiscs and then had their clothes delivered by conveyor belt. A music video was even produced for the launch of Coca-Cola Clothes. It was a retail "experience," something that most retailers are focused on today (see Chapter 12).

1990s

By 1990, after craze status for several years, sales went flat, Murjani suffered financial difficulties, and the clothing line disappeared. But the strength of the groundbreaking concept was never forgotten among the licensing professionals at The Coca-Cola Company. A new collection of fashion apparel was launched in Germany in the early 1990s with direct-mail giant Otto Versand. Based in Hamburg, Otto was the largest direct-mail catalog company in Germany, at the time mailing more than 13 million catalogs annually. Items ordered out of the catalog were delivered directly to the home by Otto Versand trucks. Clothing could be tried on when delivered and, if the customer wasn't satisfied, returned immediately. This time around The Coca-Cola Company exercised even more control over the product assortment. The company retained an outside design firm to design the seasonal collection. Those designs were presented to Otto Versand, which then handled the manufacturing, marketing, and distribution—thirty years after that rudimentary Sears apparel program!

Initially, freestanding 52-page catalogs were created and distributed by Otto Versand. Later in the program, those catalogs were discontinued and 10 to 15 pages of Otto Versand's main catalog (two inches thick) were devoted to Coca-Cola fashions. Although initial sales were very strong, the program was short-lived, lasting only several years. But The Coca-Cola Company established that a corporate brand name could be licensed for a fashion line of apparel, all to support one of its overall marketing messages. And this is a licensing strategy that has been adopted by many other brand owners over the years (e.g., Jeep, Kellogg's, and Caterpillar).

2000 to 2015[8]

By 2015, The Coca-Cola Company's licensing program consisted of more than 300 licensees worldwide. Products include all sorts

---

8. The Coca-Cola Company is ranked #150 with estimated retail sales of $1 billion."Top 150 Global Licensors" *Id.*

of drinkware, home goods, housewares, toys, school supplies, gifts and novelties, and health and beauty products. By 2013, retail sales of Coca-Cola licensed products jumped to $1.3 billion with more than 500 million Coca-Cola licensed products purchased annually.[9] From 2010–2015, the business had tripled due to strong partnerships, creative execution, and geographical expansion. By 2014, international markets accounted for 70 percent of the brand's licensing business. In 2015, Kate Dwyer, Group Director of Coca-Cola Worldwide Licensing, articulated what Asa Candler knew so many years ago, saying that the mission of the licensing program is to design and market branded merchandise that extends the brand experience and connects with consumers. "Our goal," she notes, "is to leverage licensing to amplify our brand messages. Licensing is a key marketing extension for the beverage."[10] History matters.

EKOCYCLE

In 2012, burnishing its reputation for innovation and creativity, The Coca-Cola Company and musical artist and producer will.i.am focused on recycling with the launch of a new lifestyle brand named EKOCYCLE (*EKOC* is *Coke* spelled backward), an entirely new direction for its licensing program and another example of how corporate licensing has evolved. This stand-alone brand is designed to encourage recycling behavior and sustainability among consumers through aspirational, yet attainable lifestyle products made in part from recycled materials (e.g., Coca-Cola plastic bottles). The brand helps consumers understand that what they consider waste today may be part of a lifestyle product they can purchase and use tomorrow. The EKOCYCLE brand identifies products, such as plastic bottles and aluminum cans, that can be repurposed into recycled materials for fashionable products.[11] In general, it's very challenging to

---

9. "The Coca-Cola Company," *Retail Merchandiser*, June 2, 2014.
10. *Id.*
11. "will.i.am and The Coca-Cola Company Accelerate EKOCYCLE Momentum with Addition of Four New Brand Partners," Coca-Cola Press Center, October 25, 2012.

launch and sustain an entirely new brand through licensing. The association with will.i.am and the sustainability mission as well as the commitment of The Coca-Cola Company have all contributed to this success story (also see the discussion in Chapter 8).

The first EKOCYCLE product was Beats headphones by Dr. Dre, made from recycled bottles. Another early product was New Era EKOCYCLE caps, which are also manufactured from recycled plastic bottles. Levi Strauss & Co. offered limited-edition Levi's 501 Waste-Less jeans, made from an average of eight recycled bottles. Case-Mate offered a smartphone case made from 100 percent recycled PET plastic. In early 2015, an EKOCYCLE shop-in-shop opened at Harrods in London. The shop offered womenswear and menswear clothing and accessories, home interiors, a 3D printer, and a portable bike, among other EKOCYCLE products. Also in 2015, W Hotels Worldwide partnered with the brand to bring EKOCYCLE to its rooms, rolling out king-size sheet sets made of approximately 31 recycled 20-ounce plastic bottles—equal to more than 268,000 plastic bottles across all W Hotel beds. And in 2014, EKOCYCLE introduced the EKOCYCLE Cube 3D printer that prints with proprietary EKOCYCLE cartridges featuring post-consumer recycled plastic commonly found in drink bottles and other everyday products. Each EKOCYCLE cartridge turns the equivalent of three recycled 20-ounce PET plastic bottles into wearable fashion, music accessories, and desktop décor.

Continuing to Stay Relevant
Naturally, with a brand as rich in history as Coca-Cola's and as pervasive in our culture as it is, the challenge for Coca-Cola is to keep the licensed products relevant, innovative, fresh, and design driven. Fashion apparel has always been a successful tactic of the company in that regard. Fashions featuring Coca-Cola iconography have recently hit the fashion runways through collaborations with famous designers such as Marc Jacobs and Ashish Gupta. In 2014, Coca-Cola collaborated with fashion designer Dr. Romanelli (known as DRx) to create a collection of vintage clothing.

The Coca-Cola Company is among the most innovative corporate brand licensors in the world, consistent with the company's long history of marketing innovation. To celebrate the one-hundredth anniversary of the iconic contour bottle in 2015, the company invited over 130 designers and artists from around the world to create artwork featuring the bottle designs using only Coca-Cola red, black, and white. The result is a collection of incredibly creative, whimsical, and sophisticated "mash-up" artwork introduced in February 2015 as part of a global anniversary campaign.

Many of the mash-up designs are featured on Coca-Cola licensed products (e.g., fashion scarves, headphone covers, backpacks, wallets and duffels, Moleskine journals, tote bags, and phone cases). Finally, in an example of The Coca-Cola Company as licensee, the company offered bottles featuring team logos and nicknames of more than 50 colleges and universities during March Madness in 2017, reinforcing the brand's strong association with sports.

As we trace the history of The Coca-Cola Company from the late 1800s to the present, we observe a brand that has always had the goal of being ubiquitous as well as a brand that has always wanted to be seen as more than just a drink, but as a lifestyle. That was Asa Candler's vision in the late 1800s, and that early vision remains incorporated into the goals of the company today. Licensing began with the promotional non-beverage products given away at soda fountains at the turn of the nineteenth century, to products that could be used in daily life in the 1920s, to toys and dolls in the 1930s and onward, to apparel at Sears in the 1960s, to fashion apparel beginning in the 1980s, to EKOCYCLE in 2012, and the fashion runways of the past several years. We can see how corporate brand licensing has evolved over the decades through the lens of this iconic brand, which has always used promotional and retail licensed products as a marketing and communications tool to help deliver its brand messages, connect with consumers, and drive beverage sales.

CHAPTER 3

The Benefits: The Advantages of Harnessing Brand Equity Through Licensing

Brand-focused licensing is not a one-size-fits-all strategy. Although brand owners should align this strategy with larger marketing objectives, tailoring it to fit specific goals is crucial. In fact, the versatility of licensing is an advantage for companies that use the strategy properly.

Licensing helps companies leverage brand equity in wide-ranging, innovative ways. Organizations sometimes don't fully realize how valuable their brand equity is and how licensing can be used for a variety of marketing purposes. For example, some companies may want their licensing program to change a brand's positioning or extend a brand's meaning. P&G's licensing program for Mr. Clean helped turn a brand known as a liquid cleaner into a broader household cleaning brand. (See Figure 3 in the photo insert.) Skechers extended its brand meaning from footwear to fashion by utilizing licensing. These types of brand redefinitions are ambitious but fully within the scope of strategic licensing.

Alhough many benefits exist for marketers who use licensing in strategically sound ways, we will focus on the following seven benefits of brand licensing:

1. To enter or maintain a presence in businesses that have strategic value, but fall outside of the company's core businesses or financial thresholds.
2. To build brand awareness and reinforce brand values.
3. To engage with consumers, strengthen the relationship with existing customers, and increase consumer touchpoints.
4. To reach new consumers and educate them about the brand.
5. To extend into new channels of distribution and new paths in the consumer shopping journey.
6. To generate new revenue streams with minimal upfront investment.
7. To protect the brand via broad trademark registration.

Virtually every brand that engages in licensing is doing so to achieve more than one benefit, so the odds are that a number (or most) of the benefits on this list apply to any brand owner. Frequently, however, one or two of the benefits are the real focus, whereas others just naturally accrue to the brand as a by-product of successfully pursuing the primary benefits.

The discussion of each of these benefits includes examples designed to spotlight specific benefits. Although one particular benefit is highlighted for each example, you will easily be able to discern the other benefits that licensing provides for the brand.

Enter or Maintain a Presence in Businesses That Have Strategic Value but Fall Outside of the Company's Core Businesses or Financial Thresholds

Unless a brand's primary licensing goal is to generate revenue (see below), the brand owner is probably using licensing to enter a business that has strategic value but falls outside the company's core business (in other words, diversification). Licensing is being used instead of other strategies (e.g., new product introduction) for a variety of reasons—financial considerations, the competitive landscape, or resource commitment. Because this is such a common goal, most of the examples in this chapter will achieve it. Baileys created a highly innovative licensing strategy that helped it gain a strong presence in an area tangential to its main business but consistent with its brand objectives.

Baileys

Baileys is among the world's best-selling liqueur brands, accounting for 50 percent of all spirits exported from Ireland. It is a mix of Irish dairy cream and Irish whiskey. The first Irish cream in the market, the brand was introduced in 1974 with the belief that women deserved a better choice of spirits at a time when spirits were targeted mostly at men. It actually took four years to perfect the "impossible blend" of smooth Irish cream with triple distilled Irish whiskey. Today Baileys is served and sold in more than 180 countries around the world, and its consumer is generally female, ages 25–50.

According to Baileys, the flavor profile is "an unapologetic liquid, part cake, part booze, pure seduction, absurdly delicious." The marketing objective of the brand is to get many more people drinking a little Baileys every year, to think of Baileys as a treat, a pleasurable indulgence. Consumers enjoy the brand but need more occasions to engage with the brand. When you want a treat, think of Baileys. When considering what kinds of products Baileys should pursue as licensed brand extensions, the brand must consider whether those products will communicate that brand

47

message and align with the brand's marketing goals. Licensing *must* support those objectives to be considered successful. This is a reframing of the brand message.

Let's consider how Baileys effectively used licensing to enter businesses that have strategic value but fall outside its core competency and as a marketing/communications tool to achieve the company's goals and reach consumers in different ways and at different occasions, making the brand more accessible as an everyday, indulgent treat.

Baileys has successfully licensed the brand to several companies on a geographically regional basis for chocolates; ice cream; whipped cream; pouring cream; flavored creamers; assorted glassware; chilled and frozen desserts; coffee pods; ready-to-drink coffee; and gift assortments that include Baileys liqueur, chocolate, and glassware. (See Figure 2 in the photo insert.) Virtually all of these products help redefine Baileys as not just an alcoholic drink but more broadly as an impulse treat. Importantly, these products cause many more people to engage with Baileys every year (i.e., reaching more consumers). And if you "eat" more Baileys, you will most likely drink more Baileys (or at least try it). These products have strategic value and give Baileys a presence in categories outside of the company's core business.[1]

In general, the licensed products help reframe Baileys as an impulse treat and more of an everyday occasion. In addition to the strategic value to Baileys, brand loyalists will be drawn to the products, strengthening their already existing relationship with the brand, which they will now be using more frequently at different times of the day. And new consumers will be drawn to the product categories in which they already engage, the goal being to educate them and drive them to try the core product. In helping to attain these goals, all of the licensed food products are delicious and strengthen the quality taste profile of the core Baileys liqueur.

---

1. Diageo, which includes Baileys and other Diageo spirits brands such as Guinness, is ranked #78 in "Top 150 Global Licensors." *Id.*

Baileys has used licensing effectively to enter new businesses and achieve many of the other benefits of licensing enumerated above. Baileys Irish Cream is sold primarily around holidays and is consumed mostly late in the day and the evening. Besides Baileys extending its brand meaning beyond a liqueur with its licensed products, those products provided consumers with an opportunity to purchase the brand at other times of the year and consume or use them during different times of the day—all designed to inspire consumers to drink more Baileys Irish cream. How did the brand accomplish those results?

First, Baileys was very perceptive about its initial tactic. Clearly, we live in a time when healthy eating is a trend that is on the rise. But there's another (some might say conflicting) trend that's been going on for some time as well. Consumers recognize that there's also a time for indulgence. With dieting in decline (see the Weight Watchers case below), consumers allow themselves a treat, an indulgent treat. Baileys recognized and capitalized on this trend; this market is dynamic.

Second, Baileys identified products that could be sold all year and be consumed during different parts of the day. Baileys' licensees support the brand with marketing at times other than holidays, giving the brand an active voice and interacting with consumers at other times of the year. For example, Baileys licensed coffee creamers are used in the morning and throughout the year.

Third, Baileys licensed products stay true to the brand's core flavor profile. Baileys doesn't simply allow licensees to use its logo, but tightly controls how the flavor shows up in the licensed products. Baileys insists that it's not just an Irish cream flavor, but that it's Baileys unique Irish cream flavor. Baileys has sensory panels that are populated by food scientists who taste every product before it is allowed to go to market. But Baileys does not just react to a licensee's proposed taste; Baileys also coaches its licensees on how to achieve the taste—what ingredients can be used and what ingredients will interfere with the taste. So the products have a real authenticity to them. Baileys understands that its licensed products must meet consumers' quality and performance expectations of the brand.

And finally, unlike many alcohol brands licensing their marks, Baileys is not in the licensing business with the objective of selling liquids to its licensees (i.e., selling the raw alcohol), although the liquid concentrate is used by many licensees. For Baileys, the goal is not about generating liquid revenue, but about making the right strategic choices and controlling the taste of the product.

These tactics all contribute to the success of the Baileys licensing program.

Building Brand Awareness and Reinforcing Brand Values

Brands generally rely on direct communication with consumers to build awareness and reinforce values—a television commercial that speaks to the brand's high quality and trust, a targeted social media campaign, an influener, an experiential event. And these are all effective tools and paths used to engage with consumers. Licensing, also a path, offers the opportunity to build awareness and reinforce values in other, often in more authentic and unexpected ways. Licensed products allow marketers to reach consumers with a genuine communications tool—a new product—increasing the impact of the messages they want to communicate and the consumer brand engagement they seek, reinforcing the brand's values.

As the following example demonstrates, with Febreze, P&G came up with an ingenious way to take advantage of this licensing benefit.

Febreze

Febreze is one of P&G's big billion-dollar brands. As a leader in the air care category, it competes with brands such as Glade and Air Wick. It is an air refresher and is the #1 fabric refresher with a majority of the market share. What really makes Febreze special, however, is its technology. It has been the pioneer in odor elimination. Febreze doesn't just mask odor (like some of its competitors), but actually eliminates odor. Accordingly, the two main equities of the brand are *odor elimination* and *scent.*

Febreze products include pump and aerosol sprays, automobile vent clips, candles, plug-in air freshener devices, and tabletop devices. Febreze is sold broadly, largely in the mass, food, and drug channels.

The brand is actively marketed by P&G with annual multi-million-dollar media plans, including TV, consumer print, digital, as well as in-store promotions. The marketing objective of Febreze is all about delivering the message that Febreze eliminates unpleasant odors and replaces them with light, fresh scents.

How can licensing support this brand message and reinforce the brand values of Febreze while also building brand awareness? The solution is surprisingly obvious: Identify products that are associated with a displeasing scent and determine whether the equities of Febreze can be used to communicate a message that those products produce a more acceptable, indeed fragrant, scent.

The brand determined that this strategy, in some product categories, is most effective when the licensed products are not stand-alone Febreze-branded products, but rather famous brands in their own right that can benefit from a Febreze co-branded message to the consumer. In this message, the equities of odor elimination and freshness deliver a benefit and feature to the product marketed under the primary brand (sort of like "Intel Inside"). Co-branded products are two brands taking advantage of the other's equities and bringing newness and a point of differentiation to a product. Consider famous branded products that, inherently, have an unacceptable scent and could benefit from an association with Febreze. The message to the consumer is on the packaging that features the easily recognizable Febreze logo.[2]

---

2. P&G has licensing programs for many of its brands, including Febreze. P&G is ranked #23 in "Top 150 Global Licensors." *Id.*

Fresh Step, a well-known brand of cat litter marketed by Clorox, licensed the Febreze brand to clearly communicate odor elimination and freshness in the product. Ditto Glad trash bags featuring Febreze freshness; carpet care products such as vacuum bags and filters, extractor solutions, spot and stain trigger sprays, deodorizing powder; and home décor candles (not co-branded). These are all products licensed by P&G, generally co-branded with the famous brand in the category (e.g., Glad trash bags,) or sometimes not (e.g., home décor candles). (See Figure 4 in the photo insert.) Most of these products are known for unacceptable smells (e.g., trash bags when they are full), whereas others are known for smelling nice (e.g., candles). All of these products are found in retail channels where the consumer also finds the core Febreze product—mass, food, and drug. And there are some additional channels in which the licensed products extend, such as pet stores and hardware stores, where the core brand may not be sold.

Again, the Febreze licensing brand strategy has other benefits, such as the one just noted—extending the brand to new channels of distribution in addition to reaching new consumers and educating them about brand values. But here's the takeaway from how Febreze built brand awareness and reinforced brand values: P&G wanted to emphasize the "odor elimination" equity of Febreze, which really distinguishes the brand from its competitors who simply "smell nice" (also an equity of Febreze). It looked for categories where odor elimination is important to consumers. And, importantly, instead of competing with the strong leaders in those categories by licensing the brand as a stand-alone brand in the category, Febreze joined them as a licensed co-brand. Keep in mind that Febreze also needs to be careful not to be associated with negative scents in a way that would tarnish the brand. The co-brand, with Febreze "freshness," was a smart way to avoid that from happening. And let's not forget the benefit to the other brand in this licensing equation. Glad is able to ride the coattails of Febreze by informing consumers that unacceptable odors are eliminated with this product. It's a win for both brands, which should always be the case in a co-branding licensing arrangement.

Reaching New Consumers and Educating Them About the Brand

Some brands are so pervasive and have such broad distribution that they feel as if they have reached just about everyone they can reach through their advertising and retail presence, or they are struggling to help consumers understand the brand beyond the common perception of the brand (and perhaps misconceptions). Licensing is capable of going beyond the reach of traditional advertising and retail distribution to expand audiences, and it can expand consumers' vision of the brand in innovative ways. Energizer demonstrates how to do this with licensing. It's not just about batteries!

Energizer

With this brand, its history is illuminating. In the 1890s, The National Carbon Company offered the first commercially available battery in the United States, pioneering the personal, portable power category. Shortly thereafter, an enterprising inventor, Conrad Hubert, connected a battery to an electric light to create a handheld lantern, now known as a flashlight. And in 1905, Hubert founded the American Ever Ready Company. The Eveready battery was characterized by many innovations over the years (e.g., the first 9-volt battery, miniature batteries, and alkaline batteries) and became a trusted value brand for consumers worldwide. The Energizer brand was introduced in 1980 as a premium line of batteries for high-tech, high-drain devices. The famous Energizer Bunny was born in 1989 and just ten years later was named to *Ad Age*'s list of the Top Ten Brand Icons of the twentieth century. As we all know, the Energizer Bunny is a symbol of endurance, representing the Energizer brand's core promise of "long lasting." In fact, the Energizer Bunny was added to the *Oxford English Dictionary* in 2006, defined as "a persistent or indefatigable person or phenomenon"—admirable equities for a battery brand.

In 1990, Energizer introduced the world's first AA lithium battery and first on-battery tester. And from 2012–2016, Energizer introduced the first battery made, in part, with recycled batteries, technology that protects devices from battery leaks, and longer-lasting lithium batteries.

What all of this history teaches us is that the company has always tried to be a leader in innovation and technology and to determine what consumers might need in their batteries, often even before the consumers knew.

With that history in mind, the consistent equities of the Energizer brand are clear:

- Long Lasting—It's all about run time when it comes to batteries.
- Quality—Consistency and low in-device leakage.
- Reliable—Works in any condition.
- Power—Supplies the power necessary for all kinds of devices.
- Innovation—In technology and in doing the right thing.
- Batteries—Of course!

All of this has made the Energizer brand alternate between the #1 and #2 battery brand (depending on the precise product) in the world,[3] sold in over 140 countries. The brand, of course, has a very diverse and broad channel and customer base, sold across many retail channels and often in more than one location in a single store.

The brand, however, wants to be recognized as more than just a battery brand. It wants to be considered a brand that delivers *Power* and *Light* and products that use power in a very *Reliable* and often *Innovative* way. A brand that delivers solutions to consumers where energy, technology, and freedom intersect.[4]

---

3. Combined Value Share Data, Nielsen Global Track, 2017.
4. www.energizer.com.

To deliver this message, the company has used licensing, reaching new and loyal consumers and educating them about the broader meaning of the Energizer brand. The Energizer brand has been successfully licensed for lighting products such as household LED bulbs and solar outdoor lighting; other types of batteries such as automotive and photo batteries; power connecting products such as cables; charging products such as automotive chargers, gaming chargers, portable power, and USB chargers; and pet LED products. Given the ubiquity of the brand at retail, its pervasive advertising and high market share and presence in so many households, it's not so easy to find new consumers and to deliver a message that Energizer is more than just batteries. Although virtually all consumers know the Energizer brand, they don't necessarily think of the brand beyond batteries. These licensed products deliver that message and educate consumers while also retaining loyal consumers and recruiting new ones.

Energizer has used licensing effectively to reach new consumers and to re-educate consumers in general about the brand's meaning. Of course, prospective licensees first had to be persuaded. For example, when potential partners were approached, their first reaction frequently was "But my product doesn't use batteries." These potential partners had to be convinced that the Energizer brand means Power and not just Batteries. Energizer was successful in licensing the brand, for example, for generators (which are gas-driven) and power inverters (which are driven by 12-volt batteries). And with many of these licensed products, the brand found new consumers by targeting men. Battery purchasing has historically skewed slightly female.[5]

One of the tactics that worked well for Energizer (and should be considered by many brands entering licensing) was to target products close to core in categories where there may be more room for expansion in the future. In the camera business, batteries are important and was a natural extension for Energizer licensing. But

5. Energizer is ranked #81 in "Top 150 Global Licensors." *Id.*

once Energizer had a presence in the category with licensed camera batteries, the brand had permission to extend into other photography categories such as flash attachments and tripods and most recently drone accessories. The same tactic worked in the automotive category where Energizer started by licensing power inverters but then was able to extend into headlamp bulbs (with, in addition, more presence at retailers such as Pep Boys and AutoZone). (See Figure 7 in the photo insert.)

Energizer also used licensing to maintain brand presence in categories it once held within its own offerings. The company's leadership realized that it could utilize licensing when a shift in strategic priority meant that a product category needed to be re-evaluated. By quickly converting such categories to licenses, Energizer has been able to maintain a presence on retail shelves and to satisfy their retail customers and consumers alike. An example is night lights, once part of Energizer's own product portfolio but now licensed to a third party. Licensing can be used by brand owners to maintain a presence in a category even when a company's priorities undergo adjustment; it's a common strategy among sophisticated brand licensors.

In short, Energizer has used licensing in a well-thought-out way to educate consumers about the brand's meaning, reach more consumers, and reach them in different aisles of the store.[6]

Strengthening the Relationship with Existing Customers and Increasing Consumer Touchpoints

The bond between consumers and brands is being challenged in our digitally sophisticated world where so much product information is available to consumers (see Chapters 1 and 11). However, that bond can be strengthened in various ways, and one

---

6. Energizer was the star of a great licensing anecdote at the 2018 Consumer Electronics Show in Las Vegas, one of the largest annual tradeshows in the United States. The central hall suffered a blackout in the middle of the day. One of the most popular booths during the blackout was that of Energizer licensee Jasco, which was showcasing its Energizer battery-operated emergency backup lights! Let there be light!

of the most effective is through licensing, even for brands with an already enviable number of brand loyalists. People come to think more highly of Coca-Cola not just because of advertising that tells them what a great product it is, but because of ancillary messages delivered by the brand—Coca-Cola sponsors Little League across the United States with associated signage, it features a famous singer in concert, it supports numerous charitable organizations— things consumers value but unrelated to the actual beverage product. Subtly or not so subtly, the brand touchpoints increase and the brand relationship becomes tighter. Creating additional touchpoints and stronger relationships can be a challenging benefit, but as we'll see from the Weight Watchers story that follows, it's achievable.

Weight Watchers

The weight management marketplace has been experiencing seismic shifts over the past decade or so. For many years, it was all about dieting as the means to lose weight. Consumers were flooded with diet plans, each one professing to have the new answer to losing weight. More recently, however, consumers moved away from dieting and became more focused on nutrition and healthy eating as a weight loss and management exercise (to say nothing about the technology and gadgets now available to monitor all of this). Weight Watchers, founded in 1963 with gatherings of women concerned about their weight, was not only about dieting but also about changing habits and sharing stories and being with other people at meetings who cared and understood.

Today's younger consumers are drawn to brands that offer an experience (see Chapter 12). And from its earliest days, Weight Watchers was in many respects an early adopter of the branded experience and still emphasizes the experiential component of the brand.

The brand has grown in size, geographic reach, and services offered. Today Weight Watchers presents itself less as a diet plan and more as a lifestyle-change program. Weight Watchers remains one of the dominant brand names in the category and is a brand worth examining in the context of licensing, which it has used aggressively to, among other things, increase consumer touchpoints.

An overweight 214-pound housewife from Queens, New York, Jean Nidetch, was desperate to lose weight. It was mid-1961. She had spent years following all sorts of diets, with no real results, certainly not any lasting results. So she attended a free diet clinic sponsored by the New York City Board of Health. She lost some weight but couldn't keep herself motivated. She decided to invite a handful of overweight friends to her house to talk about being overweight and confess some of their eating habits that contributed to their weight gains. They shared their food obsessions (Jean's was cookies). The friends started gathering at Jean's house each week, and soon she was cramming 40 people into her living room. They all lost weight. Word spread. What these women soon realized was that it wasn't just about dieting; rather, as noted earlier, it also was about changing habits, sharing stories, and being with other people who cared and understood. Jean started setting up meetings at other people's homes. Soon she would move to a business location. Those early meetings were the beginning of the weight loss and management brand Weight Watchers—a brand that offered no products, just a service; an experiential brand.

Although the Weight Watchers Food Plan became the centerpiece of the diet, the secret sauce was the psychological benefits reaped by members—meetings, journaling, diets with goals that could be met, motivational speakers, magazines, and books.

Under the Weight Watchers plan, you can eat anything you want. Every food is assigned points, and you need to stay within your maximum daily points. The program is called SmartPoints (formerly PointsPlus). Nutritious, low-calorie food has low points; junk food has high points. Members are assigned daily points based on their gender, weight, and activity level. And you are allowed some flexibility from day to day to account for how you eat on different days and different occasions. You figure out what to eat—just stay within your weekly point allowance. Exercise is also emphasized in the program. And data shows that it works. In addition to the meetings, there are a variety of other support mechanisms, including personal coaching, an online plan and community, a magazine, and a content-rich website.

Estimated annual revenue for the weight loss market in 2016 was $66 billion, with almost 100 million Americans on diets at any particular moment.[7] Weight Watchers is a giant of the industry, leading all of its competitors (e.g., Nutrisystem and Jenny Craig) in the weight loss program business. The industry, however, has been in transition, and Weight Watchers has struggled to keep up. People have criticized the company's food plan, claiming that it allows consumers to eat a significant amount of bad food. To make matters worse, the company now must compete with fitness and health apps as well as gadgets such as Fitbit and the Apple Watch. And the company must contend with younger generations who view the brand as old-fashioned. In 2011, Weight Watchers was worth $6.2 billion; in 2015, that number dropped to $400 million.[8] However, in 2015, Oprah Winfrey acquired 10 percent of the company,[9] became a minority owner with a board seat, and started promoting the brand on television, on Twitter, and elsewhere. Although the company had a difficult 2016 with competitors gaining share, Weight Watchers surged ahead with significant growth in 2016 and 2017 with increased earnings, significantly more subscriptions and memberships, and members staying in the program longer.[10] Undoubtedly, Oprah Winfrey's involvement has helped.

---

7. *The U.S. Weight Loss & Diet Control Market* (14th edition), Marketdata Enterprises.
8. "Holistic or Horrifying? Not Everyone Loves Weight Watcher's New Program," by Caitlin Gibson, *The Washington Post*, December 24, 2015.
9. In March 2018, Winfrey sold about 25% of her stake for a significant profit of about eight times what she paid.
10. "The Oprah Effect Is Stronger Than Ever at Weight Watchers," by Nathaniel Meyersohn, @CNNMoneyInvest, November 7, 2017.

Despite the brand's ups and downs, the equities today remain the same as when Jean Nidetch founded the company in the early 1960s:

- Empathy
- Rapport
- Mutual understanding
- Healthy living
- Weight loss and weight control
- Let people eat what they want
- Diet without pain
- Enjoy the food you eat

Weight Watchers is basically a service and experiential business. It provides online services to its members, as well as group meetings and coaching. Members get customized diet programs based on the point system and a great deal of support should they choose to avail themselves of those support offerings. Weight Watchers reported 1.1 million meeting subscribers around the world in 2016 who attended approximately 32,000 meetings and 1.5 million active online subscribers.[11]

Licensing became one of the tools Weight Watchers turned to in order to strengthen the relationship it already had with its customers (its members), as well as a mechanism to interact with those customers at new and different touchpoints. Morover, licensing is reaching new consumers who never signed on to the program but are intrigued.

Licensing also allowed Weight Watchers to offer products to consumers that would help them succeed with the program and make it easier for them to follow it.

The licensed products include scales and dining restaurant menus (e.g., Applebee's) as well as food products, including baked goods, bread, yogurt, chilled meats, cheese, ice cream, and ready-

---

11. www.weightwatchersinternational.com.

to-eat meals, all featuring SmartPoints on the packaging. Licensed products have been available at ShopRite, Price Chopper, Walmart, Safeway, Publix, and Kroger, among other retailers, in the United States. Notice, too, that all of the products align with many of the brand equities.

As of 2013, in the United States alone, Weight Watchers offered 400 SKUs of licensed products in 15 categories. In the United Kingdom, the offering was 240 SKUs in 44 categories. And licensed products can be found in other European countries as well as in Australia and New Zealand. The company estimated that retail sales of Weight Watchers licensed products in 2016 was $1.6 billion (a decline of over $1 billion since the estimate in 2014).[12]

Although this chapter is about the benefits of licensing, be aware that at times, benefits have costs. Licensing has been such an effective tool and revenue generator for Weight Watchers that it may have obscured its purpose for developing licensed products in the first place. Its focus on another benefit of licensing—*generating new revenue streams with minimal upfront investment*—may have led the company to put its brand on too many products. By offering consumers all sorts of sugar-free and points-emblazoned sweets and desserts, which they also aggressively sell on their website and at their meetings, are they tarnishing their image? Are they encouraging the opposite of what they want to encourage— unhealthy living? Are they risking their reputation? Licensing has helped the company strengthen customer relationships and increased touchpoints as well as revenue, but at what cost? Stay on strategy. Licensing can be a double-edged sword. For Weight Watchers and every company that embarks upon ambitious licensing programs, the lesson is to keep track of the benefits versus the costs. Monitoring and assessing licensing programs regularly will help marketers maintain the correct benefits and minimize the costs. (See Chapter 6 for more on the risks of licensing.)

---

12. Weight Watchers is ranked #36 in "Top 150 Global Licensors." *Id.*

Extending into New Channels of Distribution

Often, well-known brands are sold in a very specific channel of distribution. Weight Watchers was a company that was once solely known as a brand that provided a service, an experience. Consumers of the brand went to Weight Watchers meetings or met with a Weight Watchers coach. But the company wanted to extend its reach to consumers in different ways, so the brand was licensed for food items that are available in the grocery aisle, a new distribution channel for the brand.

Brands are always seeking new ways to reach consumers, and there are many more paths to delivering a brand message to consumers today (see Chapter 12). That's what marketing is all about—reaching new consumers and inviting them to participate with the brand by purchasing a product or a service. But licensing offers an organic tool for brands to branch out into new distribution channels. Sometimes a "new channel" is just a different aisle of the store where the core product is already sold. Black & Decker makes and sells power tools, the company's core product, that are sold in the power tool aisle at Walmart, for example, whereas Black & Decker–licensed small kitchen appliances are sold in the home appliance aisle of the same store as well as at other retailers where the power tools might not be available. And all of the Black & Decker products, both core products and licensed products, are seamlessly featured together on Walmart.com. In this way, Black & Decker reaches consumers, perhaps consumers of the power tools or perhaps new participants in the brand, in different ways and at different locations and presents a much broader opportunity for consumer engagement and connections. (See Figure 5 in the photo insert.)

Licensed products in different channels are also a way to engage new consumers with the brand, consumers who would not otherwise be engaged with it. Caterpillar makes large earth moving equipment. Not many of us need to go out and purchase a Caterpillar asphalt paver or a multi terrain loader. But we very well might purchase Cat clothing, footwear, or accessories. And we usually find those licensed products at entirely different retail channels than the ones that carry the core Caterpillar products.

Following is a good example of a brand using licensing to enter new distribution channels—Briggs & Stratton.

Briggs & Stratton

Briggs & Stratton is primarily a manufacturer of small engines. Although it makes branded products that are sold to consumers, its main business is supplying engines to other companies for the branded products of those companies, and indeed, Briggs & Stratton is chosen by eight out of 10 leading power equipment brands in the United States for its power equipment.

Founded in 1908 to service the rapidly growing automotive industry, today the company is the world's largest producer of gas engines for lawn mowers, snow blowers, portable generators, pressure washers, and other outdoor power equipment. The vision of the brand, according to CEO Todd Teske, ". . . is to be the global leader of supplying power for use on power equipment, and to be a relevant supplier of high value powered products and service solutions designed to make work easier and improve lives." The brand equities with which licensed products must align are:

- Durable and Dependable
- Easy to Start, Run, and Maintain
- Tried and True, Known
- Responsible, Innovative, and Intuitive
- Small Engines

And yet for all of its fame, Briggs & Stratton is known primarily as a brand that is inside other branded products—the engine inside all sorts of outdoor power equipment. Generally the products that incorporate Briggs & Stratton engines are available at outdoor power equipment dealers and at retailers such as The Home Depot, Lowe's, and Sears. Because the brand is so famous and reliable, other brands frequently feature the Briggs & Stratton brand name on their products as a sign of quality. Both consumers and retail buyers are aware of and trust the brand. Consumers of products using Briggs & Stratton engines are generally men who own homes and work in the yard.

In 2001, the company determined that it wanted to reach consumers with new Briggs & Stratton–branded products in new distribution channels. The goal: Briggs & Stratton wanted more consumers to choose and use the brand, driving more brand loyalty and awareness. Using licensing as its tool, the company now has Briggs & Stratton–branded engine oil, fuel containers, premium fuel, lead acid replacement batteries, garden and air hoses, electric- and gas-powered air compressors, air-conditioning tools and accessories, and work gloves, among other products. (See Figure 6 in the photo insert.) These licensed Briggs & Stratton–branded products are available at retailers such as Lowe's, Tractor Supply, Walmart, AutoZone, The Home Depot, and Costco. Besides succeeding in developing fully branded products for consumers that are logically associated with the equities of the brand, Briggs & Stratton also is reaching consumers in new distribution channels (or different aisles of stores where the engines are sold as part of other branded products) and burnishing the reputation and breadth of the brand's meaning, through licensing.[13]

Reaching consumers with the brand message through licensed products is frequently the goal. However, developing the right channel strategy for licensed products is not as easy as it may seem. Generally, upscale brands should have their licensed products sold only in upscale channels with the exception of products that are sold only at mass. Conversely, mass products cannot demand that their licensed products be featured in the upstairs channel.

By way of illustration, just because a brand is a premium priced brand doesn't necessarily mean that the licensed products belong solely in premium channels. Some products are generally sold only

---

13. Briggs & Stratten is ranked #95 in "Top 150 Global Licensors." *Id.*

in the mass channel; therefore, if that category was targeted for the licensing program by a premium brand, the mass channel would need to be acceptable; otherwise, the brand should abandon the potential category entirely. For example, if DeWalt, a premium tool brand, were to license sunglasses, those products would belong in upscale sunglass specialty and department stores. However, if that same premium brand were to license DeWalt toy tools for children, they would need to be sold at Walmart and Target, the mass channel, because that's where toys are sold. An upscale restaurant brand or food brand seeking to license the brand for frozen foods or ice cream, for example, would likely have to accept the big supermarket chains where the volume is meaningful and where frozen foods and ice cream are largely sold.

Sometimes channel strategy and reality simply don't meet, in which case the risks and rewards need to be balanced. Jaguar is an upscale luxury automobile. Product categories that come to mind are casual apparel, small leather goods, and apparel accessories to be sold in the upstairs channel of distribution (consistent with the brand image). That makes sense. However, department and specialty stores, particularly in the United States, don't need a Jaguar apparel collection, for example, because they have access to legitimate and well-known designers for those categories. The only channel available to Jaguar in this example would be the mid- or mass market, where designers are less available to the retailers in those channels. So does the reward of a successful apparel program outweigh the risks to the brand image? The answer is "no," and Jaguar has not proceeded in those categories in the United States. That being said, if Jaguar wanted to launch a fragrance in the United States, it would probably accept the drugstore channel because so many prestige fragrances are sold in that channel (often in locked displays).

If you want to capitalize on this particular benefit—extending into new channels of distribution—these are the questions to answer:

1. Is the channel strategy (both offline and online) for the licensed products aligned with the channel strategy for the brand's core product?
2. Are there channels for the licensed product that, although not aligned with the core product channel strategy, are still acceptable because that's the only channel where those products are sold or where similarly situated brands are sold?
3. Is there a specialty store channel strategy that makes sense?
4. Is there a retail exclusive channel strategy that makes sense? (See Chapter 7.)
5. How will the products be displayed or featured in a particular channel?

Generating New Revenue Streams with Minimal Upfront Investment

Let's talk about money. How many marketing disciplines can you name that generate revenue directly? Put another way, when do companies *get paid* for marketing their brands? Licensing is a marketing tool that generates revenue for the brand owner in the form of royalties or fees or both. Royalties are paid by the licensee and generally are based on wholesale sales, or if the licensee is a retailer, they could be paid as a percentage of retail sales. Fee arrangements can also be negotiated. Royalties can be based on all sorts of sales transactions—for example, the manufacturer's sale of the licensed product to the retailer, the retailer's sale to the consumer, ticket sales at a licensed event, meal checks at a licensed restaurant, and transactions on a licensed credit card. And advance payments are frequently made when contracts are signed to be credited against future royalties. In short, money is coming in, not just going out as a marketing expenditure.

However, to generate revenue through licensing, the brand owner must make certain investments; it's not just "free" money. Before the revenue starts flowing, expenses must be incurred by the brand owner, including research, design guidelines, artwork, talent, travel, and legal. But eventually, even with a mildly successful program, the revenues will catch up and exceed the expenses. Licensing revenues are, or should be, in a mature program, high-margin revenues.

Whereas taking a strategic approach to licensing mandates looking beyond revenue to the six other benefits, revenue is still a significant consideration, particularly for in-house licensing professionals who have budgets to achieve. However, for most large, successful brands, the actual royalty revenue will often be a very small percentage of their topline revenue. Nevertheless, licensing revenue can easily be meaningful using other financial metrics. Here's an example. Let's say that an iconic, large brand, company ABC, has a successful licensing program generating $1 billion in retail sales of licensed product. Those retail sales are driven by $500 million in wholesale sales.[14] If we use an average royalty rate of 7 percent (royalty rates can range from one or 2 percent on the low side up to 15 percent on the very high side), these sales will generate $35 million in royalties (i.e., 7% × $500 million)—and with very high margins. But to a company that is generating $10, $30, or $80 billion in top-line revenue, this doesn't make a significant contribution to the bottom line. Of course, it's also a question of how a company uses this revenue. Is it just deposited in the company's general account? Does it go toward the brand marketing budget? Is it used to further promote the licensing program and licensed products? Perhaps it's used to support a charitable endeavor. In other words, the royalty revenue can become meaningful, even at a multibillion-dollar company, depending on its

---

14. In the 2017 "Top 150 Global Licensors," the following was reported, by way of example as retail sales of licensed product: General Motors, $3.5 billion; Procter & Gamble, $3 billion; Caterpillar, $2.82 billion; The Hershey Company, $1.5 billion; Stanley Black & Decker, $1.5 billion; The Coca-Cola Company, $1 billion; Volkswagen, $280 million; and John Deere, $260 million. *Id.* One cautionary note: Most brand licensors do not have access to precise retail sales of licensed product. Therefore, the sales reported are generally estimates based on royalty payments.

use. The U.S. Army, for example, by federal law uses licensing revenue from its approximately 240 licensees to support its program (the Army Trademark Licensing Program) with the net revenue devoted to U.S. Army Morale, Welfare and Recreation programs.

There is another important way to look at royalty revenue, and this is where it becomes really meaningful. Let's say that the core product of company ABC above generates a 15 percent profit margin. And let's say that licensing revenue is operating at a 75 percent margin (which is not unreasonable), or approximately $26.25 million to the bottom line (using the earlier example). How much sales of the core product are required to generate $26.25 million? It will take $175 million of core product sales by company ABC to generate $26.25 million for the bottom line. Now the numbers start grabbing attention. And let's not forget the other benefits that redound to company ABC from those in-market licensed products.

Royalties also provide another underappreciated but increasingly meaningful benefit: the data that comprehensive royalty reports provide. Consider the following data that can be gleaned from a substantive royalty report:

- Learn in what countries the products are selling. A brand owner may not know how popular its brand is in a particular country. Now the brand owner gets data about that without having to conduct any market research.
- Learn gaps in rights that have been granted. Frequently licensees don't use all of the product or territorial rights they have been granted.
- Find evidence that products are being sold in countries or channels of distribution in which they should not be sold.
- Learn which SKUs of licensed products are selling well or poorly and in what parts of the country or in what countries.
- Learn in what distribution channels the licensed product is selling and sometimes which retailers, brick-and-mortar as well as online retailers.

The license agreement between the brand owner and the licensee determines the information contained in a royalty report. Clearly, the more information required, the more useful data there will be (see Chapter 5).

Nonetheless, some famous companies still seek a purely financial benefit from their licensing programs; here is one example.

Westinghouse

Westinghouse was founded by George Westinghouse in 1886. For much of its history, it competed with General Electric in the power generation industry and in long-distance power transmission and high-voltage AC transmission. The company encountered severe financial challenges in the early 1990s due to bad loans made by its lending division. During the 1990s, Westinghouse shed most of its traditional industrial operations and made acquisitions in the broadcast industry, including CBS in 1995. The company name was changed to CBS Corporation in 1997, and in 1998, CBS established a brand-dedicated licensing division named Westinghouse Licensing Corporation. Today Westinghouse does not make any products. Everything is licensed, including lightbulbs, decorative lighting, ceiling fans, portable generators, small and large motors, pressure washers, small home appliances, air conditioners, and night lights. Products that Westinghouse once made are now licensed, as are others. Certainly, Westinghouse is attempting to use the trademark in as many product categories as possible that will resonate with the consumer in terms of its legacy. However, given that licensing is the sole source of revenue for the brand owner, generating revenues may be the priority for this brand's licensing program.[15]

In conclusion, revenue should *never* be the sole objective for any brand to enter licensing. If that's the case, mistakes will be made. Opportunities that might be revenue-rich but detrimental to the brand will likely be pursued. The product might be wrong,

---

15. Westinghouse is ranked #16 in "Top 150 Global Licensors." *Id.*

the quality might be inconsistent, the brand promise might be damaged, the distribution might be wrong, a targeted demographic group might become disenchanted with the brand, or a number of other considerations will take a back seat to the revenue opportunity. Moreover, in general, purely revenue-generating opportunities won't be proactively pursued in accordance with a brand strategy, but will be coming in over the transom to which the brand owner is simply reacting. This is a recipe for disaster. Brands can be severely damaged when revenue is the overriding goal. This remains true in the Westinghouse example above, where the brand is no longer in the market except for licensed product, where revenue is very important inasmuch as licensing is the sole source of revenue. Still, the brand can't make mistakes that will damage the brand meaning. If it does, the rest of the licensing program is at risk as the brand gets damaged and declines. Be careful not to be blinded by a ringing cash register!

Protect the Brand via Broad Trademark Registrations

Licensing has a legal benefit that many brand owners don't even realize, certainly not the marketing professionals (although the lawyers certainly know). Licensing allows a brand owner to register its famous (or not-so-famous) brand name and logo (its "Marks") in classifications outside of the core product category. The International Trademark/Servicemark Classes contains 46 classes of goods and services. Generally, when registering a Mark, companies register in the class that corresponds to the goods the company is selling (or the services it is offering). For example, The Coca-Cola Company registers in Class 32, which covers non-alcoholic beverages.

Understand, however, that registrations (either federal or state) are not necessary in order to gain ownership in a Mark. One's right to use a Mark is conditioned on being the first to use the Mark in commerce for one or more categories. Registering a Mark in the United States will neither automatically permit a company to use it, nor will a failure to register a Mark by itself prohibit a company from using it. Registration does serve valuable purposes, however. It serves as formal notice to the world that the Mark is owned in the category in which it is registered. There are other procedural and legal advantages that won't be discussed here. Suffice it to say, registration is a good thing to do and licensing is a route to registration in other classes outside the core category.

But whether or not the Mark is registered, one must actually and continuously use the Mark in commerce in the relevant category in order to secure, finalize, and retain ownership rights (there is also an "intent to use" provision that allows a brand owner to file a registration before actual use commences). If a category is never used or if an owner abandons its use in a category, third parties may claim rights to use the Mark in the unused or dormant categories (see the discussion about White Cloud in Chapter 9). For purposes of our discussion of benefits, what's important is that in the United States, the required "use" can be by the owner of the Mark itself or by an authorized licensee.

Famous brands can use licensing to protect themselves without having registrations in multiple categories.

The Coca-Cola Company

Although the brand "Coca-Cola" has been registered for a long time in Class 32, if it were to be used in other product categories without permission, the company could stop such usage based on the fame of the brand and the dilution of the Mark by the unauthorized user. But what if The Coca-Cola Company wanted the extra benefit and protection of registrations in other classes of goods? Given that it makes only beverages, how would it accomplish that? As mentioned in Chapter 2, in the late 1970s and early 1980s, the Legal Department at The Coca-Cola Company decided that's exactly what they wanted to do and licensing was the solution. The Legal Department determined in which classes the company should register its Marks and directed the Marketing Department to seek licensees in those categories of goods.

But there's a bit of a twist here. To qualify for registration, the brand must be used in a trademark capacity, not just as decoration. In other words, in the case of The Coca-Cola Company, the product must be "Coca-Cola brand" towels or sweatshirts or glassware. This is as opposed to products whose origin is another company's name simply featuring Coca-Cola (or any other brand's) iconography as decoration. And The Coca-Cola Company was very strict about this. Neck labels on shirts featured the words *Coca-Cola brand*, not another company (i.e., the manufacturer) name although the name of the licensee can be featured on the product (or the packaging) as the authorized licensee of the brand owner. As a result, The Coca-Cola Company has been able to register its Marks successfully in classes outside of Class 32 because of its use on licensed products.

The Coca-Cola Company has and continues to use licensing effectively to protect and strengthen an already exceptionally strong trademark and brand with use in other categories and registrations. It's a benefit of licensing that should not be overlooked.

Harley-Davidson Motor Company
Harley-Davidson Motor Company realized the value of this protective benefit the hard way. In the late 1970s/early 1980s, Harley-Davidson was not doing particularly well as a motorcycle brand due to competition from less expensive imports, but the brand remained extremely popular. It was so popular that there was a good deal of unauthorized use on all sorts of products of the Harley-Davidson brand and its associated slogans, artwork, and icons (i.e., counterfeiting). Although Harley-Davidson was successful in stopping many of these unauthorized uses, the warning bells were ringing—the company was allowing too much unauthorized use to continue. Harley-Davidson needed to begin using the Mark in other categories outside of motorcycles and related accessories. Licensing was part of the solution to the trademark challenge that Harley-Davidson faced at that time. The program

was officially launched in the early 1980s, and the legal benefits were among the reasons Harley-Davidson launched its licensing program. Today the Harley-Davidson licensing program is among the most successful in the United States and is expanding overseas. And the Marks of Harley-Davidson are aggressively protected, with the help of licensing.

Many brand owners don't think about trademark protection as a goal of their licensing program, but it is a benefit, even for famous and well-protected brands. And this is a fairly easy benefit of which to take advantage. Brand owners need to communicate with their intellectual property counsel. They must be given the opportunity to recommend categories where there may be legal reasons to license the brand (provided that those categories are brand-aligned). They must have the elements that they need, and the products must be designed in such a way to enable registrations, if that's important to the company. Sometimes it won't be realistic because the brand is being used simply as decoration. But make certain that stakeholders are being consulted. And always make sure that you (and not someone else) have rights to the trademark in the targeted category before licensing in that category (ownership doesn't require registration, as mentioned earlier). This is particularly true when U.S. brands are licensing their marks overseas (see Chapter 10).

CHAPTER FOUR

A Strategy, Not a Tactic

You would be surprised to learn how many companies fail to think strategically about licensing opportunities. It's surprising on many levels, not the least of which is that licensing is about allowing a third party to use a company's most valuable asset—its brand. When licensing is reactive and tactical, it's implemented in a vacuum—objectives haven't been determined, product categories haven't been vetted, and management is not in place to oversee the process, among other shortcomings.

Would an iconic brand launch a new product without well-thought-out goals and a strategy to achieve them? Probably not. Organizations will fail to take advantage of licensing's marketing power if they treat it as a tactic, as an opportunity to which they can react. Being proactive, strategic, creative, and managerial (i.e., operationally ready) are requirements for any licensing program. To meet these requirements, best practices and processes must be used to develop an executable strategy. Those as well as illustrative examples will be discussed next.

Every company has its variables that need to be addressed in a licensing plan, but certain elements are critical to establishing and then executing any plan, including:

- Licensing Goals and Objectives
- Description of Brand Equities
- Licensing Positioning Statement
- Target Consumers
- Distribution Channel Strategy
- Market Dynamics and Trends
- Product Categories and Competitive Landscape
- Design Guidelines
- Financial Forecasting
- Program Management and Support (addressed in the next chapter)

The majority of these elements involve a comprehensive evaluation of the brand—the identification of the brand's equities and the brand's marketing and licensing goals. Without a clear understanding of the brand's equities and what the brand wants to accomplish through licensing, a company is essentially licensing in the dark. Following a comprehensive analysis of equities, goals, and objectives with which licensing must be aligned, the brand needs to evaluate appropriate product categories through a variety of filters—for example, distribution channel strategy and market dynamics—before finalizing the plan and moving forward. And to ensure that licensed products meet the quality expectations of the brand, the company must be operationally ready to handle oversight of product design, development, and production.

Several brands will be used as examples in this chapter— mostly Cracker Barrel Old Country Store and content provider HGTV,[1] although other examples will be sprinkled throughout.

---

1. Cracker Barrel is not listed in "Top 150 Global Licensors." HGTV is ranked #69 in "Top 150 Global Licensors." *Id.* HGTV HOME has won five prestigious LIMA International Licensing Excellence Awards that are awarded each year in various categories by the industry following voting by the membership and expert judges. Two of the awards, in 2013 and 2014, were for the Sherwin-Williams program (paint), one in 2014 was for the Bassett program (furniture), and HGTV HOME won Best Corporate Brand Program of the Year in 2013 and 2015. For more on HGTV HOME in the context of retail exclusives, see Chapter 7.

First, here's a a brief history on both brands that will provide some context for the discussion of the nine strategic elements (the tenth to be covered in the next chapter) listed above and that follow.

Cracker Barrel Old Country Store

While working in the family gasoline business in the 1960s, Dan Evins began thinking of ways to better meet the needs of people who lived life on the road traveling through the small towns of America. This community of travelers was growing on the heels of the rapid development of the interstate highway system in the United States. He thought about the "country store" he remembered from his childhood, a place to buy all sorts of gifts and candy as well as a place to get simple home-cooked food. Evins also believed that the "real flavor of America" was being pushed out by the rise of fast-food restaurants. So in 1969, Evins opened the first Cracker Barrel Old Country Store in Lebanon, Tennessee, next to the interstate. His vision was to replicate the country store experience and offer quality home-cooked, simple food at reasonable prices. Evins was right about the opportunity. The company went public in 1981, and by the end of 2017, Cracker Barrel owned and operated close to 650 stores in 44 states with annual revenue just under $3 billion. Cracker Barrel serves breakfast (all day), lunch, and dinner and prides itself on its "Southern hospitality," friendly home-away-from home and good "home-cooked" food, and memorable guest experience. The restaurants are housed alongside a unique retail shop offering apparel, food items, home goods, and seasonal items. Sales in the store exceed industry averages for that type of retail location.

Cracker Barrel claims many loyal customers and has been consistently praised for excelling in meeting customer expectations; for providing an experience, not just a meal; and for remaining committed to a consistent business strategy. But over time, the competition in the "casual, sit-down, family restaurant" segment became fierce with other strong players entering the market, such as Applebee's, Olive Garden, Chili's, Red Lobster, Outback Steakhouse, Denny's, Ruby Tuesday, International House of Pancakes (IHOP), and TGI Fridays. With suburbs expanding and neighborhoods getting closer to highway intersections, travelers had many more options from which to choose. In or about 2009, Cracker Barrel was facing the challenge of how to grow the venture. Licensing was under consideration.

HGTV

The idea for HGTV grew from the personal experience of Ken Lowe, HGTV's founder. A self-styled amateur architect moving up the broadcast management ladder at Scripps Networks Interactive, he and his family moved around a lot and found themselves building or repairing houses. There were many home improvement challenges, and he wondered why there wasn't more television programming that could help people like him. In 1992, he pitched the idea to Scripps by drawing a house in which every room from attic to basement was its own TV show. Scripps liked the idea and agreed to invest $75 million. Two years later, in May 1994, Scripps announced its plans to launch Home & Garden Television (the original name of HGTV). With cable television experiencing explosive growth, HGTV was one of more than 100 networks introduced to the industry that year. HGTV is only one of three announced that year to reach full distribution in the United States.

In December 1994, Home & Garden Television went on the air as a new cable network devoted to all things related to the home and garden. The goal of the network was to use experts on whom viewers could rely "to inform, inspire and lead them to better buying and how-to decisions."[2] A year after launch, HGTV was available in 10 million households. In 2016, the network was available in close to 100 million households and in all television markets in the United States. HGTV.com was launched in 1996 and by 2016

---

2. Burton Jablin, then-HGTV president and at the time of publication president of Scripps Networks.

had 370 million visits and 3.3 billion page views.[3] In addition, in a joint venture with Hearst, *HGTV Magazine* was launched in 2012 and today remains one of the most successful magazines in the home category.

Licensing Goals and Objectives

Every company that engages in marketing its brand has a clear understanding of what its marketing is designed to accomplish. The objectives of any licensing program must align with some or all of these marketing goals, and those licensing objectives must be clearly stated and understood. Whether a licensing strategy is, for example, designed to reach a new group of customers or redefine the meaning of the brand or make inroads in global markets, a company must establish the objectives in advance and use them to inform all licensing activities and decision making. Without such an understanding, the company runs the risk of creating licensing that is not aligned with the brand's overall marketing goals.

For example, to address the issues of fewer people dining outside of their homes and increased competition, Cracker Barrel's marketing goals included raising awareness of the brand to drive people to the restaurants. To that end, its licensing program strategy was focused on identifying opportunities that would build credibility for branded products that could be sold outside of the Cracker Barrel retail stores. Doing this would create brand awareness, drive traffic to Cracker Barrel stores and restaurants, and generate new revenue streams.

As for HGTV, the alignment challenge was somewhat different. This brand is a content network featuring cable television and digital and print content. The brand doesn't sell products; it offers a service—television and digital programming that is entertaining and offers advice and design and style solutions, with advertising being the source of revenue. Entering the consumer product space would be an entirely different business model for HGTV.

---

3. Data provided by HGTV.

With that in mind, the goals and objectives of HGTV would need to be largely specific to licensing but at the same time aligned with its corporate goals, such as:

1. To extend the HGTV brand beyond broadcast television and the Web to provide new touchpoints for existing and new viewers, further driving loyalty to the brand.
2. To maintain relevancy with HGTV's core viewers and attract new ones.
3. To increase viewership through the sale and exposure of licensed product.
4. To reinforce HGTV's positioning as a solutions-based, style-driven brand for the home.
5. To leverage consumer brand permission (supported by research) to enter categories that are prevalent within HGTV's programming.
6. To leverage existing advertiser relationships with both manufacturers and retailers and build the enterprise value of the brand.

The two examples above illustrate how to articulate very clear objectives for a licensing program. Any brand considering licensing must state exactly what the brand wants to accomplish with the licensing program at the very inception of this process. These words are very important and must be crafted carefully. They must align with overall brand objectives. And, importantly, all stakeholders within the company must support and understand these goals. Internal consensus on the licensing goals should precede any other strategy development. Once that is accomplished, don't file the document away somewhere. Instead, pin it on your bulletin board so that you look at it every day. Every decision you make must be in furtherance of these goals. A successful licensing program is not about luck or about relying on licensees to be successful. It's about being loyal to the goals and making the right decisions based on those criteria. Otherwise, you run the risk of your program going off the rails.

Description of Brand Equities

Every brand has equities that are widely associated with the brand and resonate with consumers. Indeed, in many respects, that's what the definition of a brand is—a set of descriptive words widely shared by consumers. Think of the words that come to mind quickly and obviously. Coca-Cola, for example, is a soda beverage, it's brown and fizzy, it comes in cans and bottles, and its brand colors are mostly red and white. It's also associated with sports and music and fun moments. People who are familiar with Coca-Cola will probably use most of these words to describe the brand. Similarly, Black & Decker is about tools, power, getting a job done, ease of use, black and orange. Brands represent commonly shared words, phrases, feelings, and emotions. The previous chapter listed the brand equities of a few of the brands examined—Energizer, Weight Watchers, Febreze, and Baileys.

When developing a licensing strategy, list and vet the equities (or attributes) of the brand and select those equities that are most relevant to the licensing process and translatable to licensed products. If a proposed product category does not connect to a good number of the brand equities, it's likely a wrong category to consider. Generally, think about identifying anywhere from six to 10 brand equities that can be associated with licensed products. And never mind about words such as *trust* and *quality*. They are too general in meaning to be of use here and generally apply to most brands (it's what makes a brand a brand). Be specific so that you can create a clear link between brand equities and licensed products. Then, when a consumer sees a licensed product, he or she will make an immediate and unconscious connection to the core brand based on identifying key attributes the consumer associates with the brand.

For Cracker Barrel, the brand equities that should apply to licensed products are:

- Country
- Authentic
- Road Travel
- Nostalgic
- Unique
- Family
- Good Country Cooking
- Hospitable

And for HGTV, the relevant brand equities to consider for licensing are:

- Solutions
- Inspiring
- Style and Design
- Home and Garden
- Trusted Expert
- Accessible
- Passionate

Licensed products must represent at least some if not all of the equities identified for each of these brands. If they don't, there will likely be a disconnect between the licensed product and the brand.

Licensing Position Statement

A Position Statement articulates what the licensing program should deliver to the brand in order to be considered successful, usually in one or two clear sentences. When writing this statement, make sure it is an expression of consensus among all of the stakeholders at the company. Surprisingly often, companies embark upon a licensing program without senior management's buy-in. In that case, when license agreements are ready to be signed, when licensed products are submitted for approval, or (and this is the worst-case scenario) when licensed products appear on retail shelves, the C-Suite is surprised. The most senior-level executives at any organization must be aware of and embrace the strategy to develop a licensing program, before implementation. No surprises. This is mission critical not only for the brand but also for the benefit of the licensees that are developing and bringing products to market.

Similarly, use the licensing position statement to secure consensus from the salespeople. Imagine the following hypothetical example: A Stanley salesperson is meeting with his buyer at The Home Depot, who he has known and with whom he has done business for years, and the buyer remarks how much he likes the Stanley work gloves on display in Aisle 6. That should be good news for the Stanley salesperson, right? But there's a problem. The work gloves are licensed products sold to the store by a licensee, and the Stanley salesperson didn't know about it. He didn't even know Stanley had licensed a manufacturer to make and distribute work gloves. He didn't even know that Stanley had a licensing program. So instead of thanking the buyer, the salesperson says, "What work gloves? We don't have work gloves." Not a good moment (again, a hypothetical moment for illustrative purposes).

This statement is an opportunity to inform and engage stakeholders about the licensing program. Make sure that all of the stakeholders within a company are aware that a licensing program is commencing and have visibility to the plan, beginning with the Position Statement. Other stakeholders might include account executives at a brand, the legal department, quality assurance people, and perhaps the board and outside agencies. Communicate intentions and progress. This is all part of "Operational Readiness," which will be discussed in more detail in the next chapter.

Following is a Cracker Barrel licensing Position Statement:

Cracker Barrel Old Country Store will provide a broad range of food and non-food products from a trusted, authentic source that celebrates the brand's country heritage and delivers the quality and honest value for which Cracker Barrel is known. The strategic distribution of these reliable, familiar products will both deepen Cracker Barrel's unique connection with its loyal guests as well as reach new consumers who have not yet experienced this popular American brand.

Let's take apart this Position Statement and look at its elements. First, the general product category is defined—*food and non-food products* (admittedly very broad but directionally clear that both food and nonfood products can be considered). Second, key word equities are used throughout the Statement—*authentic, country heritage, honest, value, reliable, American.* Third, distribution is mentioned. And, finally, the consumer target is stated—*loyal guests and new consumers of the brand.* That's a lot to pack into two sentences, but it's all there for stakeholders at Cracker Barrel to see and understand. Yes, it's very general and covers a broad swath, but the overriding goals are there. And more details are available in the plan for whoever is interested. It's the beginning of a stream of regular and ongoing communication within the organization about the licensing program as it unfolds.

The same evaluation can be done for HGTV, where the Position Statement might read as follows:

> The HGTV brand will be used as an umbrella to leverage its core solutions and style equities to offer innovative, design-driven, functional products that solve problems and educate consumers to simplify the purchasing decision.

Again, let's look at the key elements of that single sentence. First, the Position Statement reflects keeping HGTV top-of-mind for consumers (viewers). Second, it leverages the broadcaster's solutions and style equities to deliver products with a unique selling proposition. Third, it leverages the various design aesthetics and styles presented in HGTV programming.[4]

---

4. Actually, this last point proved challenging. Given that so many design aesthetics are

Target Consumers

No licensing strategy is complete without a full understanding of what consumers the brand owner wants to reach with its licensed products. And don't assume it's the same consumer the company reaches with its core products. Perhaps the core products are sold primarily to men and the licensing program is designed to focus more on women. Black & Decker sells its power tools primarily to a male consumer, but the licensed small domestic appliances are sold primarily to women, a target of the brand. Or the brand may want to reach a consumer in a specific region of the country or age group or a specific ethnicity. Or, and this is most likely, the brand wants to further engage its already loyal consumer base and, at the same time, reach new consumers who don't generally use or engage with the brand. By identifying the target consumers, you are better able to guide the licensing program's channel and retail distribution strategy as well as the product categories selected.

In the case of Cracker Barrel, a brand that is available at its fewer than 650 restaurant/store locations at highway intersections, the brand considered licensing as a tool to reach a fairly wide-ranging group of consumers—some familiar with the brand, some users of the brand, and some unfamiliar with the brand.

Making licensed products available at potentially thousands of other store locations where the target consumer shops could have broad ramifications for the brand in terms of reaching consumers at new touchpoints.

Similarly, HGTV's viewers are more female than male and most of the licensed products are targeted at that female consumer. However, in the case of HGTV, the only way the brand reaches its target audience is through its television, digital, and print vehicles. There were no products, as noted earlier. So by choosing the right

---

presented on the various programs broadcast by HGTV as well as HGTV's digital and print formats, the network needed to develop an overall design point of view to inspire licensed products. As a result, several design themes were created by HGTV specifically for use in the licensing program. Even a special logo had to be developed for the licensing program, a stylized version of "HGTV HOME."

licensed products targeted at the right consumer, HGTV will reach its loyal viewers, occasional viewers, and others in entirely new ways and consumer touchpoints—the aisles of brick-and-mortar stores, and online and digital retail.

Product Categories and Competitive Landscape

To create an effective licensing strategy, you must, by definition, look "outside" the brand's core products to appropriate product categories that will align with the strategic elements described above and resonate with consumers. Selecting product categories will likely lead to success (if they are the right ones) or failure (if they are wrong). Don't waste time pursuing categories that might sound great but really don't make sense for your brand because they are not consistent with the strategic elements described above. Introducing the wrong product category to the market can actually damage the brand instead of achieving the desired objectives. And with social media, online peer reviews, and expert opinions readily available, these "wrong" choices can hurt a brand quickly. Invest the attention and research necessary to create a strong list of target product categories and prioritize the most compelling opportunities.

It's okay to start with a broad list. Brainstorm ideas and get them all down on paper. No idea is a bad idea—yet. Look for products that are logically associated with the brand, satisfy the stated goals and objectives, and touch some or all of the identified equities. Then vet the categories identified through a number of filters that will result in a final, smaller list that has the highest likelihood of success. And, by the way, "success" means finding the right partner, developing the right product at the right price, ensuring that quality and performance expectations are met, having the right retail strategy, and then selling through at retail.

Many companies considering licensing are leaders in their core product category (or close to the leader). If you're in a leadership position, be wary of arrogance (or ambition) that prevents you from evaluating the category objectively. Leadership in your core category doesn't mean that you can enter any other category successfully. Other companies in those categories are already category leaders with whom you must compete. At the time Coca-Cola Clothes made such a big splash (see Chapter 2), I was called by one of the most famous pizza chains in the United States. It was convinced that it was second only to Coca-Cola in terms of fame and that it could successfully license its brand for a line of fashion apparel, the same way Coca-Cola had done. The effort never panned out. The company let its unrealistic perception of its brand cloud its judgment.

A company can winnow its list based on consumer perceptions of its brand and which categories might diminish perceptions. For example, Cracker Barrel might not want to consider frozen meals (a category that could easily be on the initial list) because it runs counter to Cracker Barrel's "fresh" and "made from scratch" associations. Or it may not want to offer "center-of-plate" (i.e., entree) meals due to a concern that matching the quality and taste of the same restaurant offering would be challenging. Perhaps HGTV doesn't want to compete with its advertisers. Although every company should establish filters specific to its brand, some general filters (with brand-specific subfilters) work for just about any brand. Here are four general filters you can use, each in the form of a question:

1. Does a compelling strategic fit exist between the brand and the potential product category?
2. Is there a relevant consumer proposition for the product category being considered?
3. Are the market dynamics favorable for the brand to enter this particular category?
4. Are the financials attractive enough to justify devoting the resources necessary to enter the category and maintain a presence in the category?

For example, in narrowing the initial list of product categories, Cracker Barrel should focus on products that resonate with current and future Cracker Barrel guests, such as:

1. Categories that embody the Cracker Barrel core equities and drive consumers to the restaurants.
2. Products already found in Cracker Barrel stores and restaurants.
3. Food ingredients, as opposed to complete meals, to allow Cracker Barrel to enhance, instead of replace, home-cooked meals.

And Cracker Barrel should avoid categories that do not fit the brand, such as:

1. Categories with limited connection to the store, restaurant, or core consumer.
2. Food categories that run counter to Cracker Barrel's "fresh" and "made from scratch" associations, such as frozen meals, as stated above.
3. Center-of-plate meals due to concerns that matching the quality and taste of the same restaurant offering would be challenging.

HGTV could be licensing the brand in categories where there is "white space" and that fit with HGTV's program goals and, of course, brand equities. In evaluating categories, in addition to the general filters identified above, HGTV should ask the following questions about each product category considered:

1. Will the category help build loyalty with current viewers and attract new ones?
2. Will the HGTV brand bring a meaningful voice to the product, offering solutions in a category that is often confusing to consumers?

3. Is the category crowded with multiple strong product lines?
4. Does the category have one or more dominant branded leaders, or is there an absence of an authoritative voice?
5. Is the category a strategic anchor that will build consumer permission and allow the program to stretch into further categories?
6. Is there a particular product or merchandising consumer need missing from the category's offerings?

The answers to those questions will drive HGTV to the right product categories and help the brand license and develop products with a selling proposition that is unique to HGTV.

Some of the key categories identified for Cracker Barrel might include baking mix, pancake mix, iced tea, jerky, refrigerated and frozen side dishes, soup, spreads, syrup, cookware, and confections and snacks. For HGTV, categories to consider might include flooring, wallcoverings, paint, furniture, storage and organization, window coverings, lighting, tabletop, and bed and bath.

Once categories are identified, a company must develop a marketing rationale that articulates how the brand can create a competitive, viable point of difference within each industry segment. Before any brand seeks partners in the identified categories, understanding the market dynamics in each category is essential. As we're about to see, these dynamics may cause a seemingly aligned category to drop off the list due to heretofore overlooked market considerations.

Market Dynamics and Trends

The retail "shelves" (both online and offline) aren't empty just waiting for your licensed products. In fact, the shelves are full and something will probably have to move off the shelf to make way for the new licensed product (although it's a bit easier online where floor space isn't a consideration). Retailers probably won't move a successful product off the shelf to make room for something else, even if it sounds like a good idea. Everything that has been done thus far in the plan has been done in a relative vacuum; you can address the earlier factors without worrying about the realities of market conditions in the product categories identified. But can the brand win in those product categories? And further, are there trends in particular categories that should not be ignored and perhaps embraced as you develop your strategy. It's time to look at market dynamics and trends to determine what's happening in the market.

This is a good time to conduct primary research (e.g., collecting new data through sources such as surveys or focus groups) and secondary research (e.g., online research to collect existing data) if you really want to gain some knowledge about consumer permission (primary research), assess the size of the selected product categories, and learn about the category growth rates and other market dynamics (secondary research). Focus groups can help in understanding whether a brand that consumers already use or engage with will be receptive to licensed products and, if so, which ones. This research might also reveal whether consumers believe that licensing could have a negative effect on the brand and if that would alter their current perception of the brand. And finally, the focus groups are likely to disclose where consumers would expect to find licensed products—what distribution channels (online or offline)—and what consumers' product expectations might be.

Don't rely just on secondary research to unearth this data (although it's definitely important). Primary research is relatively inexpensive and can easily be accomplished online, so undertake it to mitigate risks. Further, brand owners conduct consumer research on a regular basis for any number of reasons. It's fairly easy to add a licensing set of questions to your ongoing or regular consumer research activities.

Visit retailers and observe what's on the shelves and scroll through relevant e-commerce sites. These retail audits, at multiple retailers in different channels of distribution and different regions of the country, can provide context for strategy development, including category trends, category fit, competitive intelligence, and price and product positioning. Also, relevant trade shows can be very useful in gaining a better understanding of what's going on in a category, and give you an opportunity to talk informally with executives who work in those categories every day.

Ask the following questions to facilitate strategy development:

1. Have other brands been successfully licensed in this category?
2. Are there market trends or unmet needs in the category upon which the brand can capitalize?
3. Is there room for another brand in this category?
4. Can the brand achieve a meaningful share in the category?
5. Will the financial rewards support long-term revenue goals?
6. Is the category large and growing?

Answering those questions is often as much art as it is science. Yes, it will require some research. But it will also require you to evaluate what you are discovering. Questions that pertain to achieving an acceptable market share in a category or determining what the financial rewards might be are a function of good research, information, and very educated guesswork. Seeing the trends that might affect a category that the brand has already identified or, the flip side, seeing a trend that drives a brand to a new category will take some marketing intuition as well.

It's important to be aware of trends so that brands remain relevant in the culture; engage with consumers where, how, and when they are shopping; and break through the clutter to meet consumers' needs and wants. For example, there's a trend today for socially conscious consumerism. It started with cleaner household products and has moved to "clean" labeling. There's a trend for instant gratification. So many meal delivery services are popping up. Giving consumers an experience is a growing trend, resulting in more pop-up shops, for example. There is a trend for healthy living and nutritional eating and a counterbalancing trend that supports indulgent treats.

Licensing strategies should also address cultural and product trends that are occurring in the licensing marketplace that might impact choices made when developing the strategic plan for a brand. For example, there has been a trend for some time now of restaurants and chefs licensing their brands and names for grocery products. Let's examine this trend, and the related market dynamics, in the context of the Cracker Barrel example.

Cracker Barrel should have been thinking about participating in this trend back in 2010 when it started to recognize the challenges it was facing as a restaurant chain. The "restaurant licensing" trend has capitalized and faced some important market dynamics. For example, consider the frozen meal category, a category that any restaurant thinking about licensing will likely evaluate.

First, the frozen meal category is growing, quality is improving dramatically, and consumer behaviors indicated that frozen meals stood as an attractive growth option for all sorts of brands. Second, consumers were eating at home more often, particularly following the recession in 2008. Third, the competition in the frozen category in particular was stiff with giants in the category that controlled a good portion of the business, such as Nestlé (with Stouffers, which appealed to consumers seeking hearty portion sizes and Lean Cuisine, which met the needs of those looking to monitor calories) and ConAgra (with Healthy Choice for weight control, Banquet for filling meals at a good price, and Marie Callender's for filling meals but with more "restaurant" quality). Fourth, some of these same major food companies were starting to grasp the power of restaurant brands and their ability to generate consumer trial; they became welcoming partners for new restaurant-licensed branded lines of product. Fifth, this trend also disproved the notion that consumers who could purchase restaurant-branded foods at the supermarket would opt to cook those foods at home instead of visiting the restaurant; eating at home and dining out are entirely different occasions. For example, partnering with Nestlé, California Pizza Kitchen launched its frozen foods line that allowed consumers to enjoy "all the flavor of the restaurant, now in your grocer's freezer." Provided that the frozen pizzas delivered on taste and quality, the licensed product was more likely to drive consumers to the restaurants as opposed to discouraging them from visiting the restaurant. These powerful market dynamics contribute to a macro trend that has been evolving for almost two decades.

And this trend is illustrated by many other examples. In 2000, TGI Friday established a partnership with Heinz and offered an initial six-item TGI Friday licensed frozen snack line that included Cheddar & Bacon Potato Skins, Mozzarella Sticks, Chicken and Steak Quesadilla Rolls, and Buffalo and Honey BBQ Chicken Wings. The depth of this program helped TGI Friday pioneer this trend (although it wasn't the first company in the category to establish this type of licensing partnership). Upon the release of the licensed products, Erica Gilbertson, Associate Brand Manager for Heinz, shared the following:

> These new options are a perfect shortcut for creating complete dinners with the same type of robust taste and flavor combinations people have come to know and love from TGI Friday. They are a flavorful and convenient alternative, and a great way to keep dinner exciting and fun, especially on those busy days when you just don't have enough time to enjoy the full restaurant experience.

Read that quote again. You can just hear TGI Friday's goals and objectives between the lines. TGI Friday was taking advantage of both trends in the market as well as dynamics in the frozen food category.

Other restaurant brands, and chefs, have entered the licensed food space (frozen and nonfrozen) as well, including P.F. Chang's (frozen meals for two), Romano's Macaroni Grill (frozen meals), Hooters (frozen meals), Panera Bread (soup), IHOP (pancake mix and syrup), Taco Bell (microwaveable entrees and taco shells), Dunkin' Donuts (whole bean and ground coffee), Wolfgang Puck (soups), Bobby Flay (sauces), and Jamie Oliver (ready-made meals) among others. So for a newcomer to licensing such as Cracker Barrel, although there was plenty of competition in the food category, the market dynamics and trends were generally favorable.

HGTV evaluated market dynamics and trends and identified categories where white space existed and where consumers generally had challenges navigating the category. Consider paint and furniture. Have you ever tried to choose and buy paint colors for your home? All of those color charts and color chips; so many different shades of so many colors. Consumers are challenged and unsure of themselves when purchasing paint and color, often without the help of a decorator. This is white space for a solutions-based paint program for HGTV. Ditto furniture. Consumers often don't have faith in their style choices for what may be a major purchase of something that should last many years. This is another white space where HGTV can offer expertise and guidance to help consumers make choices, confidently. And by the way, with Millennials aging and starting families, more consumers are decorating their first homes, a trend of which HGTV needs to take advantage.

After vetting each category through the market dynamics filters, as illustrated above, a brand owner will have a final list with which to move forward and seek licensing partners. The brand will have a lot of intelligence about what is going on in the market, making partner decisions much more informed and the sales pitch to potential partners much more compelling.

The market, occupied by a multitude of competitors, is a richly woven fabric populated by micro and macro trends; rapidly evolving consumer behaviors, tastes, and needs; and innovation. You need to study the landscape of the categories you have identified to determine how and if your brand can make a statement, how and if you can win. Then articulate that in your strategy.

The final piece is to establish the distribution channel and offline/online strategy for the licensed products you have identified as part of your plan.

Distribution Channel Strategy

Having done primary and secondary research and having examined the market dynamics and relevant trends, you know a great deal about each category—how and where the category is sold at retail, consumer behavior in the category, the competition, and consumer expectations.

Based on this knowledge, you can align distribution channels with the core brand and the licensed product category, leveraging the brand's equities and reaching the target customers where, when, and how they shop. In some categories, leading brands are sold to a wide range of retailers—Energizer and Coca-Cola are examples—and licensed products are likely to follow suit. Other brands such as Baileys are sold in more specialized channels, requiring a more selective assessment of where the licensed products can be sold. High-end luxury brands must be even more careful about licensed product distribution. And some brands have a very particular consumer base, such as Pantone with a mostly professional and business consumer, and need to distribute their licensed products where those consumers are likely to shop.[5]

Consider distribution channel strategy from Cracker Barrel's perspective. Most leading food brands are sold in all grocery and mass channels of distribution, although some brands, of course, are sold in high-end and specialty grocery stores. But for Cracker Barrel to secure a best-in-class licensee and generate meaningful revenue, brand impressions, and consumer touchpoints, its licensed food products must be made available to the entire grocery and mass channels. The only other alternative is to develop an

---

5. In the United States, Pantone licenses products such as journals for Pantone chips, sketch pads, and color cards as well as the popular Color of the Year Mug and note pad blocks. Pantone is much more active licensing its brand in overseas markets, which will be discussed in more detail in Chapter 10.

exclusive partnership with a single large retailer that will devote heavy resources to promoting its exclusive line of Cracker Barrel licensed products.

For HGTV licensed products, the natural channel for the brand is home improvement stores, specialty stores, catalogs, and online retailers. Again, retail exclusives turned out to be an appropriate strategy for HGTV licensed products. (For more on retail exclusives see Chapter 7.)

The channel will, of course, dictate the pricing of the products, but even within channels, "good, better, and best" pricing strategies are options. Each brand must consider what pricing strategy best suits its brand and its licensing strategy in general. As for Cracker Barrel, it should seek products that are priced consistently with the core brand—a fair price and a great value. In other words, those products should have accessible price points across retail channels (i.e., prices that appeal throughout the Cracker Barrel guest segmentations). Artisinal grocery products at high-end specialty stores would be the wrong channel strategy for Cracker Barrel.

Financial Forecasting

This might be a little more art than science, but it is doable as long as you accept that there are many caveats and variables. Any brand considering licensing wants to understand what the potential revenues might be, whether costs will be covered, whether there will be a profit, whether the time and resources devoted to the enterprise will be worth the financial return. Although revenues should not be the primary objective for embarking upon a licensing program, a forecast should be included in every plan, probably for the first three years. How is this accomplished? The best forecasting method is to follow the steps listed below. Keep in mind that depending on the category, there are rarely any significant sales in the first year of a contract. It takes awhile to design and develop product, with all of the required brand approvals, and then get it to market. A three-year projection is more likely looking at sales for years two, three, and four of a license agreement. And remember, these projections are designed to help guide your Strategic Plan. Once you start soliciting potential licensees, they will provide you with more informed sales projections.

1. Identify the market size of the potential category.
2. Estimate the share of market that you hope to achieve (resulting in sales projections).
3. Assume an appropriate royalty rate and apply it to the sales projection.
4. Factor in a growth percentage for each subsequent year.
5. Develop low, high, and medium projections for each potential category.

By addressing distribution channels and the seven other factors, you connect all of the dots. Rather than approaching licensing reactively and in a vacuum, you have created a well-thought-out, integrated approach.[6] You are now almost ready to begin the

---

6. *Cracker Barrel—Results.* In 2012, Cracker Barrel signed a license agreement with John Morrell Food Group, a subsidiary of Smithfield Foods, Inc., for food products to be sold in the grocery channel, such as ham, bacon, lunch meats, glazes, jerky, and sausage. But there was a roadblock. Kraft Foods Group already sold products in the grocery channel under its own Cracker Barrel brand (primarily cheese products), and the licensed products from Cracker Barrel Old Country Store sold outside their restaurants would, Kraft asserted, encroach on Kraft's trademark in the grocery channel. Kraft won a preliminary injunction against Cracker Barrel Old Country Store, and the products were not allowed to be launched. In late 2013, Kraft and Cracker Barrel Old Country Store reached an agreement that allowed the licensed products to be launched under the brand CB Old Country Store.

HGTV—Results. Beginning in 2011, HGTV launched a collection of licensed products for the home that translated the rich content, inspirational voice, and great style that consumers liked about the network. Over the next several years, HGTV HOME included products such as paint and paint accessories, wallpaper, flooring, furniture (indoor and outdoor), lighting (indoor and outdoor), and decorative fabrics, among others. In particular, the paint program by Sherwin-Williams (an existing HGTV advertiser) was initially launched exclusively at Sherwin-Williams stores; then a second exclusive program was developed specifically for Lowe's (also an existing HGTV advertiser). The paint program offers not only paint colors and proprietary paint formulations but also an entire merchandising system that helps consumers choose a color palette for various rooms of their home to match their decorating style. Similarly, the indoor furniture collection by Bassett Furniture is sold at top furniture retailers, but also at

search for the right licensee partners. But before embarking on that portion of the process, you have one more task. Referring back to the list of ten factors at the beginning of the chapter, you may recall that the last item on the list—Program Management and Support—will be addressed in the following chapter. This is a critical topic: What does it mean to "manage a licensing program"? Does your company have the infrastructure in place to manage the licensing program, and does it have a clear vision for how it will support its licensees once they are on board?

Bassett Furniture stores, which feature the "HGTV HOME Design Studio only at Bassett," offering home makeovers by design experts who consult with consumers in the stores and in their homes to develop the right custom furniture choices. HGTV HOME products successfully communicate a unique, fresh design aesthetic while providing consumers with expert "know-how" through packaging, marketing, and POS materials, all consistent with the goals and objectives HGTV had stated for its licensing program.

CHAPTER 5

Managing and Supporting a Licensing Program

If you are taking a strategic approach to licensing, you will be (*must* be) involved and engaged through the entire process. This means that after you have signed a license agreement with a licensee, the work doesn't stop—you don't stop paying attention. Instead, you become an active manager of the relationship and support the licensee.

As you may have noticed, this step was listed under the strategic actions of the last chapter. But it is such an important subject—and so often a neglected or misunderstood responsibility—that it requires its own chapter. Being diligent about managing and supporting a program can be the difference between good and great results, failure or success. This process begins before a license agreement is even signed.

Let's start with a discussion of the information you will need to gather during the potential licensee due diligence phase in order to later support and manage the program consistently and effectively.

Preliminary Information Goes a Long Way

Ideally, brand owners begin collecting information before a license agreement is signed. Assembling data about targeted product categories and implementing other information-gathering tactics are part of the strategic approach. A great deal of useful knowledge about how to manage licensees can be obtained during the prospective licensee vetting process. The term *due diligence* applies here. Brand owners often fail to vet their licensees rigorously, an early and important step in the process that helps mitigate risks and avoid problems later on (a subject that is discussed in greater detail in the next chapter).

But before risks can be mitigated, information must be gathered. Keep in mind that you might be collecting this type of information from several potential licensees in the same category before you make a decision on which company might be best. Here's a critical caveat: Be wary of potential partners who intend to use your famous brand as a way to enter a new market in which the partner has never sold a product. Also watch out for those who want to use your famous brand to develop a product or product line that is entirely new to the partner. Your famous brand should not be used as a guinea pig by a potential licensee. If this is the case, your due diligence process should reveal it.

During this process, brand owners discover information that will help drive success of the licensed product and can use this information when managing the licensee and holding the licensee accountable for its actions in support of the brand license. When conducting due diligence, the following preliminary questions are important when vetting potential licensees:

1. What are the company financials, including current and historical operating results, credit information, and business growth potential? Also, is there other historical information about the company that may be useful?

2. What is the management strategy, including long-term vision, staffing and infrastructure, licensing experience, partnership mentality, and brand insight?

3. What is the organizational structure? This includes identifying key individuals within the organization who have important roles and roles that might affect the licensee's performance. In particular, sales and marketing infrastructure will be important, including sales network, retail distribution channels appropriate to the licensed brand (both offline and online), advertising, promotion and public relations capabilities, market research capabilities, and customer support.

4. What are the potential licensee's manufacturing capabilities? These include expertise in the product categories relevant to the proposed license agreement; commitment to innovation if that's important to the brand owner; health and safety standards and protocols; distribution systems and product failure and repair capabilities, if relevant; location of factories; and factory oversight. Will information about manufacturing, supply chain, and cost transparency be available to consumers? That last question is increasingly important to younger consumers as well as retailers (see Chapter 12).

5. What are the research and design capabilities, including historical product development success and technical expertise?

6. What is the company's quality philosophy—in particular, the company's demonstrated commitment to quality in its product and its adherence to local laws and regulations? Is there an in-house quality control department? An outside testing laboratory? Is there a recall procedure in place?

7. Is there any legal and regulatory history, including product liability claims, recalls, and regulatory violations?

8. What is the product development process, and does the prospective partner use consumer research as part of this process?

9. Does the company have a social responsibility program in place at all facilities manufacturing the product? If so, what are the details? Brand owners often have their own policies on social responsibility and require their licensees to adhere to those policies. The Mary-Kate and Ashley case study in Chapter 8 is illustrative. In that example, the brand owner insisted, contractually, that licensees adhere to Walmart's very strict social responsibility guidelines and attached those guidelines to the license agreements.

10. What does the product category and the competitive landscape in which the product is sold look like? Some of this research will have been done by the brand owner as part of the strategy development, but prospective licensees are always a good source for this information, either confirming what you already know or modifying what you thought you knew about the category. Licensees know a great deal about their categories (e.g., size, sales by channel, trends, and margins). Licensees can often identify their own category market share and list their top competitors along with their market share. They also have a good sense of where there is "white space" in their category. The HGTV case study in the previous chapter is a good example of this point. Although HGTV conducted substantial research in the paint and furniture categories, it learned a great deal more about these categories from then-potential licensees Sherwin-Williams and Bassett Furniture.

That's a significant amount of information to get from a licensee *prior* to signing a license agreement during the vetting stage, and every potential partnership will have different requirements. But this is the kind of information that will be of great help in the brand owner's decision-making process. The last thing any brand owner wants is a surprise down the road when course corrections are more difficult to make. Get all of the information you can up front and, if necessary and possible, incorporate relevant requirements into the license agreement.

Adopt Best Management Practices Post-Signing

Let's assume that the brand owner has completed the due diligence, gathered the necessary data, negotiated business terms, and signed a contract. The match has been made; the licensee is now ready to begin product design and develop its go-to-market plan. This is not a time to sit back, relax, and look forward to royalty revenue. That would be a big mistake. Don't forget that you have allowed a third party to use your most valuable asset—your trademark, name, and logo—on a product it will be developing, manufacturing, and selling to retailers or directly to consumers. There is no way to avoid a loss of control, but that loss of control can be mitigated with management. The success of a strategic licensing program is directly proportional to the continuous involvement of the brand owner. From inception, the program must be managed, and "management" includes supporting the licensees. This doesn't necessarily mean spending a great deal of money; a brand owner can do plenty without incurring a significant expense to help a licensee develop and sell great product. It's a partnership. Both the brand licensor and the licensee must understand and embrace that relationship.

To that end, the following discussion provides suggestions for best practices—highly effective tactics for a wide variety of brand licensors and licensees. You do not have to implement all of them. Instead, select the ones that will work best for your organization.

Introductory Information
Send new licensees a packet of information about how they can comply with the license agreement and detail the brand owner's expectations.

It is essentially a "welcome kit". The licensee can refer to this document throughout the relationship but particularly during the early stages of the partnership. Licensees may have their own tools for managing their business, but brand owners must emphasize that the licensees are to use the tools the brand owner provides. This will be particularly important when the brand owner has multiple licensees. Accordingly, information, forms, and templates for the licensee to use should be included. It can contain information such as the following:

1. Identification of the contact executives for account management, approvals, finance, and legal.
2. The calendar timing of key deliverables the brand owner expects, such as royalty reports, forecasts, business plans, and other contractual requirements.
3. A description of the product approval process.
4. How to access packaging, brand, and design guidelines.
5. How and when to provide sales and royalty projections.
6. The contents of royalty reports and the process for making payments.
7. Regular update expectations.
8. Contents of business plans.
9. Tools and support that can be provided by the brand owner and are available to the licensee (e.g., online support through the brand owner's website and social media activations, industrial design, technical innovations, joint sales opportunities, and retail connections).

Although brand owners must let licensees drive their own businesses, a brand owner's management and support can increase the success of a program significantly and ensure that the brand owner's goals and objectives for using licensing as a tool in the first place are being achieved. To provide this management and support, I will focus on five managerial areas: (1) Business plans, (2) Brand immersion, (3) Product development,

(5) Licensor support, and (5) Business reporting.[1] Let's look at each area in detail.

Business Plans

Brand owners must insist that licensees create a business plan for the launch, marketing, and ongoing sales of the licensed product.

This might sound like a natural step that any brand owner would take before launching a product, but don't assume that your licensee develops business plans in the regular course of its business. Many, although not all, licensees are privately owned companies, and many of them operate more out of instinct and past business experience than by a formal and well-thought-out business plan. Be prepared to help your licensee or prospective licensee develop the business plan. Many brand owners require such a plan before entering into a license agreement (that's certainly a way to gain confidence that you are choosing the right partner); others don't ask for the plan until after the agreement is signed (it can actually be required under the agreement). Admittedly, you will be asking a prospective licensee to do a good amount of work, so you should assess the circumstances before making this request pre-signing. If the brand is very famous and the opportunity is significant, the brand owner will likely have more success requesting the business plan prior to negotiating the business terms and signing an agreement. To a large extent, it's a question of leverage. So before or after the license agreement is signed depends on the circumstances and the quality of the prospective licensee as well as the power of the brand owner. If it's a big, risky opportunity, then you should ask for the business plan before the license agreement is signed. If you collect useful information before a license agreement is signed, some of that information might be relevant to the agreement negotiation or be included in the agreement. In

---

1. Companies that meet a certain revenue threshold can join SPLiCE, a trade organization of licensors devoted to sharing best practices. Members include brand licensors such as The Coca-Cola Company, Crayola, General Motors, Harley-Davidson Motor Company, Stanley Black & Decker, and Meredith Corp.

any event, the license agreement can require that a business plan be submitted for approval prior to any product being developed or approved for sale. You will find that having a licensee-submitted business plan will facilitate your management of the licensee throughout the term of the agreement.

Keep in mind that business plans are dynamic documents. They should be updated by the licensee on a regular (probably annual) basis and reviewed with the brand owner. Annual business plan meetings are a best practice and a good time to review progress against the last plan and discuss updates to the plan for the year ahead. It helps if you can provide licensees with a template business plan rather than rely on licensees to use their own format. A template ensures that the brand owner will receive all of the information that it needs and wants.

You may have acquired some or all of the information you need through the due diligence process described above. If so, great. If not, then here's what to ask for:

1. **Company Data:** Structure of the company, public/private, principal owners, years in business, number of employees, description of primary business, size in dollars, year established, locations, manufacturing locations, territory coverage, management team.
2. **Financial Background:** Bank references, credit references, product liability insurance, bankruptcy filings, annual sales.
3. **Legal and Regulatory History:** Claims, pending issues, recalls.
4. **Competitive Market Share:** Market share by manufacturer, by retailer, and by category; market trends; historical market growth/decline rates; licensee competitive advantage; consumer needs in the category; competitive brands.
5. **Retail Distribution:** Licensee's top retailers with percent of sales at each; retail expansion opportunities with the

license; overall retailer strategy, both offline and online strategy.

6. **Licensing Strategy:** Licensee's objective in obtaining the license, strategies to support the use of the brand (e.g., positioning at retail).

7. **Licensed Products:** Overview of product category including product mix currently offered, features/benefits of the licensed product, warranty and quality data, retail price position, cost and pricing structure, anticipated introductory date.

8. **Competitive Comparison:** Winning against the competition in the category, territory, distribution channel; positioning against the competition; price point; resources for research and development to ensure competitive superiority.

9. **Manufacturing Plan:** Product development process and manufacturing operations, location of manufacturing plants (identified as owned or third-party manufacturers), quality control protocols, social responsibility requirements.

10. **Quality Assessment:** Product certifications, product warranties, customer service capabilities, return data and processes.

11. **Sales and Distribution Plan:** Explanation of how products will be sold (i.e., own sales force, manufacturer reps, other); size of sales force; distribution capabilities by region of the United States and outside the United States; location of distribution centers; digital strategy, if any.

12. **Marketing Plan:** Launch plan for licensed products; promotional media used to support the licensed products (e.g., magazines, other press, point-of-purchase, direct mail, catalogs, social media, and trade shows); annual marketing budget for licensed products; marketing agencies used by the licensee; design capabilities.

13. **Sales Projections** (a topic that should be addressed during the licensee vetting stage): Total company sales and sales of similar product for most recent year and prior year, projected sales of licensed product (three years), proposed annual minimum guarantee of royalties to the licensor, proposed royalty rate. Proposals for business terms can be included in the business plan or in a license application the brand owner might develop for prospective licensees.
14. **Brand Opportunity:** What the licensee is trying to accomplish with the licensed brand with what consumer demographic and with what retailers.

The license agreement is ready to be signed, or perhaps it was already signed, with some of this information collected before signing and some after the signing. Either way, with all of this information, the brand owner is much better equipped to confirm that the licensee and the proposed licensed products, distribution, marketing, target consumer, and all other factors are aligned with the strategy you developed. All of the dots must keep connecting. This will facilitate the hard work, which is about to begin. You must be involved in every stage of product development through the time the product appears on retail shelves. Some licensors call this the "critical path"; others, the "licensing process"; still others, all sorts of names. I'll call it the "licensing journey": the journey from product development to the final three feet—from the retail shelf (or screen) to the consumers' hands.

Brand Immersion
Although you get to know your licensee during the vetting and negotiation stages, brand owners and licensees need to learn to work together as partners. The licensor/licensee relationship should not be an adversarial one. Sadly, many licensors and licensees treat it that way. Your goal is a true partnership with aligned interests and goals—to sell the most brand-right, well-designed,

competitive product in the category to the right consumer in the most appropriate channels of distribution. The licensee achieves sales and revenues, and the licensor achieves those objectives that it articulated in its strategy as well as generates revenues. Managed properly, the relationship can work seamlessly.

Schedule a "brand immersion" shortly after the license agreement is signed—it's a way to provide the licensee with the information about the brand that it will need to succeed. Immersion means a comprehensive study of the brand led by key brand stakeholders and teams, preferably at the brand owner's offices. Of course, the number of attendees from the brand owner will depend somewhat on the importance of the particular license. However, some level of brand immersion is necessary for any licensee.

At this meeting, the brand owner and licensee introduce their key players to each other (in person, by phone, or by document) and determine who is responsible for what. And by inserting a strong confidentiality provision in the license agreement, the brand owner can share brand history, goals, objectives, opportunities, and challenges as well as upcoming product releases, marketing plans, and competitive analysis. Brand owners can communicate to the licensee how the brand is organized. You might also include a core product review, if relevant. Sales data, trends, and demographics are other types of information to consider sharing.

This is a time to educate the licensee about all things brand. Without this education, the licensee can easily take off in a wrong direction and waste everyone's valuable time.

This is also a time for the licensee to further educate the brand on the licensee's category, opportunities, challenges, competitors, retailers, trends, and anything else relevant to making sure the brand owner understands the licensed product category, which is outside of its core product offering. Retail distribution and key account information can be shared by both licensor and licensee.

Hold a meeting to review the approval process for product and collateral materials, the legal process regarding trademarks, intellectual property notices and other issues, how counterfeiting and infringements are handled by the brand owner when brought to its attention, the royalty reporting process, and other steps in the licensing journey with which the licensee must comply (more on those steps later in this chapter). At this meeting, share documents and templates for the licensee to use—royalty reports, annual business reviews, and retail status reports, for example. Every licensor will have its own unique requirements.

This is also a meeting where the brand owner can explain how the licensee accesses various support mechanisms provided by the brand owner, such as the brand's website, the social media strategy, the sales force, retail contacts, trade shows, and creative and industrial design departments. There might be a style/design guide review. And it's a good time to talk about product expectations, including price points and innovation, as well as other product equities. Finally, review how you expect communications in general to flow. In short, everything should be shared and discussed up front if things are to run smoothly.

Product Development

Play an active role in reviewing and approving all product and collateral materials. Every stage in the licensing journey is very important, but approvals are vital. This is about what the product will actually end up being when it reaches the marketplace—its design, product features, functionality, quality, and performance.

Licensees are contractually required to submit all product, packaging, web pages, and marketing materials (e.g., advertising, public relations, and collateral materials such as trade show signage and letterhead) to the brand owner for approval (including trademark usage and notices). Generally, submissions are made at various stages of development. For example, with respect to product approvals, the licensee might submit initial design sketches, followed by prototypes, followed by production samples. The brand owner's approval is required at each stage. The earlier you comment on a submission, the more you control the final product; this early involvement also results in less disruption to the product development process. As long as the licensee can follow your directions and comments, each stage of the approval process will build upon the previous one. This will, of course, take resources from the brand owner. Licensees have timetables and usually want to get products to market quickly. Brand owners don't want to throw a wrench in the works and then be blamed for preventing the product from being released on a timely basis, with all sorts of consequences. Conversely, licensees need to respect the demands they are placing on the brand owner for approval—they should be giving the brand owner sufficient time to comment. Either party can be responsible for delays if either is not respectful of the other's needs.

Sometimes brand owners will miss something in the approval process that needs to be corrected later or an approved sample turns out differently when it goes into production. Brand owners need to be diligent about this. Two examples are provided here (without naming the brand owners). A well-known brand owner approved a pre-production sample of a licensed microwave oven. Unfortunately, the production run didn't align with the pre-production approved sample. The letter *L* was dropped from the word *CLOCK*, and the product went to market that way. In another instance, a brand owner approved a collection of baseball style hats featuring logos as well as "fanciful" design elements. Only after the licensed product was available at retail was it discovered that the "fanciful" design elements were actually gang logos.

Not so long ago, licensees would send hard copies of their submissions for licensor approval, and there's nothing wrong with that method. But these days most sophisticated brand licensors use online options. These approval portals facilitate communicating information about the submission, uploading artwork, photos, and renderings; and obtaining licensor approval or disapproval along with comments for resubmission. Importantly, these systems allow for products, associated packaging, and associated collateral materials to all be connected in one record. Of course, actual physical samples (certainly final samples) will always be necessary for the brand owner. There are many moving parts to any approval system, and over time, countless stages of various products, packaging, and collateral materials have been approved, disapproved, or commented upon. The available online systems (or ones brand owners can create and customize) are the best way to maintain all of these records. Often, royalty administration online systems connect to the approval portal to ensure that royalties are being paid for approved products. Prior to the development of online approval systems, lost or misplaced approval/disapproval records plagued virtually every licensing program.

Licensor Support

Without spending a great deal of money, brand owners are often surprised at how much help and support they can provide to their licensees.

For many programs, brand owners can support licensees with decorative or packaging design guidelines and updates. Brands benefit when there are established guidelines for what the products or the packaging might look like. Every brand will already have comprehensive guidelines for how its trademarks can be used and how its packaging should look, and these guidelines are helpful to licensee partners. But more is needed for licensing. The packaging guidelines for Coca-Cola (e.g., the bottle, the can, and the carton) probably won't be all a licensee needs to develop its product or licensed product packaging or meet the brand's design expectations, for that matter. Brand owners should, as appropriate, develop specific licensed product packaging, labeling, hang tags, point-of-sale, and collateral materials guidelines for licensee use. And when licensees are looking for decorative elements for a product, brand owners can create a set of approved graphics for them to use.

Indeed, the most successful programs probably need to go beyond packaging and trademark guidelines, however. What about the product itself? Clearly, some products have no design elements other than trademark guidelines, such as Cracker Barrel pancake syrup and baking mix (although they do have product specifications that Cracker Barrel might want to consider providing to its licensees to ensure quality). But frequently the product itself incorporates design elements. This is certainly true of apparel, but of many other product categories as well. Brands shouldn't always rely just on their licensees to develop their own designs. That's the best way to ensure that products from different licensee partners don't look consistent. Instead, develop those design guidelines independently and ensure consistency across product categories. Licensees will probably need to make modifications based on market needs and dynamics and specialized knowledge of their product categories, but the design guidelines are a good starting point.

HGTV faced a particular design challenge, as mentioned in the previous chapter. First, because HGTV is a broadcast network (i.e., a service, not a product), it had no name or logo or packaging guidelines for a line of products. Those had to be developed specifically for the licensing program. A stylized logo, HGTV HOME, was created as well as packaging guidelines. An entire brand architecture had to be developed specifically for consumer licensed products.

Second, and even more challenging, was the fact that although HGTV as a broadcaster represented expertise, style, and solutions for the home in its television programming, it did not represent any particular design aesthetic. So what exactly would HGTV products look like? What should the furniture look like? What is the style of HGTV? HGTV had to create a design vocabulary and aesthetic for solution and style-based products that would achieve a variety of objectives: defining the look and tone of products, creating a recognizable aesthetic for the HGTV HOME brand, driving differentiation in the marketplace, and so on. HGTV invested in the development of a comprehensive brand architecture of consumer products and seasonal design aesthetics to help guide its licensees.

Your licensees will appreciate these efforts, and it will help sell them on the partnership. It also provides the brand owner with greater control and facilitates the approval process, particularly when the licensee follows the guidelines.

In addition to design guidelines, there are many other ways that brand owners support product development and design. For example, many brand owners have industrial design departments (e.g., Stanley Black & Decker helps a licensee redesign paint sprayers), innovative technologies (e.g., P&G occasionally licenses innovative technology it has developed in addition to its intellectual property), technical expertise or even patents (e.g., brands such as AT&T and Kodak have substantial businesses licensing their technology and patents, often without any trademark license), or ingredient expertise (e.g., spirit brands may allow licensees to use their raw alcohol). Depending on the nature of the specific licensed product, these areas can often be very helpful to licensees as they develop their licensed product.

Brand owners can also help licensees by using their marketing and promotion capabilities. For instance, brand owners can feature licensed products on the brand's website, if not for e-commerce then just to help promote the products. Or a brand may allow licensees to link their websites with the brand's website. Websites of brand owners frequently have a much wider audience than those of their licensees. Licensed products can be featured at a brand owner's tradeshow booth, in its catalogs, and in marketing materials provided to retailers. Brand owners can also support co-promotions on retail floors, online, and in advertising materials. Licensed products can be featured together in on-floor displays at retailers. And brand owners can incorporate licensed products in their social media, digital, and experiential activities to engage with consumers.

For example, retail displays featuring Gain laundry detergent's licensed Gain sponges along with Dawn liquid soap cleaner (two P&G brands) housed together in the same display on the floor of Walmart is a good example of licensor and licensee cooperation for the benefit of both as well as the retailer. The HGTV Design Center at Bassett Furniture stores, discussed in Chapter 4, is another example of a brand owner (in this case, HGTV) and its furniture licensee (Bassett Furniture) working together.

Stanley Black & Decker offers a third example of licensor support for a licensee. Black & Decker developed an end cap for Walmart that featured the brand's handheld and cordless upright vacuums and invited its licensee for corded upright vacuums also to be featured in the display. Black & Decker also developed a Father's Day promotion with Amazon and invited licensees to participate.

Keep licensees informed of brand activities as well as the progress of other licensees. Perhaps you can distribute regular newsletters to all of your licensees containing information about the brand as well as licensee success stories. Licensees want to know which retailers are successfully selling licensed product. If a brand owner has a group of licensees, the brand owner may want to gather them together at least once a year for brand updates, retail education, networking, and collaboration discussions. Some of these "licensee summits" can be held several days in interesting locations, and some are shorter and all business. But licensees usually come away from these meetings with a productive to-do list.

Business Reporting

As mentioned earlier, there are many moving parts in any licensing program, even if there is only one licensee. But the work that must be managed is multiplied exponentially when there are multiple licensees. At the time of publication, Stanley Black & Decker had more than 100 licensees worldwide. P&G works with more than 20 external partners as licensees worldwide. In each instance, that could mean hundreds of products to track, to say nothing of new product development, quarterly royalty reports, marketing, and everything else that goes into building and sustaining a line of licensed products.

If you have multiple licensees, be forewarned. In fact, even if you only have one or two, this advice applies: You must be organized. You must have strict requirements about gathering up-to-date information from your licensees. Otherwise, the licensing program will spin out of control and the risks of something going wrong will increase.

Following are the kinds of information and data that any brand owner should receive regularly throughout the licensor/licensee partnership. Some of the data can be provided weekly via phone, whereas other information can be provided monthly or quarterly in more formal reports. Provide licensees with templates to satisfy formal data requirements. That way data provided by different licensees will be consistent and easily usable. There is power as well as control in the data.

Overwhelmed? Recognize that these lists are very comprehensive, and many licensees will protest (sometimes rightly so) that it's too much work. Every program is different. Some brands have more leverage than others. Some licensees have more leverage than others. This is a dynamic process, and it is a partnership. Brand owners need to be reasonable in what they request, but they also need to make it clear that they expect their partners to be responsive.

The following comprehensive list of information can be shared in a regularly scheduled phone call:

1. **Topline Sales Data.** Talk about sales trends at current accounts. Are they up, down, or flat since the last conversation? What, if anything, can the brand owner do to help? Have there been any changes in distribution strategies? Are there any upcoming retail presentations? Can the brand owner provide any support for those presentations?

2. **Marketing.** Review the up-to-date promotional calendar for both the licensee and the brand owner. Is marketing aligned? Review specific promotions, social media, and consumer marketing activities. How can the brand owner support the licensee?

3. **Licensed Products.** Have there been any consumer inquiries? Are there any new brands or competitors entering the category?

4. **Innovation.** Does the licensee have anything in the works? Have there been any changes to the timeline since the last conversation? Does the brand owner have any new products or features in the works that can be shared with the licensee?

5. **Approvals.** What is the status of pending submissions? Are any new submissions about to be submitted or processed?

6. **Concerns, Challenges, and Issues That Are Specific to Any Licensing Program.** Are there any? If so, what are the solutions?

7. **Expectations.** Is the program meeting both the licensor's and licensee's expectations?

More formal reports can be required monthly, quarterly, or annually (depending on the information requested) and can include the following:

1. Summary of product categories granted in the license agreement and which of those products are in market and the territories where the products are being sold.

2. Sales summary by channel (e.g., mass, club, drug, grocery, midmarket, department stores, and e-commerce) and change compared to a year ago.

3. Royalty summary by product category.

4. Rolling monthly net sales for the past 12 months.

5. Quarterly net sales compared to projections.

6. Distribution update including notable distribution gains and losses, upcoming retail account presentations, and retailers at risk, if any.

7. Marketing support including promotional calendar, recent retailer specific promotions and those in the works, recent consumer marketing activities and those planned, and recent and upcoming trade shows.

8. New product pipeline including products under devel-
    opment, projected in-store or online date, and projected
    submissions for approval. This should include any innova-
    tions that the licensee might be considering.

Brand owners might also want to solicit some additional information from licensees annually. (This is really getting into the
weeds, and many licensees will not have this data or the resources
to retrieve it):

1. Product/category consumption trends.
2. Market share/dollar share.
3. Retail share.
4. Map of locations and identity of websites selling licensed
    products.
5. Category penetration (i.e., percentage of households pur-
    chasing product).
6. Consumer profile including trial and demographics.

As previously noted, staying on top of royalty reports and the
data included in those reports is essential. Brand owners need to
have processes in place to ensure that royalty reports and payments are made on time and that systems are in place to input
and evaluate the data included in those reports. Licensees should
be audited every three or four years (with some licensees, perhaps
more frequently). Audits frequently discover underpayments by
licensees. Generally, these are not intentional underpayments, but
mistakes being made in reading, interpreting, and implementing
contractual provisions relating to the calculation of royalties. One
of the provisions that often confuses those charged with calculat-
ing royalty payments is with respect to the definition of net sales
(i.e., the sales dollars off of which royalties are calculated). Every
contract allows certain deductions from gross sales, and it is in
the interpretation of those deductions that mistakes can easily be
made. And that's just one example. Audits can also confirm that

licensees are selling in the right distribution channels, selling in the right countries, and selling only approved product, among other contractual provisions. Audits are important, licensees expect them, and there is no reason they have to be adversarial. Brand owners must take the position that audits are undertaken to enhance the licensor/licensee relationship and not drive a wedge into the relationship. It's a process that must respect the business partnership between the brand owner and the licensee. Make it clear that there is no hidden agenda; questions can be asked by both sides, and the results of an audit should be shared and explained to the licensee. When an audit is done properly, licensees often appreciate the audit because it improves their systems and processes.

Managing Retailers

Managing a licensing program sometimes requires managing retailers. This can be challenging. The retailer generally has the leverage. This is true for online retailers as well as brick-and-mortar retailers. After all, without the retailer, there are no product sales. When the brand already has a strong relationship with a retailer, more opportunities exist to work with the retailer on specific programs or promotions. For example, a brand whose core product is important to a retailer (e.g., Tide at Walmart, Black & Decker at The Home Depot, Heinz at Kroger's, and Kellogg's at Publix) can frequently work with a retailer to support on-floor opportunities to sell licensed product.

Managing a retailer becomes particularly important, however, when the brand owner has developed an exclusive, contractual relationship with a retailer for the entire licensing program or specific categories of licensed product. The challenges, opportunities, advantages, and disadvantages of a retail exclusive or direct-to-retail program will be discussed in greater detail in Chapter 7. That chapter will also address the management responsibilities and roles of the brand owner and retailer.

As brand owners consider these managing and supporting responsibilities, keep in mind that every licensing program has many moving parts. Things can become complicated and often challenging. To keep things relatively simple and running coherently, communication is crucial. Maintain a continuous dialogue about timelines, schedules, forms, and templates for reporting. All of these best practices will go a long way toward maximizing the benefits that brand owners and their licensees reap from a given program.

Yes, there will be risks despite these best practices. But operationally ready brand owners can mitigate the risks in many ways and enjoy the benefits of licensing. The next chapter will identify some of those risks and the steps (in addition to those identified in this chapter) that brand owners can take to avoid them.

CHAPTER 6

Understanding and Mitigating the Risks

Licensing always carries a certain degree of risk. That's why this chapter uses the words *mitigating the risks* and not *eliminating the risks*. You cannot completely eliminate risk. But brand owners can assess risk and reduce the likelihood of problems, which will help with category identification and licensee selection, as discussed later in the chapter.

Be aware that potential risks are sometimes what cause a brand owner to turn away from licensing entirely. Organizations worry that the risk isn't worth the benefits that licensing provides. Sometimes they may be right. Many times, however, most of the risks can be mitigated through some simple and relatively inexpensive best practices.

Virtually all of the risks mentioned in this chapter pertain to a loss of control. Despite a high degree of oversight, organizations still are, through licensing, allowing a third party to produce and market a product using what has already been described as the brand owner's most valuable assets—its trademarks and other intellectual properties. In the product journey from product development to the consumer, many stops exist where there is risk. Those risks as well as how to mitigate them will be discussed in this chapter. Many of the examples provided are real-life examples, but without the brand owner's name being mentioned. Most brand owners want to keep their missteps to themselves.

Identifying Risk Types

There are three general types of risk. First are "internal risks": issues that arise and problems that occur between the brand owner and its licensee. For example, internal risks include the risk that a licensee doesn't fulfill its financial commitments on time or refuses to fulfill the commitments at all or doesn't launch the product as agreed. Internal risks are generally contractual or simply relationship risks. Perhaps the partnership was wrong from the beginning, and this becomes apparent before any product reaches the market. These risks are kept "within the family"; in other words, they generally occur behind the scenes and the consumer is unaware of them, particularly if the product never makes it to the retail "shelf."

Second, there are "external hard risks." For example, a licensee sells a product that has not been approved by the licensor (a contractual breach, but still a major headache for both parties). The consumer may or may not be aware that something went wrong; it would likely depend on the quality or design elements of the unapproved product.

Third are "external soft risks," and these can be significant. For example, the licensee may damage the brand owner's reputation due to a faulty product. More than likely, these risks will reach the consumer's attention.

Beyond loss of control, bad publicity and reputational damage are the risks that brand owners generally fear most. One might say that these result from a loss of control. This can be the outcome of poor product, bad marketing by the licensee, manufacturing conditions, supply chain issues, even reputational challenges faced by executives of a licensee. A myriad of activities by a licensee can redound to the brand owner's detriment. And in this age of transparency and social media, these risks are even greater. For example, Millennial consumers seek supply chain transparency and many manufacturers and retailers are providing it. What will they discover? Despite all of the potential pitfalls, however, the odds of reputational damage to the brand owner are small. If you look at the long history and evolution of brand licensing and the hundreds of thousands of brand licensed products that have reached the market, very few brands have endured damage to their reputations from licensed products. And when it has occurred, the effect is usually short-lived. Moreover, smart brands will move quickly to contain the damage—in the most serious cases, dropping the licensee and terminating the license agreement.

All of these risks can be greatly reduced or caught and corrected early by engaging in the best practices described in the previous chapter. Having the right strategy and choosing the right partner is the first line of defense against risk. Organizations must vet prospective licensees thoroughly to make sure they are a good fit with the brand, not only in terms of strategic objectives but also in terms of less tangible factors. For example, ask questions such as these: Is the licensee a good corporate citizen? Are its products innovative? Does it have strong retail relationships? Are there competing products in its existing portfolio? Is the licensee aligned with the brand owner's vision?

All of this information, gathered in the early stages, will help brand owners make the right decision, choose the right partner, and thereby mitigate risks. Also, operational readiness to manage the licensees will help brand owners implement the best practices described in the previous chapter and utilize the information collected to their advantage. Alhough this probably goes without saying, if you are not ready to manage a licensing program (i.e., not prepared to devote the necessary resources), you should not proceed until you are ready.

Internal communication, too, is crucial to managing risk. Creating regular updates to senior management about licensing plans and activities ensures no (or greatly reduced) surprises. It also facilitates senior management's buy-in and support.

Now let's focus on the specific risks that any brand owner might confront when engaging in licensing. Keep in mind that every brand owner has its own distinct characteristics and ways of doing business that must be understood when considering risks, but what follows next will generally apply to any brand owner considering licensing.

Licensed Product Failure

A licensed product might fail for many reasons, and some of them are beyond a brand owner's control. No one can force consumers to buy a product. Maybe the price/value relationship is wrong. Maybe the retail channel is wrong. Maybe retailers don't need a new product in that particular category. Maybe the competition is stiffer than anticipated. Maybe the product is not viewed by consumers as being aligned with the brand. Maybe the product misses the demographic target. Maybe what was thought to be a trend turns out to be a short-lived fad. That's a good many "maybes." There is not much a brand owner can do about some of these market dynamics, but some can be corrected (e.g., develop a new channel strategy). Perhaps some course corrections will fix the challenges the product is facing. It will take time and attention. If initial failure cannot be corrected, the product will fade from retail shelves and online screens and the brand owner and its licensee will figure out a way to disentangle themselves from each other.

At this stage, you need to evaluate what went wrong, why it went wrong, and how that might inform future decisions. Maybe the idea was just a bad one. And this is where a brand owner can exercise some forethought. Do the research. Do the market evaluation. Do the necessary strategy work. And listen to what potential licensees have to say about the opportunity. They know much more about their category, their consumer, and the market dynamics in that category than you do. Talk to retailers. Understand their perspective on the category and product being considered. Brand owners can easily mitigate the risk; gathering this information will give them insight into a licensed product's potential—or lack thereof.

Let's look at some licensing failures. Perhaps these head-scratchers could have been avoided. Indeed, by examining them, you will see how risks could have been mitigated with a modest amount of research and analysis.

In 1999, *Cosmopolitan* (the magazine), introduced a line of Cosmopolitan yogurts in the United Kingdom. Perhaps you don't see the connection. Well, the folks at Cosmo, the story goes, saw a connection between the magazine's "sexy" appeal and a study that concluded that Brits liked to use edibles in the bedroom during sexual activities. Huh? The line was discontinued fairly quickly. You might argue that research wasn't needed to see that this was a risky proposition, but it certainly would have helped.

Smith & Wesson is over 150 years old and an iconic American brand. The company has always been a leader in handguns, but its consumers wanted other products from the brand, products it didn't manufacture. So the company turned to licensing and successfully extended its brand to close-to-core categories that its research revealed consumers wanted from Smith & Wesson. The products included handgun grips, holsters, concealed carry purses, tactical gear (mostly apparel), and (perhaps a bit of a stretch) monitored home security alarm systems (an attempt to take advantage of the brand's equities in "security"). But the company reached too far with Smith & Wesson mountain bikes for consumers (the company made mountain bikes for police departments), leather jackets, and a Smith & Wesson men's cologne. With these last products, in particular, the company also faced distribution challenges with many nonsporting goods retailers not interested in carrying the brand. In any event, you won't find those products anymore. They quietly disappeared from the market.

Famous brands, often leaders in their category, frequently get arrogant or, perhaps more kindly, "ambitious" about where their brand can extend, and that causes them to make flawed decisions.

Other examples of famous iconic brands extending their brands past the breaking point include Life Savers soda (yes, in the colors and flavors you would expect), Coors Rocky Mountain Spring Water (yes, Coors uses spring water in its product, but it's a beer company!), Colgate Kitchen Entrées (what?), Frito-Lay Lemonade (it must go good with snacks), Bic disposable underwear (I'm speechless), Ben-Gay aspirin (perhaps the company thought it owned pain relief) and, of course, Trump Steaks (no, they weren't successful).

So one way to mitigate the risks of sales failure is not to go where you don't belong. Know the market and understand your true brand equities and where you will have consumer permission.

Cannibalizing Sales of the Core Product
Be mindful of not going forward with licensed products that might cannibalize the sales of your own core products or compete with other products or brands in your own portfolio. For brands that are engaging in strategic licensed brand extensions (rather than decorative licensing), this is particularly true. The closer a licensed product gets to the brand owner's core product, the more likely this could happen. At the same time, you don't want to turn away from important licensing opportunities out of misguided fear. Does Crest Scope licensed disposable, pocket breath freshening spray cannibalize sales of P&G's core Crest Scope mouthwash? P&G correctly determined that it did not. Consumers purchasing the licensed product seeks convenience, something to carry with them. P&G's core product comes in a plastic bottle and is kept, mostly, in the bathroom (except for the travel sizes).

Cannibalization can also occur in multibrand companies. P&G, with such an extensive product portfolio, must be careful not to license one P&G brand into a category where it will be competing with another P&G brand. For example, a logical extension for P&G's laundry detergent Gain might be dishwashing detergent for the dishwasher. But wait! P&G owns the leader in that category, Cascade. So despite the connection between "detergent" for your clothing and "dishwasher detergent" for your dishes, this is a nonstarter for P&G. It is not likely to be granting rights to a third-party licensee to make a Gain licensed product that will be competing directly with another one of its brands. Of course, sometimes there are exceptions to this concern. For example, perhaps a channel strategy that differentiates price and target consumer for the product will justify a decision to proceed with the license. And, of course, many multibrand companies often have brands that compete with each other but have different profiles (such as price or target consumer). P&G, for example, offers both Dawn and Gain dishwashing liquids, positioned differently in the market.

Cannibalization can occur indirectly as well as directly. And it doesn't always mean that a licensed product is distracting the consumer from purchasing the core product. Sometimes the licensed product is categorized similarly to the core product and placed on the same shelf in the store or on the same page online. Although sufficient difference exists between these two products, so that consumers don't choose one over the other, the core product may receive less shelf or page space to make room for the licensed product. Long term this might help build a larger product assortment at a particular retailer and communicate a stronger brand message, but for the short term, it could mean lower sales of the core product. Again, be careful.

Cannibalization has been most hotly debated in the restaurant licensing category. The question is: Do restaurant-branded licensed food products sold in the grocery channel mean that consumers will visit the restaurant less? If you purchase Arby's frozen French fries in the supermarket (a license with ConAgra), are you less likely to visit an Arby's for a snack of French fries? If you can buy Subway-branded lunch meats at a supermarket (not currently a license) and make your sandwich at home, are you less likely to visit a Subway restaurant for a Subway sandwich? A good many restaurants have shied away from licensing because they fear this form of cannibalization. And this fear intensifies when franchisees are involved. They don't want to see anything in the grocery aisle that *might* prevent a customer from visiting their franchise, despite all of the brand-building benefits such a licensing program might bestow upon the brand and upon them. An extreme example of this is Dunkin' Donuts coffee. When Dunkin' Donuts licensed packaged coffee to The J.M. Smucker Company in 2007, many franchisees were angry. They sell packaged branded coffee at their locations. Isn't it possible that a customer who purchases the coffee at a supermarket would have come to the franchised location for the packaged coffee? In this case, they may be right. But it's also possible that a customer would get hooked on buying Dunkin' coffee at the supermarket and be driven to the franchise at another time, increasing franchisee sales of coffee and doughnuts. Also, are they separate buying occasions? People do most of their food shopping at supermarkets, and that's where they will purchase their coffee. If they like Dunkin' and it's not available, they are likely to buy something else.

Was it a mistake when Cracker Barrel decided not to license frozen meals, particularly center-of-plate meals, for fear it would cannibalize restaurant attendance or fail to meet the same quality standards as the food served in the restaurants? (It's doubtful that consumers expect the quality of a store-bought frozen meal to equal the quality of a similar meal cooked at a restaurant.) It's a tough call, but one that illustrates the difficult decision companies must make when the threat of cannibalization looms.

Other restaurants have forged ahead without any noticeable cannibalization (as already noted, it's been quite a trend in licensing over the past several years). The prevailing opinion seems to be that purchasing food at the supermarket to prepare and eat at home and going to a restaurant to eat a meal are entirely different dining occasions. One doesn't replace the other because the brand is the same on the grocery product and on the restaurant sign. There are many success stories: TGI Friday's Mozzarella Sticks and other frozen foods, IHOP frozen breakfasts, P.F. Chang's frozen meals, Panera Bread soups and salad dressings, Taco Bell meal kits and sauces, Fat Burger frozen patties, and Cinnabon's comprehensive licensing program that includes Pillsbury cinnamon rolls (pretty close to a Cinnabon bun, right?). In fact, the Cinnabon chain has experienced exponential growth over the past several years, and undoubtedly, a host of licensed products and co-branded products with companies such as Kellogg's and Taco Bell have greatly helped extend and expand the Cinnabon brand and its meaning.

It's doubtful that licensed restaurant retail food products will negatively impact the restaurant's own market and cannibalize sales, and the theory has been largely debunked by the many successful examples discussed here and in the category. In fact, these products keep consumers engaged with the brand when they are not going out to eat.

To mitigate the cannibalization risk, evaluate what impact the success of a licensed product might have on core sales and make certain the licensed products are not directly competitive with the core offering or, in the case of restaurants, the core occasion (eating out).

Consumer Complaints

If a consumer has a complaint about a licensed product, he or she is going to contact the brand owner and not the licensee. You can be fairly confident about that. After all, the consumer purchased the product because it bears the licensor's brand name and because the customer believes in the brand promise and trusts the quality of the product because of the brand. And most of all, the product looks as though it came from the brand owner, not some third-party licensee whose name appears in the "fine print" somewhere on the packaging (unless it's a co-branded product, in which case either brand may get the call or e-mail). Of course, given how easy online and offline retailers are making it for consumers to return goods, for any reason, consumers may choose simply to return the product, registering a direct complaint. And many of these return mechanisms provide the consumer with the opportunity to register his or her complaint as part of the return process.

However, be prepared for consumer complaints. There may be just a few, or there may be many, but there are usually some (as is generally true of the core product). Make sure there's a way for consumers to contact the brand owner and have their communication routed to the licensee for resolution and that the licensee is set up for this. In one incident, a brand licensed its name for outdoor power equipment, one being snow blowers. Unfortunately, the snow blowers didn't work and broke down easily. A consumer complaint made it all the way to the brand's CEO. That's something that needs to be handled right away. However, despite any brand licensor's best efforts, sometimes a clunker gets through the process. So set up (contractual) arrangements with your licensees to handle consumer complaints.

Of course, sometimes a product can cause harm or be subject to a recall. Contractual requirements must stipulate that licensees notify brand owners right away when these circumstances arise. In another example, a licensee received a warning from the U.S. Consumer Product Safety Commission about the performance of a product, didn't fix the problem, and was threatened with a recall. The brand owner wasn't advised until much later. That should be a contractual breach. And as for actually causing harm, it can happen, although quite infrequently. And guess who the injured consumer is going to sue? The brand owner, of course. So make sure license agreements have strong indemnification running from the licensee to the brand and that the licensee has product liability insurance in the proper amounts with the brand owner named as an insured.

The world of character licensing provides good illustrations of this risk because recalls and potentially injurious products are often found in the toy category where products are destined for children. In 2007, a company named RC2, a licensee of the popular "Thomas the Tank Engine," was compelled to recall 1.5 million "Thomas" wooden trains and accessories that were contaminated with paint containing lead. The toys, made in China, were sold in all of the major retailers that sell toys (e.g.,

Walmart and Toys"R"Us). This was a voluntary recall when the licensee discovered the problem on its own. But the recall covered products made over a two-year period, indicating that the licensee failed to notice the problem for quite some time in one of its best-selling items. The recall was covered by a number of media outlets, including *The New York Times* and *National Public Radio*. Parents were outraged, many expressing fears of buying any "Thomas the Tank Engine" toys. The image of HIT Entertainment, owner of "Thomas the Tank Engine," and its popular brand was severely damaged (it did recover; "Thomas" remains a popular children's property today). The problem was exacerbated by the absence of immediate and transparent communication by the company (both the licensee and the brand owner) to consumers. Consumers need to see that the problem is being addressed aggressively.

Contractual Risks
As mentioned earlier, contractual breaches are risks. Many can be handled and resolved between the parties and don't affect consumers, such as failure to make timely payments, market the products on time, and follow the agreed business plan. But there are contractual breaches that cause mishaps in the marketplace.

For example, a licensee may sell an unapproved product (or, even worse, a product entirely outside of its contractual grant). There was a licensee that deviated from the style guide provided by the brand owner, didn't submit the product for approval, and went to market with an unapproved product featuring the wrong design. The brand owner demanded that the product be pulled from the market and required the licensee to remit all of its profits from the sale of the unapproved product to the brand owner.

Licensees might sell products in countries that are not included in their contract; online sales increase this possibility. They may also sell through channels that are not included in their license agreement. This often occurs when licensees sell to off-price or discount retailers contrary to contractual prohibitions.

Brand owners can catch these mistakes early in the process by requiring certain data in royalty reports that will expose these errors, reviewing those reports when they are submitted to identify errors. Formal audits of licensees will also reveal these oversights. Licensees who know that brand owners are carefully reviewing the data in royalty reports and who have a formal auditing process are likely to be more careful themselves. Regular communications and status reports will also help monitor the situation.

In addition to e-commerce complicating cross-channel and cross-territory sales, social media has complicated brand oversight of licensees. Your licensees may use social media effectively to promote their licensed products, but it happens in real time and it happens fast. And it can go viral. Licensees don't consistently seek brand approval for this kind of marketing, but they should. And if they proceed without brand owner approval, it constitutes a contractual breach.

Make this potential violation clear to your licensees. Brand owners mitigate the risk when they share comprehensive processes and procedures with licensees up front. But to be fair to the licensees, brand owners need to respond to these kinds of approval submissions very quickly. Brand owners can't take days or weeks to respond to a licensee's request regarding marketing through social media. That's how opportunities get lost.

Be aware that licensee employees who implement the licensed product program (including, for example, product development, launch, marketing, and royalty calculations) are not likely the same people with whom the brand owner negotiated the contract. They may not even be aware of the key, relevant contractual provisions, or if they are, they may not understand their implications. At the very start of a relationship, make contractual requirements clear to the licensee—particularly the people involved in implementing the program—and have processes in place to ensure compliance.

Nonperformance

Nonperformance can result for many reasons—perhaps just a bad product idea or financial challenges at the licensee. Often, however, it means that products fail to reach the shelf (or do so only briefly and incompletely). But sometimes the product just can't get on the retail shelves even if it is a good idea and a well-designed and priced product. There's just no room even if the brand owner and licensee have done everything right (online has less space restrictions, of course).

Consider a famous brand in the "baby" category that targeted baby health and beauty products for licensing. It seemed like a winning idea—baby shampoos, lotions, creams, and powders, for example. The brand made sense in the category. One big challenge: Johnson & Johnson (J&J). That company "owns" that category. It is virtually impossible to compete with J&J on a large scale, particularly in the Food, Drug, Mass channel. The licensed product, no matter how good it might have been, would have failed, not because it wasn't a good idea or couldn't have been well executed, but because retailers don't need another brand in the category. The competition was just too tough, and the brand decided not to proceed. Despite the strength a brand owner might have at a particular retailer, brand owners in other categories, categories in which the brand owner might want to enter, have leverage with retailers as well. In this example, nonperformance was averted. That being said, perhaps a different strategy would have worked. Perhaps the brand could have developed a strategy focused online or with a product that was clearly differentiated from J&J's product assortment and where the licensed product didn't have to contend with J&J's power with important retailers. The Honest Company (founded by actress Jessica Alba and three business partners) did just that. It successfully competes with companies such as J&J with its own new brand of household and baby products focused on ingredients that promote sustainability and manufacturing transparency. The products are sold online on the company's controlled e-commerce site, with virtually no traditional brand advertising.

In another instance, a well-known brand was licensed in the tape category (i.e., packing tape, duct tape, masking tape, and painter's tape). All of the products were of great quality, were packaged beautifully, and were aligned with the brand's equities and objectives. The licensee was extremely passionate about the brand and committed to the program. Too bad Duck brand tapes and Gorilla brand tapes filled the shelves of important retailers. The licensee simply couldn't get any traction. The competition was too tough, and the licensee failed to perform. Ditto a famous pet brand that licensed its name for all sorts of innovatively designed pet products such as bowls, leashes, and collars. But Walmart, PetSmart, and Petco, the leaders in the category, need only three or four brands in these products and they already had them on their shelves, selling successfully. They don't need any more brands in the category (occasionally, a celebrity brand of pet products breaks through; more on that in Chapter 8). The licensee failed to perform.

However, times have changed, in many respects dramatically, in recent years. Brands can now be launched online, rely on social media for marketing, control their supply chains and distribution, offer a unique selling proposition, and avoid competing directly (certainly in the early stages) with the traditional competition in brick-and-mortar-stores (see the discussion of digitally native vertical brands in Chapter 11). This changes the equation and opens up new opportunities for licensing that didn't exist prior to this transformation of the retail landscape.

Nevertheless, you would think that a prospective licensee would know whether the competition is going to be too stiff, and often they do. However, just as often they are blinded by the fame of the brand owner and the doors they believe an association with the brand will open for them, despite the competition. Be aware that a licensee may approach you with stars in his or her eyes rather than a realistic business perspective. If your evaluation is that the competition is too stiff, you need to communicate that point to the licensee. If the licensee can't make a convincing argument that you're wrong, then you shouldn't license the product to the company. In this way, you can avoid this kind of risk with proper market evaluation.

Retailers Have the Power

Unless a brand owner has a direct contract with a retailer (see Chapter 7), once the product is in the retailer's hands, there's not much a brand owner can do about what is done with the product. This includes how the retailer markets the product—in advertising, in promotions, in freestanding inserts (i.e., coupon offers that come with a newspaper), in social media, or on a web page—and how the product is displayed on the retail floor or online. It also includes how the product is priced, discounted, marked down, or put on sale. This is also true, naturally, of the brand owner's own core products.

Of course, if a brand has clout with a retailer because the brand is a major vendor, then that brand might have some influence on how the licensed product is offered—but not much. The retailer is the gatekeeper and holds most of the cards. The best the brand owner can do is to evaluate how and to whom the licensee intends to sell the product (and at what price point) before signing a license agreement. Through this evaluation, the brand owner ensures that it's moving forward with its eyes wide open, which lessens the "retailer" risk to some extent. Understanding what is going on in a category on the floor or screen pages of key retailers, learning about trends that affect retailers, will also help brand owners understand or anticipate how the proposed licensed product might be treated by retailers.

The *marykateandashley* program (discussed further in Chapter 8) exploded, exclusively, on Walmart's floor in 2000 and continued successfully for seven or eight years in fashion apparel, accessories, health and beauty products, and a host of other categories. The *marykateandashley* brand was owned and controlled by Dualstar Entertainment. Dualstar did a remarkable job of trying to control how the brand was presented on the floor of Walmart; it created the photography and graphic designs for signs that would appear on the racks or shelves or near the licensed products in the store. Dualstar went so far as to provide Walmart with camera-ready artwork for signage, and Walmart produced beautiful signage for the products. Unfortunately, as executives from Dualstar visited Walmart stores around the country, they often saw the wrong signs (actually signs of other Walmart brands) featured on the racks displaying the *marykateandashley* licensed products, their signs not being used at all. They complained to Walmart, and the company responded: We don't always get it right in each of our 4,000 stores, but we get over 100 million customers in our stores each week; don't worry, they'll find the product. Case closed. What this illustrates is that sometimes, even with a commitment of brand owner resosurces, doing all the right things to ensure that the product and brand message is delivered to the consumer as intended by the brand owner, the retailer simply cannot be controlled. But that's still no reason not to do whatever might help and support a retailer, as often it will make a difference and have a positive effect on the program.

Counterfeits and Infringements

Sometimes the mere existence of a licensing program, particularly a successful one, can encourage counterfeiters and infringers to violate the law. An infringement is the unauthorized use of an intellectual property in any medium (such a use could be on a product or in an advertisement, for example). Counterfeits are the actual product using the trademark without authorization. Counterfeits are always infringements too because they are using the trademark without authorization. But let's focus on counterfeits. Counterfeiters see branded licensed product selling in the marketplace and decide to follow the lead and introduce their own product featuring a brand owner's intellectual property without any contract or permission. Maybe it's innocent (i.e., they didn't know the intellectual property is protected). Maybe not. Maybe a company in another country is copying what it sees an authorized licensee doing somewhere else. And e-commerce and social media have made counterfeiting even easier. In any event, it's a risk and it needs to be managed.

Many people might think that "the U.S. Army" is in the public domain. It's not. The word and image is an intellectual property owned by the Department of the Army, an agency of the U.S. government. And the U.S. Army has a formal licensing program with hundreds of successful licensed products. Counterfeiters, however, take advantage of this "misperception."

Managing risk doesn't always mean taking legal action. Frequently when counterfeiters are identified by a brand owner, if the product is acceptable and meets all of the other requirements, the brand owner "converts" them to an authorized licensee, and the former counterfeiter pays royalties and adheres to all of the other standard license agreement provisions. In the U.S. Army example, that would include allowing the company to use the official U.S. Army hang tag and packaging hologram.

In other cases, the brand is so famous that it becomes the subject of counterfeit goods without any reference to authorized licensed product that may or may not exist. Consider, for example, a famous unnamed U.S. laundry detergent sold in China, where it is also a very famous brand. Using the laundry detergent brand name, some enterprising Chinese company decided to launch face whitening cream in China. This product is not only a counterfeit but also a misunderstanding of the brand meaning (which is frequently true of counterfeiters who are trying to take advantage of a famous brand). Laundry detergent whitens your clothing, so why not the skin on your face?

Promises by the Brand Owner: Don't Make Them If You Can't Keep Them

Brand owners can mislead their licensees as well. This is rarely malicious. But in the "selling phase," when a brand owner is enthusiastically persuading a potential licensee about not only the value of the brand but also all of the benefits flowing to the licensee by being associated with the brand, these benefits may sound like promises but are really only possibilities. Perhaps the brand owner talks about helping the licensee with marketing or co-promotions as something that *might* be possible. Or the brand owner talks about its great relationships with key retailers and how it *might* be able to help a licensee with those retailers. Or the brand owners speaks of its great design department or industrial design department that *might* be able to help with product development. Or the brand owner raves about its great website and social media campaigns in which the licensee *might* be able to participate. And so on. The word *might* is emphasized because there's no commitment or promise (contractual or otherwise) that has been made by the brand owner, just possibilities. But "it's not what you say, it's what they hear."[1] Later on, when the brand owner is not able to deliver on these "promises," the relationship can sour; certainly, the licensee can become frustrated. It won't matter that none of these "promises" were formalized in the contract.

To manage this risk, don't say things that might be construed as a promise or a commitment. Be clear on expectations and reiterate them.

In addition, make sure the intellectual property you are allowing your licensee to use on its product will still be relevant when the product comes to market. Clearly, that's not an issue with the brand name itself. Presumably, it's famous enough that it's not disappearing. But what about sub-brands, slogans, advertising imagery? The brand might be using these properties successfully in the marketplace, enthusiastically including them in the "sales" pitch and offering them to licensees to use on or in association with the licensed products, but by the time the licensed product comes to market, those properties have been discontinued or replaced by something else. Again, this will, at the very least, frustrate licens-

---

1. This quote is the trademarked founding idea of maslansky + partners, a research-driven messaging firm specializing exclusively in language strategy for its clients.

ees. It may also drive them to seek financial relief or other forms of relief.

One classic example of this took place in the mid-1980s. Wendy's, the third hamburger chain in the nation back then (following McDonald's and Burger King), wasn't having much luck getting companies interested in licensing its trademarks (they wouldn't license any food products for fear of the cannibalizing risk mentioned earlier in this chapter). At the time, Wendy's had a successful television commercial featuring an elderly woman, Clara Peller, who, when ordering a hamburger at a fictional competitor, was given a burger with a very large bun but an exceptionally small burger. She angrily demanded, "Where's the beef?" This was designed to compare Wendy's large single beef patties to the burgers offered by the two leaders in hamburger fast-food restaurants. At the time the popular commercial was airing on television, Vice President Walter Mondale was engaged in a 1984 Democratic Presidential primary debate with Colorado Senator Gary Hart and challenged Hart on his alleged lack of substance and supposed "new ideas," asking, "Where's the beef?" Well, overnight Wendy's had an explosive licensing program built around the image of Clara Peller and the now famous phrase. Hundreds of products were soon on the market, from watches, to T-shirts, to mugs, to caps, to school supplies (i.e., decorative licensing). The licensees couldn't make products fast enough, that is until they picked up the weekly edition of *Ad Age* one morning and learned that Wendy's was discontinuing the "Where's the Beef?" advertising campaign. Soon products were collecting dust on the retail shelves, products were heavily discounted, and licensees as well as retailers were angry. Wendy's should have been more careful and better at communicating its plans. Although Wendy's was clearly delighted with licensees that managed to get product to market quickly to take advantage of this burst of fame, the company didn't consider what would happen if they ceased using Clara Pellar and running the ads. It wasn't only licensees stuck with inventory, but also retailers that needed to mark down products quickly in order to get rid of them. As for Wendy's, deeply discounted products featuring the company's famous name didn't exactly burnish Wendy's reputation. With a little bit of foresight and better communication this could have been largely avoided.

It's difficult for brand owners and licensees to take advantage of fads that might be short-lived (either market fads or brand-generated fads). Although on the one hand e-commerce and social media may have made this easier by offering a path to get products to market quickly and get them off the market quickly, on the other hand social media has also made it easier for a fad to rise quickly and then descend into flames just as quickly. Licensors and licensees should beware of the "promise" of potential short-lived opportunities.

Reputational Damage

Even when bad things happen because risks weren't managed properly, the damage is usually private rather than public, brief rather than long-lasting. Product sales failures, for example, just fade away in most cases—the products disappear from shelves and websites without much fanfare. But remember the biggest risk that licensors fear: damage to the brand's reputation. Recalls, injuries from products, design or quality flaws, deep discounting, for example, can all result in reputational damage. Some of these risks occur from the licensed product itself, and these risks can be mitigated by many of the steps already discussed. But even more importantly, brand owners must be sure they are not making decisions that will damage the equities of their brand or consumers' perceptions of their brand. Decisions that will disappoint consumers or affect their purchasing behavior in a negative way rather than the intended positive effect. This is entirely in the hands of the brand owner when evaluating licensing and product categories. What follows is a good case study of a brand that has struggled with the licensing decision and the potential for damaging its brand meaning—L.L.Bean.

L.L.Bean[2]

In 1911, an avid hunter and fisherman named Leon Leonwood (L.L.) Bean returned from a hunting trip with cold, damp feet and a revolutionary idea. He asked a local cobbler to stitch supple leather uppers to waterproof rubber boots, creating a comfortable, functional boot for exploring the Maine woods. This ingenious invention—the Maine Hunting Shoe—changed outdoor footwear forever and a year later began one of the most successful family-run businesses in the country.

In hopes of selling his newly created boot, L.L. obtained a list of nonresident Maine hunting license holders and created a descriptive flyer that he would send through the mail. Selling out of his brother's basement in Freeport, Maine, Bean used his four-page mail-order catalog to launch a nationwide mail-order business. The 1912 flyer proclaimed:

> You cannot expect success hunting deer or moose if your feet are not properly dressed. The Maine Hunting Shoe is designed by a hunter who has tramped the Maine woods for the last 18 years. We guarantee them to give perfect satisfaction in every way.

The L.L.Bean satisfaction guarantee, a cornerstone of the brand's reputation right up to today, was born.[3]

---

2. This material was taken from a case study written for a class at Boston University, titled: "L.L. Bean Case Study: Leveraging an Iconic Brand Through Licensing," by Susan Fournier, Michael Stone, and Adam Cooper, April 30, 2011. Much of the history is from *L.L.Bean: The Making of an American Icon*, by Leon Gorman, Harvard Business Review Press, 2006.

3. The 100% Satisfaction Guarantee, a return policy that allowed customers to return an item at any time, in any condition, during the lifetime of the customer, was changed by L.L.Bean in February 2018. The change was motivated by a growing abuse of the policy, such as people buying old items on eBay and returning them to L.L.Bean for full credit. Now, L.L.Bean customers have one year to return a product (with a receipt), still a generous return policy. That being said, the case study still represents a good example of a brand struggling with how licensing might affect its reputation.

Defects in the initial design of the Maine Hunting Shoe led to 90 percent of the original production run being returned. However, L.L. made good on his money-back guarantee, corrected the design, and continued selling his boot to the masses. It was here that Leon Leonwood Bean would institute L.L.Bean's Golden Rule: "Selling good merchandise at a reasonable profit; treating your customer like human beings, and they will always come back for more." Another cornerstone of the L.L.Bean brand was born— customer service.

Over the years, L.L.Bean has remained steadfast in its commitment to the equities established by L.L. so many years ago— 100 percent customer satisfaction and service as well as a product that is of superior quality. This distinction has led L.L.Bean to be recognized consistently as a retailing leader for customer satisfaction and service worldwide.

Importantly, L.L.Bean is a multichannel retailer that controls all of its distribution and sales to consumers. In 2016, it has been reported that L.L.Bean achieved $1.6 billion in sales (L.L.Bean remains a private, family-owned business) through an expanded three-prong distribution approach: a direct mail-order business fueled by its catalog, an e-commerce business, and retail outlets. Still as relevant as ever, L.L.Bean mails catalogs to consumers in every state and over 150 countries with various titles, including seasonal variations of Women's, Men's, Kids, Outdoors, Fishing, Hunting, and Home. In 1996, L.L.Bean created www.llbean. com to attract Internet-savvy shoppers to its merchandise. To drive business to llbean.com, the company sends weekly promotional e-mails to reach its large consumer base. In 2000, L.L.Bean extended its retail operations beyond Maine for the first time when it opened a store in McLean, Virginia. From 2001–2008, the company opened additional stores in Maryland, New Jersey, New Hampshire, Massachusetts, Connecticut, New York, and Illinois. As of 2017, L.L.Bean operated 30 retail stores and 10 outlet stores in the United States,in addition to its flagship store in Freeport,

Maine, and 25 stores in Japan (which started out as a license in 1991 and became a wholly owned subsidiary in 2001).

The L.L.Bean brand story has evolved over time as the company has grown. Over the past 107 years, L.L.Bean has offered consumers additional products and ways to purchase the product. But the imperative has always been moving ahead with the times and growth while remaining faithful to traditional L.L.Bean core values and maintaining the brand character. The L.L.Bean mystique has been debated, analyzed, and defined repeatedly throughout the company's history. The ongoing balancing act of keeping L.L.Bean recognizable has been agonized over at every material crossroads the company has faced.

According to the brand doctrine, some things have and must always remain the same:

1. The values of trust, reliability, and service.
2. Products that add value to people's lives.
3. Products that do what they are supposed to do, every time, and for a long time, all for a reasonable price.
4. Products that are functional, durable, and safe.
5. Products that cater to the lives of outdoor-oriented people and those who live an outdoor lifestyle.

Two defining attributes represent the unique character of the company and its way of doing business:

1. **Customer Service:** L.L.Bean has always been proud to be close to its customer and strives to be "the best, most consistent and most caring customer relations company anywhere."
2. **The 100% Satisfaction Guarantee:** You can return a product anytime during the lifetime of the consumer, for any reason. No questions asked. "You have our word." (See footnote 3.)

The Licensing Opportunity

As L.L.Bean's business has grown, so too have the company's aspirations. L.L.Bean started considering not only new geographical markets and growth through expanded distribution but also new product categories and consumer markets that can be tackled with the L.L.Bean brand. In 2009, the company launched L.L.Bean Signatures, a clothing collection targeting a younger customer, another goal of the company. In 2000, in the company's first-ever licensing initiative, L.L.Bean became the official outfitter of Suburu, collaborating on an L.L.Bean–edition Outback and Forester for the U.S. market (the license ended in 2008). A second license created an L.L.Bean credit card now offered through Barclays Bank of Delaware.

Other additional licensing opportunities, however, have been the subject of much debate, including categories such as camping equipment, dog accessories, children's sportswear, adventure travel, and bedding and bath. Each area represented a unique opportunity for L.L.Bean to leverage its impeccable brand image and enviable reputation and to reach both loyal and new consumers at fresh touchpoints. Deciding which opportunities, if any, to pursue involved deep analysis of potential ramifications for the brand from both opportunity and risk perspectives—or in the terms used in this chapter, brand gain versus potential reputational damage.

As with all strong brands, L.L.Bean has struggled over the years with the challenge of maintaining its brand heritage in the face of aggressive growth. By all accounts, L.L.Bean's success over the past one hundred–plus years has been a function of changing things that needed to be changed but maintaining those values that should never change. This kind of analysis in all likelihood was conducted when considering whether to add additional stores beyond the iconic store in Freeport, Maine; to launch an e-commerce site without the support of store personnel; and to add to the product assortment.

As a result, L.L.Bean needed to ask itself some tough questions when considering licensing: Was product licensing a good business decision? Which categories offered the best balance of risks and rewards? At the end, it came down to an oft-repeated phrase inside the company: "What would L.L. do?"

As the company evaluated licensing opportunities, it confronted several significant reputational risks. What would happen to the two iconic pillars of the L.L.Bean brand—the 100% Satisfaction Guarantee and customer service, to say nothing of the overall loss of control on the presentation of the brand at retail locations not owned by the company? How would other retailers selling the licensed product handle the 100% Satisfaction Guarantee? If a customer purchased an L.L.Bean–licensed product at a specialty retailer or a department store and was dissatisfied with the performance of the product, would that retailer accept the return like L.L.Bean would? And how could L.L.Bean take back the product when it didn't sell it? And what of L.L.Bean's reputation for customer service? Could L.L.Bean rely on retailers that were selling its licensed product to help customers the way L.L.Bean employees help them? To answer questions about the product the way L.L.Bean answers the questions?

Although licensing might have benefits to L.L.Bean, such as reaching new consumers, reaching important demographic groups, and expanding geographically, the risks to its core equities are also significant. Perhaps those risks could be overcome. Perhaps a strong licensee partner would agree to accept returns consistent with L.L.Bean's policies. Perhaps a single retail partner (as opposed to broad distribution) would agree to train its sales staff and customer relations department to provide customer service that would meet L.L.Bean's high standards. And perhaps a strong, exclusive retail partner would agree to present the L.L.Bean product assortment in an impactful manner that would respect this iconic brand. The challenges to L.L.Bean's reputation could, conceivably, be overcome.

As of today, L.L.Bean has made the decision not to proceed with licensing, presumably because the reputational risks (i.e., the risks to those very important brand equities mentioned above) are too great. However, circumstances change and L.L.Bean may someday embrace licensing to achieve brand objectives. Challenges such as the 100% Satisfaction Guarantee and customer service can be solved. (The new return policy will, undoubtedly, make this part of the decision easier.) Presentation at retail can be addressed. Or perhaps L.L.Bean develops a licensing plan that is limited to an online retail strategy where there can be more control. Because so much change is going on today with respect to reaching consumers with product, at such an accelerated pace, brands such as L.L.Bean should continue to evaluate the benefits and risks of licensing as a brand marketing and communications tool to achieve brand objectives.

CHAPTER 7

To Be or Not to Be at a Single Exclusive Retailer

Looking to buy HGTV HOME paint? You can buy it only at a Sherwin-Williams store or at Lowe's. How about *Better Homes & Gardens* sheets and pillowcases? Only at Walmart. You want that Food Network pot and pan collection? Only at Kohl's. Adam Levine's menswear is just your thing? Only at Kmart. "Something Navy" by blogger Arielle Charnas? Only at Nordstrom. And this isn't limited to brick-and-mortar retailers. Looking for Simple Joys by Carter's, a line of baby and children's clothing sold in multipiece bundles? Only at Amazon. Ditto Starter apparel, only at Amazon. Direct response TV retailers such as QVC and HSN frequently offer exclusive licensed products. Often, a single retailer is the sole destination for a brand's licensed products or for certain categories of licensed products from that brand.

Yet one size doesn't fit all. Before embarking upon this strategy, brand owners need to consider a number of factors that will determine whether a single retailer strategy is right for the brand's licensing program (or a portion of it). As you make this assessment, keep in mind that the retailer is the "gatekeeper." No one will buy your licensed product if it's not on the shelf (or on the screen), and in a retail exclusive model, the retailer has some very strong incentives to support your licensed products. Most major retailers today, across virtually all types and channels, have developed retail exclusive programs with licensors. And in the future, we can expect to see more of this in the e-commerce space. To determine whether this strategy is right for your licensing program, it helps to think about this strategy from a historical context.

A Brief History of the Single Retailer Strategy

Working with a single retailer is by no means a new strategy. It's been around a long time. Celebrities, music icons, athletes, corporate brands and designers, among others, have been pursuing and implementing this strategy for decades. Chapter 2 mentioned an exclusive arrangement The Coca-Cola Company had with Sears & Roebuck Co. back in the 1960s for a line of music-themed T-shirts. In fact, Sears was a pioneer in retail exclusives. In 1981, it launched a collection of licensed fashion apparel branded by then-supermodel Cheryl Tiegs, selling almost a billion dollars in its 10-year span. Shortly thereafter in 1983, Sears introduced another active apparel collection licensed by the #1 tennis player in the world, Australian Evonne Goolagong. At about that same time, in 1985, Kmart launched an exclusive apparel collection licensed by then-star of the television hit *Charlie's Angels*, Jaclyn Smith (a program that is still going strong, but more on that in the next chapter).

And in 1968, Macy's developed an exclusive relationship with the United States Lawn Tennis Association (now the United States Tennis Association). It was the first year that an event, called the Nationals, limited to "amateurs," became the U.S. Open Tennis Championship, open to all players (one of the Grand Slam events of tennis to this day). Macy's opened exclusive USLTA "Headquarters" shops in all of its stores with USLTA-branded apparel and other merchandise as well as tennis equipment, promoted the concept shop in advertising and other marketing vehicles, and sponsored sanctioned USLTA tournaments. In addition, Macy's introduced its own brand of USLTA licensed tennis balls for sale at its stores. The Macy's licensed tennis balls were used for the first U.S. Open that year (temporarily replacing longtime partner Wilson). To this day, Macy's continues to rely heavily on retail exclusive programs such as the Martha Stewart Collection, Ryan Seacrest menswear, and Tommy Hilfiger apparel.

Besides there being historical precedent for the single retailer strategy, in recent years, the number and caliber of brands signing exclusive agreements with retailers has increased. There are, of course, pros and cons to working with a single retailer, and illustrative examples will be provided. But first, we need to define some terms.

Two Exclusive Options

Exclusive is a relative term. Some companies may offer exclusives to one retailer in a given category that is particularly relevant to that retailer but not other categories. For example, Martha Stewart has an exclusive program at Macy's for home décor and other home products. The brand, over time, has also been exclusive at the specialty retailer Michaels limited to arts and crafts products, specialty store Staples for office supplies, and The Home Depot for home improvement products. Clearly, Martha Stewart recognized that each of these retailers was particularly strong in the licensed category, motivating the company to pursue this strategy.

Exclusive arrangements can take two forms, with hybrids, of course. First, there's Direct-to-Retail, or DTR. In a DTR program, a brand is licensed, by contract, to a single retailer in defined product categories. In this model, the retailer is responsible for sourcing the licensed products on its own and commits to floor space and launch as well as ongoing marketing. The retailer is the licensee and the contracting party with the brand owner, responsible for paying royalties based on its retail sales or its cost of goods (all part of the negotiation with the retailer).

The second type is the Retail Exclusive, where a single retailer also is the sole destination for a brand in a defined category of licensed goods. Similar to a DTR, in a Retail Exclusive, the retailer also commits to floor space and marketing. But here the difference is that the brand owner enters into license agreements directly with manufacturers to develop the licensed products and to sell them solely to a single identified retailer who, of course, can purchase those products only from those licensees. In this instance, the royalty is paid by the manufacturer to the brand owner based on its wholesale sales to the single retailer.

The DTR scenario creates better margins for the retailer (they are purchasing directly from their manufacturing sources in most cases) and, as a result, may create a stronger commitment to the product assortment and the brand owner. The Retail Exclusive scenario provides more confidence to the brand owner that the products are best-in-class (because the brand owner is working with its own manufacturing licensees) and the brand has more control (it's much easier to control manufacturing partners than it is to control a retailer). But in the end, both provide the result that a retailer is the single destination for the entire program or for specific categories of products. For purposes here, I'll use the term *retail exclusive* to refer to both types of arrangements.[1]

Benefits of a Retail Exclusive

The following three benefits motivate brands to consider retail exclusives:

- *Gaining real, focused attention from a retailer.* After all, it's the only store where a consumer can buy these goods; the retailer has a powerful incentive to support and do right by the brand.

---

1. Sometimes without retail exclusivity, a retailer will make a major commitment to a brand in terms of product assortment and marketing. An example is Craftsman. Following Stanley Black & Decker's acquisition of Craftsman in 2017, Stanley Black & Decker partnered with Lowe's to offer the brand across multiple product categories, many of them licensed, in the areas of Garage, Automobile, Lawn and Garden, and General Construction, with a Lowe's heavily backed launch in 2018. Licensees may sell products to a limited list of other, approved retailers.

- *Building the business together.* The brand owner and retailer (as well as the licensee if there is one) are motivated to work together every step of the way from product development and design to on-floor merchandising, to design of online pages, to launch marketing, to ongoing support by both parties. The retail exclusive helps build a true partnership and meet the consumer's expectations.
- *Being able to analyze sales performance and take corrective actions where necessary, quickly.* With a single retail partner, much data is available about sales and purchasing behavior. This data can help drive corrective action when a product doesn't sell as expected.

Brand owners realize another related benefit when they choose to launch a product with a retail exclusive for perhaps a limited period of time. They gain some traction with a new product category or program and, if successful, have a story to tell other retailers when the product is offered more broadly. For example, in early 2017, Energizer teamed up exclusively with QVC to sell licensed solar lights. On the third day, when the product was offered as a QVC Today's Special Value, consumers purchased 1,400,000 lights! That's over $21,000 in sales per minute! This far exceeded QVC's expectations and established the category in particular and Energizer licensed products in general as highly desirable by consumers—a strong selling point with retailers in the future.

Retailers, too, benefit from exclusive partnerships, including:

- *Allowing the retailer to differentiate its product offering from those of its competitors.* With so much retailing parity, this differentiating ability is a major advantage and helps draw consumers into the store or to the website.
- *Providing greater control over the quality of the product.* They are sourcing the product themselves, or if the product is purchased from a third-party licensee, the retailer

can make quality demands that cannot be ignored (the retailer is the single customer for the licensee).

- *Offering the retailer a stronger path to reach a particular demographic group,* such as younger consumers.
- *Controlling the sourcing of the product (in DTR situations).* In other instances, the retailer might "advise" the brand owner whom to license as the exclusive supplier, recommending preferred vendors. In any event, the retailer is likely relying on preferred sourcing resources.
- *Negotiating favorable costing, resulting in very competitive retail prices and margins.* A retail exclusive results, of course, from negotiation between brand owner and retailer or between retailer and manufacturer. Of great importance to the retailer will be the cost of goods. The lower the cost, the lower the retail prices. Better costing results in better margins for the retailer. Retail exclusive combined with great value is a winning combination.
- *Managing the category more effectively.* With an exclusive brand in the category and the control that it bestows on the retailer, the retailer is better able to manage the entire category, which will include other brands and private-label product, on its floor or website. For example, there is likely to be less overlap in product and design.

And let's not forget the consumer, who benefits from all of this focus on product design and quality, price, and value. To understand these benefits in action, for all parties, let's look at some representative examples of retail exclusives and the different ways they are structured and implemented.

The Food Network[2]

The Food Network is a good example of the benefits of a straightforward retail exclusive (in this case, a DTR) to both brand owner

---

2. *Id.* "Top 150 Global Licensors," *License Global.* The Food Network is #109.

and retailer. Launched in 2006, this authoritative voice in cooking and food preparation helped Kohl's strengthen its position in a category in which it was weak. In other words, it filled white space (i.e., a product need at a particular retailer), one of the key ingredients of a successful retail exclusive program. Kohl's had identified kitchen products (such as tableware, cookware, table linens, and kitchen gadgets) as a key growth category for its stores. The relationship with The Food Network and the development of the product assortment helped Kohl's move forward with this strategy faster than if the retailer had tried with its own private-label brand or other brands generally available at retail. Although Kohl's sourced virtually all of the product on its own, the experts at The Food Network were very involved in the design of many of the products, always trying to bring innovation to the category and to offer solutions and special features to consumers. For the brand owner, this relationship was a way to establish the brand outside of broadcast television, allowing it to engage with its already loyal viewers in a new way as well as to attract new consumers who shopped at Kohl's. This award-winning line grew to cover a dozen or so food and cooking categories and occupied a substantial amount of floor space at Kohl's stores. In this example, the brand owner and the retailer were able to use licensing to fill a gap in Kohl's product assortment in the category in a shorter period of time due to the use of a famous brand. In addition, it allowed The Food Network to reach potential viewers and existing viewers of the network in a new way that was totally aligned with the brand values.

Better Homes & Gardens

Meredith Publishing[3] signed a DTR license agreement with Walmart in 1998 for its flagship magazine, focusing on a line of patio furniture and garden tools sold in the store's garden center. In 2008, the program expanded to products for the bed, the

---

3. *Id.* Meredith Publishing is ranked #2.

bathroom, tabletop, and home décor. As an example of a sustainable, long-term partnership, the agreement has been renewed and expanded many times since inception (today the brand is in virtually every "home" category at Walmart stores). From the first expansion of the program in 2008 and through 2017, the number of SKUs of *Better Homes & Gardens* products at Walmart had increased sevenfold from 500 to over 3,500 (depending on the season), and the licensed products are sold at all Walmart stores and at walmart.com.

Consumer research showed that readers of *Better Homes & Gardens* are frequent Walmart shoppers. Moreover, some of the magazine's largest advertisers sell a significant amount of product at Walmart. For Meredith, the magazine connects with its readers through its comprehensive content. That content creates a great deal of credibility for the *Better Homes & Gardens* brand and helps it establish relationships with consumers in a broad array of products and product categories. Walmart recognized all of those advantages.

Both Walmart and Meredith also had their eye on competitors. For Walmart, the brand offered an excellent opportunity to compete with other well-known brands sold at its competitors— particularly Martha Stewart then at Kmart, now at Macy's— drew new customers (who might otherwise go to department or specialty stores for these products) into its stores, and filled a white space at Walmart, which had been mostly offering its customers private-label brands in the category. Meredith, too, competed with Martha Stewart for readers and advertisers in the home space.

Given that this is a DTR, Walmart pays royalties to Meredith based on its retail sales (which also means that Meredith's royalties decrease when Walmart places goods on sale or markdown, something that doesn't happen in the Retail Exclusive model). Walmart also sources all of the manufacturing and is responsible for all design and product development (which, in this case, it outsources to an independent design firm). Meredith approves all product at the concept stage, and Walmart and its design firm handle all final product approvals. Meredith also tracks and analyzes sales and manages other aspects of the license agreement to ensure compliance by both parties. Under the agreement, Walmart is obligated to sell the product and Meredith is obligated to advertise the line. Meredith accomplishes this in the tone and manner of the magazine's editorial voice. But the "editorial" must be earned and meet all of the editorial requirements of any other brand. Meredith also engages in co-branded advertising to support the Walmart program. For example, Meredith might team up with Kraft Foods that is advertising Kraft cheese on hamburgers being served on *Better Homes & Gardens* licensed dinnerware. For Walmart, this is an "across the box" solution helping Walmart move consumers from the grocery aisles of the store to the general merchandise aisles of the store. This DTR is one of the most successful in the United States for many reasons, not the least of which is a strong sense of partnership. However, it's also successful because Meredith realized that, in many respects, it needed to play by Walmart's rules and align its vision with that of Walmart's, all while enhancing its brand. (See Figure 8 of the photo insert.)

The Coca-Cola Company
In 2012, The Coca-Cola Company announced a multiyear license agreement with retailer HSN that included licensed products sold on its cable channel, online at hsn.com, on mobile devices, as well as through social media such as Twitter. The partnership represented the most extensive collection of Coca-Cola merchandise sold through a single retailer in the world. The HSN assortment, which at launch consisted of more than 275 items, included popular Coca-Cola–licensed products that were already being sold by licensees to other retailers, as well as never-before-seen exclusive products developed by the brand owner and HSN. To support the program, The Coca-Cola Company promoted HSN on My Coke Rewards through the company's website that at the time had over 14 million members. Members were able to redeem rewards points when making purchases on hsn.com. To further enhance the part-

nership, both Coca-Cola and HSN used the program to help raise money for HSN Cares as well as charitable organizations supported by Coca-Cola. The program was designed, in particular, to take advantage of holidays and seasonal efforts that are particularly important to Coca-Cola's marketing campaigns.

At the time, Coca-Cola said that it was attracted to HSN because of the cable network's expertise at telling a story. That's often a compelling reason for brand owners to be attracted to the retail exclusive model—the retailer can make a statement and tell a more comprehensive story, either online or on the retail selling floor. Online this means space commitments by the retailer on the web page; offline it means investment in hang tags, packaging, store signage, among other communication tools, to tell the brand story. It is a much bigger challenge for either a brand owner or a retailer to make these kinds of investments without the benefit of a retail exclusive, unless the brand is absolutely compelling for the retailer (e.g., the Lowe's/Craftsman example cited earlier in footnote 1).

InStyle *Magazine*

In mid-2015, JCPenney announced an exclusive license agreement with *InStyle* magazine, a popular fashion and beauty magazine published by Time, Inc., to rebrand physical in-store salons in their stores and to name the salons The Salon by *InStyle*. This isn't exactly a product license; rather, it's the licensing of an experience. (See Chapter 12 for a discussion about licensed experiences.) The collaboration grew out of an advertising relationship between the two parties and a mutual desire to work together in a more impactful way. *InStyle* is paid a flat fee for the branding rights as well as a share of the revenue. The JCPenney concept was to reinvent its existing salons and to create an experience featuring the latest beauty trends curated by the editors at the magazine. The totally redesigned and refurbished salons offer hair care services and include a retail space offering tools and products from already well-known beauty brands. And in late 2017, the salons also started offering *InStyle*-branded licensed products, including hair accessories such as clips and bands as well as hair accessory kits that include advice tied into the styles featured in the magazine. From a legal perspective, this arrangement represents a product license (e.g., the *InStyle*-branded products) as well as a service license (*InStyle* has licensed the retailer to provide hair care services under the magazine's brand name). JCPenney was careful to avoid overlap with its Sephora collaboration, which offers other beauty products and services. The Salon by *InStyle* and the Sephora shop generally sit right across the aisle from each other with health and beauty products sold in the aisles near both shops.

The goal of JCPenney partnering exclusively with *InStyle* was to help the retailer gain relevance with female shoppers of all ages, but particularly younger shoppers, who identify with the fashion, hair, and beauty trends curated by *InStyle*, and to drive them into the store. It was also a way for the retailer to invest in its employee stylists, improving their morale and their work. For the magazine, the brand owner, this project enables *InStyle* to deliver on the inspiration its readers see in the magazine. It gives their readers, and others who are aware of the magazine, products and services they can embrace. Also, it should drive more people to read the magazine and further entrench the magazine in the beauty space with affordable products and services (often the features in the magazine are outside the price range of the readers). This last point is one that both brand owner and retailer have had to focus on. It's always important for the brand and the exclusive retailer to be aligned on vision (see the comment in the Meredith example above), price points, and target customer. For *InStyle* and JCPenney, this has required compromises by both parties. Perceptions need to be blended, and in this case, the magazine is perceived to speak to a higher-end consumer (as well as an aspirational consumer) than the JCPenney customer. It's very important, particularly for the brand owner, *InStyle* magazine, that the products and services offered in the salon are consistent with what's being featured in the magazine and will meet readers' expectations of the brand but also be affordable for the JCPenney customer.

Other than the customary brand owner approval rights, in order to exercise greater control over the offerings of the salon and to ensure brand consistency, *InStyle* regularly provides JCPenney with style books and a "Look Book" for the store and the stylists. *InStyle* also creates ads for JCPenney that the retailer then runs in the magazine. And *InStyle* promotes the salon in its magazine and on its website. As the concept expands (by the end of 2018 there should be salons in over 130 JCPenney stores), there will likely be more cross-marketing opportunities for the brand owner and the retailer. One such cross-marketing activity under discussion at the time of this writing is contests for stylists, with the winner being promoted in the magazine.

JCPenney is using the *InStyle* brand name, exclusively, to gain credibility as well as to serve its customers and its staff and to reach a younger demographic. The magazine benefits from the marketing support, in-store presence, and presentation of *InStyle* as the authoritative voice in beauty care. This retail exclusive license agreement is a win-win for both parties.

As you may have noticed in all of these examples, both the brand owner and the retailer determined that each was the right fit for the other. Brand owners need to do plenty of upfront work to demonstrate to a retailer that the brand has the right components for success. No matter how great your brand might be, to get in the door, it needs to fit the retailer's needs. That requires homework. Many famous brands have charged into a retailer to sell the merits of their brand without even knowing what's on the retailer's floor or website. If a retailer already has several brands that are performing successfully in the same category targeted at the same consumer as your brand, why put yours on the "shelf"? Even as an exclusive? Why move a performing brand to make room for your brand?

Too often, brand owners don't do their homework and pay for it later. Dedicating the time and investment necessary to develop an intelligent and comprehensive positioning to pitch to a potential retail partner is a necessity, not an option. Retailers want to know that you have evaluated their floor or online presence and the brands they are offering. Even if you aren't 100 percent accurate, they will be impressed that you made the effort and will be more likely to share their thoughts about their needs and how you might (or might not) fit in.

The crucial question to ask yourself before meeting with the targeted retailer is how to get your brand to stand out among the many brands that are presented to a retailer as opportunities (or the brands already on the floor or online). It's all in the details.

HGTV

Let's take a more comprehensive look at a retail exclusive developed by HGTV and what made it successful. As you read this case study, consider that HGTV, a television broadcaster and content provider that sold no products, determined that to win at retail, it had to tell the story of what makes the brand so successful. It is a story (also discussed in Chapter 4) about allaying viewers' fears about decorating their homes, about providing them with solutions to design decisions that are often intimidating and confusing, about giving them the confidence they need to make the right decisions for their homes—in categories such as paint and furniture where consumers often feel challenged. In other words, the products had to offer information and solutions, and the story needed to be told. (See Figure 9 in the photo insert.) Without a deep commitment from a retailer, it would be difficult to provide consumers with this educational experience, to tell the story. HGTV determined that in select categories, a retail exclusive arrangement would best accomplish its objectives. Further, HGTV recognized that with a single retailer, the network would be in its strongest position to support the retailer with both on-air and online marketing, a home advantage for HGTV as a brand licensor.

HGTV entered into retail exclusive relationships with Sherwin-Williams (owner of about 3,000 stores) for paint, paint accessories, and wallpaper, which was later expanded to include an exclusive at Lowe's for paint (supplied by Sherwin-Williams). Both retailers provided substantial floor space to the HGTV HOME paint program, offering consumers easy tools to determine what color palettes they should be using in their home. The palette program provided colors for the entire room, not only the walls but also other features of a room such as the furniture and window treatments. It offered a "whole home" color palette. The program delivered solutions and knowledge along with style. Each palette was inspired by a particular style curated to work in various rooms of the home. Often, paint brands were about style, such as Ralph Lauren or Martha Stewart, or about solutions, such as *Real Simple*. But no retailer or brand had merchandised paint, combining both solutions and style, in this fashion before HGTV HOME. And it was the retail exclusive model that allowed both brand owner and retailer to make the investment necessary to offer the branded products this way.

Similarly, HGTV HOME was licensed exclusively to Bassett Furniture for custom upholstery furniture. Bassett, in its approximately 100 stores, offered an assisted, customized sale with salespeople who had design experience (in the HGTV HOME Design Studio, generally located in the center of the store). Further, Bassett design associates make home visits to be part of the design process as well as to help set up new furniture that had been purchased at the store. The HGTV HOME Design Studio basically provides a makeover experience in the consumer's home. Again, this is a commitment by a retailer that is driven by the retail exclusive nature of the relationship. (See Figure 9 of the photo insert.)

Each of these retailers was able to differentiate themselves from its competitors by offering a valued brand available only at its stores.

For a retail exclusive program such as HGTV's to be successful, most if not all of the following factors must be part of the strategy:

1. An innovative or fresh idea.
2. Great product design that solves a problem or addresses a consumer need.

3. A retailer that is not addressing that problem or need effectively with its current product assortment (white space).
4. Strong on-floor or online presentation.
5. Multiple touchpoints in the store and coordinated product when appropriate.
6. Consistent guidelines to which all stakeholders must adhere.
7. Retailer sales training.
8. Marketing by the retailer.
9. Marketing by the brand owner. Items 8 and 9 together can create omniplatform marketing, often the "secret sauce" in a retail exclusive program.
10. Cross-partner marketing if there is more than one licensed partner or category in the store or across retailers.
11. Data and more data. With your success rising or falling with the single retailer, sales and performance data are very important and the data is available.

Let's take a look at how the HGTV HOME paint program, exclusively at Sherwin-Williams stores and subsequently at Lowe's stores, satisfied these requirements (with some callouts for Bassett as well).

1. **Innovative idea:** Consumers are overwhelmed by color choices in the paint section and don't have the confidence to choose the right colors that will work together in their home. The fresh idea was to provide consumers with paint products along with educational information and materials that guide them through the process. Very comprehensive point-of-purchase displays and take-away brochures, along with small sample cans of paint, provided this educational experience to confused consumers.
2. **Product design that addresses a consumer need:** HGTV used its expertise to develop color stories for different

styles of homes that consumers could rely on so that their paint choices coordinated with the other elements of their home décor. And Sherwin-Williams, knowing that it was the sole destination for this product, committed serious research and design to creating the right paint formulations. Bassett provided a customized design experience for the consumer.

3. **Retailer white space:** No retailer was effectively providing the consumer with this type of comprehensive solution in the paint category. Bassett was already offering the customized design service, but partnering with HGTV HOME helped consumers truly understand the offering.

4. **On-floor presence:** Both Sherwin-Williams and subsequently Lowe's embraced a new and innovative way of merchandising paint by offering displays featuring paint colors in whole home color palettes for not only painting but also decorating in general—in short, painting for the faint at heart. For Bassett, the HGTV HOME Design Studio is the hub of the entire store.

5. **Multiple touchpoints and coordinated product:** The assortment included indoor and outdoor paint. Naturally, the retailer controls the in-store experience, but collaboration is important. The brand needs to come to life on the floor as consumers are trying to make their brand choices. Both the retailer and the brand owner have a role to play. Sherwin-Williams created a totally new merchandiser specifically for the HGTV HOME brand that not only represented the innovative product offering (e.g., each color chip provides "know-how" tips) but also utilized the powerful attributes of HGTV as a design authority, solution provider, and inspirational guide.

6. **Consistent guidelines:** The HGTV HOME paint products were frequently offered in different aisles of the store, but always coordinated with uniform packaging and

product design. To accomplish this, HGTV created a comprehensive style guide for the use of its HGTV HOME logo, packaging, display, and other consumer-facing elements. And HGTV's licensees and retailers (in the paint as well as other categories) were not only delighted with the guidance but also successful in execution.

7. **Retailer sales training:** Sales associates who understand how to sell the brand are crucial in this type of program. Sherwin-Williams, a specialty retailer, relies heavily on in-store sales associates as an integral part of the customer experience, a key differentiator for the company and one of the reasons HGTV chose it as a partner. Sherwin-Williams developed a rollout plan to train its store managers and sales associates about the brand story, the features and benefits of the new product lines, and why these product lines were different from what it currently offered its consumers. Although Lowe's is a different type of retailer (a big-box retailer), it too trained sales associates to understand the HGTV HOME unique selling proposition with both direct and online training.

8. **Marketing by the brand owner:** HGTV supported the HGTV HOME brand, in general, with TV and print advertising as well as in *HGTV Magazine*. The network created custom specials that aired on HGTV featuring HGTV HOME and provided public relations assistance. HGTV also promoted the HGTV HOME, Sherwin-Williams, and Lowe's programs on its website.

9. **Marketing by the retailer:** Sherwin-Williams, Lowe's, and Bassett all committed to television campaigns (often on HGTV but also on other networks) as well as digital and print campaigns.

10. **Cross-Marketing:** There have been cross-partner marketing events where most of the HGTV HOME products were on sale, across retailers, for a limited period of time, with media support for the event. And Sherwin-

Williams worked with other HGTV partners to cross-promote each other's licensed lines. For example, Bassett Furniture features the HGTV HOME color palette, available at Sherwin-Williams, in its stores.

This discussion about retail exclusives warrants a brief further word about online and direct response TV exclusives (which include apps and online shopping). Amazon clearly recognizes the benefits of offering products exclusively on its site. That's why the company offers Amazon Exclusives to its Prime customers. It's a way to attract more consumers and to compete with other online exclusive e-commerce sites. Moreover, as of this writing, Amazon enjoys a growing reputation as a place to go for fashion trends. And in an early stage of a retail exclusive strategy, this e-commerce juggernaut introduced eight fashion brands (for women, men, and children) under a private-label strategy (i.e., Amazon owns the brand names). As we have witnessed at brick-and-mortar retailers over the years, a private-label strategy often leads to a complementary exclusive licensed brand strategy. This is probably where Amazon is heading. Amazon already looks to brands for retail exclusives, having signed Starter as an exclusive brand in 2017 when Walmart dropped its exclusive with Starter, and launched Dear Drew (from Drew Barrymore; more on that in Chapter 8) in 2017. There's more to come from Amazon and retail exclusives. As for HSN and QVC, they too look for exclusives (see Coca-Cola above). For example, HSN offers an exclusive collection of cookware, utensils, kitchen appliances, and more under the licensed magazine brand *Food & Wine.* And QVC offers Martha Stewart–branded products ranging from fashion to gardening tools (some exclusive and some nonexclusive). Of course, floor space is not an issue with online retailers, but the eleven factors noted previously remain applicable. Online and direct response TV retailers may not be restricted by physical space, but they still want compelling stories to tell, differentiation from their competitors as well as among the brands they offer.

The Risks: Be Aware of the Exclusive Pitfalls

With the success enjoyed by HGTV and the other companies discussed, you may wonder why anyone wouldn't choose the retail exclusive option. But before opting for this strategy, recognize that five potential disadvantages exist:

- *You are putting all of your eggs in one basket.* This can be very risky, particularly if the retailer doesn't support the brand as strongly as you would like or takes on other competitive brands that make it more difficult for you to succeed or the retailer has financial difficulties. Or the retailer might simply have a change in strategy. After ten years as a retail exclusive at Walmart, the Danskin Now brand, with hundreds of millions of dollars in retail sales annually, will be dropped by Walmart when the contract expires in January 2019, making way for a brand that Walmart probably believes has a broader audience (as of this writing, the brand has not yet been identified).
- *It's difficult to find a single retailer to support all categories.* The lead retailer might want more categories than it can actually handle, or it may demand categories where it is not particularly strong, limiting a brand's sales potential in those categories.
- *If for some reason the relationship ends, it can be challenging to find another home for the licensed product line.* This is particularly true for a brand owner who wants to move the retail exclusive up the retail channel (e.g., from midtier to department stores), which is rarely accomplished (Martha Stewart moving from Kmart to Macy's is a rare exception). Furthermore, retailers are not inclined to take on something that has been left behind by one of their competitors. (Amazon taking on Starter after Walmart dropped the brand is an example of an exception.)

- *Brand owners may risk design integrity if the retailer is designing and sourcing the product.* Unless the retailer can demonstrate its design and product development capabilities in a particular category, you may have to lead the design process on a sustained basis so that it isn't ceded to the retailer.
- *Brand owners can be prevented from working with other retailers as part of their licensing programs.* The exclusive retailer in one category may contractually prohibit a brand owner from offering licensed products in other categories to direct competitors. Working with retailers who don't otherwise compete with each other can help diminish this risk. That's why Martha Stewart has had retail exclusives at noncompetitors such as PetSmart, Office Depot, Michaels, and Macy's.
- *Finally, quite simply, you may not find a retailer that is right for your brand and the strategy that you have developed for your licensing program.* A finite universe of potential retailer candidates exists with retailers that are strong enough in brand-aligned ways to make this a worthwhile strategy.

Be aware, too, that brand owners do not want to alienate any of the retailers to which they sell their core products. For example, as mentioned in Chapter 3, Energizer is sold at all of the mass merchants (as well as many other types of retailers), usually in a very good location or locations in the store. Should Energizer offer a category of licensed products exclusively to Target? How would Walmart (also a major retailer of the core product) react? The retail exclusive strategy worked for Energizer with HSN because it was for a limited period of time and Energizer's other retail customers wouldn't be threatened by the arrangement with a direct response TV retailer. In fact, most retailers understand that products sold on direct response TV retailers such as HSN are generally considered a strong form of brand advertising, actually helping the brand at other retailers. Perhaps that's the reason Coca-Cola didn't believe that an exclusive program with HSN would be threatening to its brick-and-mortar retailers (of course, it could also be that Coca-Cola is such a strong brand that no retailer would risk being without it). But, in general, if you are distributing a core product broadly, you need to be very careful about granting an exclusive in a licensed product category to a competitor of your other retail accounts; it may feel to the "excluded" retailers as though you're thumbing your nose at them. That's why you don't see retail exclusives for licensed products from Stanley Black & Decker or Fabreze or Energizer. The retail exclusive road map for those brands is too risky.

The majority of retail exclusives seem to fall consistently into several types of brand owners: celebrities (see the next chapter), fashion brands, entertainment properties, and media brands. Conflicts are less likely in these categories. Celebrities are not present at all at retail, so parking the brand at a single retailer doesn't risk existing business at other retailers. Fashion and designer brands can make a strategic decision to be at a single retailer (e.g., Tommy Hilfiger at Macy's and the several Martha Stewart exclusive retailers). Sometimes what are termed "diffusion" lines (a different but related name generally at a cheaper price point) can work for a fashion brand (e.g., C9 Champion at Target and Danskin Now at Walmart, both of which apparently have not materially cannibalized the core Champion and Danskin brands). However, sometimes creating different sub-brand names to satisfy different retailers ends up confusing the customer. Consider the Liz Claiborne brand. For a time, the brand had different competing labels at Macy's and JCPenney. With such a similar customer base, the same consumer could be shopping at Macy's and then cross the street or walk to another part of the mall to JCPenney only to find a similar style with another Liz label and a cheaper price. Eventually, Liz Claiborne focused exclusively on JCPenney, diminishing consumer confusion.

In the true brand space, media companies seem to gravitate to the retail exclusive model or limited retailer model much more than consumable brands (e.g., *Better Homes & Gardens, HGTV, InStyle, The Food Network, Southern Living, Food & Wine, Glamour, Epicurious,* just to name a few, including some discussed above).[4] And this is a trend that will probably continue. Why is this true? It's all about communication. Magazines and broadcast networks as well as other types of media brands are communication vehicles. Licensing is another way for them to communicate with consumers (and their readers) on the retail selling floor or online. They already have a relationship with the consumer built on the content featured in the media vehicle. That content generates credibility and authenticity; it establishes the media company as an authoritative voice. It's like exercising a muscle constantly, generating organic reinforcement with consumers regularly. Retailers are attracted to that. And media companies don't generally have to worry about competing retailers given that so little of their sales are at the "newsstand." But media companies do need to ensure that they are not angering their advertisers (including retail advertisers) by competing with them.

Retailers, too, need to recognize that exclusive arrangements may not always serve their purposes. First, the retailer is making a potentially large commitment to a single brand in a category or categories—a commitment that may be too large to deliver the profits they seek and may have to be made to the detriment of other brands or private labels in the same category. Second, it adds incremental work for internal resources and teams across multiple departments, time commitments that may be too taxing. Instead of buying from the lines offered by vendors, buyers and others must get involved in product development, design, and marketing. Third, brand marketing opportunities may be too limited. In other words, in many product categories, retailers rely on the brand's

---

4. That's not to say that magazines always gravitate toward this model. Several magazines, for example, have licensed their titles in the furniture category and have not limited the collections to a single retailer—*Coastal Living, Real Simple,* and, most recently announced in March 2018, *Esquire. EatingWell* has licensed frozen foods for sale at supermarkets nationwide.

marketing program (e.g., the health and beauty category), but with a retail exclusive, the marketing burden will fall equally on both partners or more on the retailer. Finally, the exclusive relationship may damage other, albeit nonexclusive, partnerships or irritate other brands that are important to the retailer.

The Checklist: Ten Elements of Successful Retail Exclusive Partnerships

The following list will help brand owners and retailers (both online and offline retailers) assess whether the elements are in place to increase the odds of a successful partnership:

1. Alignment on the brand vision and the reason the licensed products fit that vision.
2. A brand champion at the retailer who will take responsibility for the program, preventing it from getting lost in the retailer's bureaucracy.
3. The retailer must be the right home for the category, meaning it must have a strong presence in the category and its geographical or online footprint fits the brand's needs.
4. The retailer must be able to make a cohesive brand statement in the exclusive categories, and the brand owner must be prepared to support the retailer with brand data, information, and collateral materials to help the retailer understand how to make that statement on the floor of the store or online.
5. Mutual agreement on a minimum buy.
6. An understanding of how much real estate on the floor or online pages will be devoted to the brand.
7. Agreement on a launch time frame and sustained marketing plan.
8. A mutual willingness to collaborate; this should be apparent before any agreement is finalized; "how it begins is how it ends."

9. Shared view of what the competition looks like at the retailer. If the retailer is strong in this category (as it should be to justify putting all of your eggs in one basket), other brands exist in the same category. Will you be able to compete?

10. The length of the agreed partnership will be a telling indicator of commitment on both sides. A short-term commitment (e.g., one year) indicates that at least one of the parties is hedging its bet. A longer-term commitment (such as five years) indicates that both parties are more likely to invest the necessary resources to be successful and not abandon the project if there are initial disappointments.

As noted at the beginning of this chapter, a retail exclusive is not necessarily the right strategy for every licensing program, but for those brand owners who are keen to jump-start their program, develop a comprehensive offering, and tell a brand story, the retail exclusive route has many advantages. But with benefits come risks. A thorough evaluation should be made before simply embracing this strategy.

CHAPTER 8

Celebrity Licensing

You may never be involved in a celebrity licensing program and may wonder why the subject is included in a book about brand licensing. The reason is that a handful of celebrities have achieved true brand status entirely through licensing. An understanding of how they have accomplished this is instructive for existing brands seeking to grow through licensing as well as new brands seeking to achieve consumer awareness. As you will discover, this subject provides insight about the dos and don'ts of brand licensing, including several best practices, and does so entertainingly.

Celebrity licensing has been going on for many years but has accelerated in recent years. This includes musicians (such as Adam Levine, Jennifer Lopez, and Beyoncé), movie stars (such as Drew Barrymore and Gwyneth Paltrow), television performers and actors (such as Ryan Seacrest), reality TV stars (such as Bethenny Frankel and Donald Trump before he became president), public figures (such as the Kardashians), supermodels (such as Heidi Klum, Cindy Crawford, Kate Moss, and Iman), chefs (such as Wolfgang Puck, Bobby Flay, and Jamie Oliver), athletes (such as Shaun White and Michael Vicks), estates of deceased celebrities (such as Bob Marley and Marilyn Monroe),[1] and influencers (such as Cupcakes and Cashmere and Michelle Phan).

Celebrities are beating on retail executive suites and the doors of manufacturers like never before, presenting themselves as the next big "brand" in a particular product category. And some are simply launching online on their own (Reese Witherspoon, for example). Hundreds of celebrities have tried to enter the consumer product space over the past 20 years. Although many of these efforts fail, some are successful and, as noted earlier, a select handful achieve true brand status.

Recently, several celebrities have decided to take a bigger stake in their consumer product program, both offline and online, by owning all or part of the company selling the products. This includes Goop (Gwyneth Paltrow), The Honest Company (Jessica Alba), L.A.M.B. (Gwen Stefani), Flower Beauty (Drew Barrymore), and Draper James (Reese Witherspoon).[2]

Fragrances have historically been an active category celebrities use to establish a product platform. However, very few lines survive long term (Elizabeth Taylor's White Diamonds being the mega exception, having launched in 1991 and still a top seller) and the celebrity is more akin to an endorser than a "brand." Recent fragrance introductions include Justin Bieber, Rihanna, Beyoncé, and Jennifer Lopez. Some say it all began with Sophia Loren in 1981; others, with Cher in 1987. But most agree that the success of Jennifer Lopez's Glow launched in 2002 was a tipping point for many celebrities to license their name for a fragrance. In 2014, 72 celebrity fragrances were introduced,

---

1. The estates of deceased celebrities, depending on legal rights of publicity, which vary from state to state, generally are licensing use more for advertising or theatrical purposes than for retail product. Nevertheless, there are some instances of licensed retail product utilizing the intellectual property of a deceased celebrity quite successfully, such as Michael Jackson and Elvis Presley.

2. Similarly, some celebrities have taken a stake in their own alcohol product line, such as Justin Timberlake's 901 Tequila, George Clooney's Casamigos tequila, Bethenny Frankel's Skinnygirl cocktails (she later sold it), Sean "Diddy" Combs's Ciroc, and, most recently, Bob Dylan's whiskey, Heaven's Door (announced in April 2018).

the number declining to 68 in 2015.[3] This chapter will focus on product categories, such as the apparel and home categories, where celebrity licensing serves as a petri dish of what does and doesn't work and why.[4]

What Makes a Celebrity a Brand?

Celebrities like to talk about their "brand." Yet few are brands. Is Tom Hanks a brand? Is Meryl Streep a brand? Both are great actors. Both are very prolific in their work and represent a diversity of roles. But are they brands like Oreo cookies is a brand? How would you describe the Tom Hanks brand? The Meryl Streep brand?

You can't describe them because they are not brands. They are celebrities. They are actors. They are artists. But they are not brands. But that doesn't mean that they can't become brands. Consider Kathy Ireland and Jaclyn Smith. And what about Paul Newman in the food category? Each has parlayed his or her original celebrity fame into a recognizable, comprehensive line of products with market staying power. And therein lies the key learnings for any brand seeking to use licensing successfully.

Kathy Ireland

Kathy Ireland was a *Sports Illustrated* swimsuit supermodel, appearing on three covers as well as being featured in the magazine's swimsuit issues for 13 consecutive years in the 1980s and 1990s. When her modeling career started slowing down, she launched her company in 1993. Departing from the obvious—a line of swimsuits—she began with socks (she got approached to endorse a line of socks, and instead, the manufacturer was persuaded to take a license using her name). Perhaps a bit ahead of her

---

3. "Trends in Celebrity Fragrance Launches Globally from 2013 to 2015," Statista: The Statistics Portal, undated.
4. There has also been a recent trend of celebrity licensed magazines (of course, Martha Stewart and Oprah Winfrey have had magazine titles for some time), including Gwyneth Paltrow's *Goop* magazine (Condé Nast), blogger Ree Drummond's *The Pioneer Woman Magazine* (Hearst), and HGTV stars Joanna and Chip Gaineses' *The Magnolia Journal* (Meredith).

time, she wanted to use a "brand" name other than her own name, but was convinced otherwise. Shortly thereafter, she got a call from Kmart. The store couldn't keep the socks in stock and wanted an exclusive. The Kathy Ireland program launched at Kmart in 1994 and grew to a full line of fashion apparel and accessories (Kmart saw it as the fashion version of their home celebrity, Martha Stewart).[5] Ireland stuck with Kmart through its bankruptcy, but following the bankruptcy, she decided that the retail exclusive strategy was too limiting. In 2004, she left Kmart and took a hiatus from selling her brand. She then embarked on an innovative strategy that remains the lynchpin of her successful business today— she moved out of fashion (where she had made a name for herself at Kmart) and focused on the home category with distribution at independent retailers.[6] Many retailers in this category (particularly independent retailers) don't have any advertising or marketing budget, so a famous name such as Kathy Ireland was (and still is) something that would attract customers. In 2011, the Kathy Ireland brand had retail sales, as reported by *Forbes* magazine, of over \$2 billion[7] with over 17,000 products,[8] from home products (the bulk of her product line), to select apparel, to furniture, wall décor, children's publishing and educational games, pet products, diamond jewelry, and more. There's a business-to-business line of licensed merchandising and display products for independent

---

5. Interestingly at the time, Jaclyn Smith, whose fashion program had been exclusively at Kmart since 1983, needed to consent to any potentially competitive program at Kmart. She allowed Kmart to move forward with Kathy Ireland and became a big supporter of Kathy Ireland. To this day, Kathy Ireland credits Jaclyn Smith with giving her the start she had at Kmart.

6. Actually, Warren Buffett, a friend, advised Kathy that she should make the transition from the ever-changing and fickle fashion category to the steadier and more consistent home category—advice that she followed. They remain fast friends to this day.

7. "Kathy Ireland: Swimsuit Cover Girl Turned \$2 Billion Business Model?," by Moira Forbes, *Forbes*, February 13, 2012. Kathy Ireland's company, Kathy Ireland Worldwide, continues to refer to that sales number as reported in *Forbes* and self-reported \$2.6 billion in retail sales for 2016 (see footnote 9 below).

8. "How Kathy Ireland Built a \$420 Million Fortune," by Natalie Robehmed, *Forbes*, May 25, 2015.

Figure 1. Stanley licensed manual garden tool and
personal protection equipment. Used with permission.
Courtesy of Stanley Black & Decker, Inc.

Figure 2. Baileys' licensed ice cream and chocolates.
Used with permission. Courtesy of Diageo Ireland.

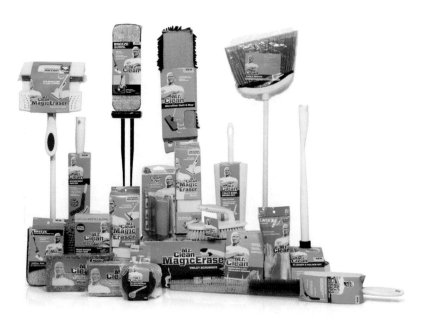

Figure 3. Mr. Clean licensed brooms, mops and other household cleaning products. Used with permission. Courtesy of The Procter & Gamble Company.

Figure 4. Febreze licensed for Fresh Step cat litter; Glad trash bags; carpet care products; laundry odor eliminator; home candles; and air purifiers. Used with permission. Courtesy of The Procter & Gamble Company.

Figure 5. Black & Decker licensed small kitchen appliances. Used with permission. Courtesy of Stanley Black & Decker, Inc.

Figure 6. Licensed Briggs & Stratton air compressor with Quiet Power Technology; non-ethanol premium fuel. Used with permission. Courtesy of Briggs & Stratton Corporation.

Figure 7. Energizer licensed 180-watt Cup Power Inverter, Digital TTL Camera Flash, i-Surge Mobile Charging Station; and Portable Watt Inverter Generator. Used with permission. Courtesy of Energizer Brands, LLC

Figure 8. Better Homes & Gardens licensed candles and melamine dinnerware. Used with permission. Courtesy of Meredith Corporation.

7

Figure 9. HGTV licensed product assortment for the home. Used with permission. Courtesy of Scripps Networks, LLC.

retailers. The Kathy Ireland brand consists of not only Kathy Ireland–branded product but also co-branded licensed product such as NuGene by Kathy Ireland (beauty products for aging skin and hair loss) and collaborations with Nicholas Walker for Jardin garden and lawn products and with Chef Andre Carthen (a.k.a., the Fit Chef) for ACafe cooking products and wedding advice as well as a partnership for diamond jewelry. These collaborations and co-brands are targeted at categories in which the Kathy Ireland brand might have some credibility but will also benefit from the expertise and brand credibility of other brand names.[9]

Ireland did many things right that are lessons for brands. She succeeded with two very different strategies. First, she used her celebrity fame to establish credibility in the fashion category (where a supermodel might have some authority among fans) through a retail exclusive with Kmart, where she received attention, focus, and commitment from the retailer. Second, abandoning that seemingly successful strategy, she turned to a category that needed an authoritative voice in a particular distribution channel—the home category in the independent retail channel. She filled a market white space. Third, she successfully utilized a co-brand strategy when she recognized the need to share credibility with another brand in a category. Finally, she has worked hard at all of this, devoting her full-time attention and making a serious commitment of resources to support her licensing program.

What's in a Name?

Some celebrities attempt to detach their personal name from their consumer products (as Kathy Ireland thought to do). They want to focus on a name that might stand on its own without relying totally on their celebrity status although still making the connection to the celebrity to, at the very least, get off the ground. The theory

---

9. Kathy Ireland is ranked #26 with reported retail sales of $2.6 billion in "The Top 150 Global Licensors," *License Global*, April 2017, Volume 20, Number 2.

goes like this: The product line will have a better chance of success if it's "powered by" the celebrity name but the product doesn't actually feature the name as the "brand" name, driving a wider consumer audience to include those who don't want to be so obviously tied to the celebrity. These are celebrities who recognize how difficult it is for a personality with little to no product category reputation to become a brand in a particular category and conclude that they can start a brand by connecting their celebrity name to an inanimate name that can live on. For example, L.A.M.B. (Gwen Stefani), Fabletics (Kate Hudson), The Honest Company (Jessica Alba), and Flower Beauty (Drew Barrymore) fall into this category. It doesn't mean that the celebrity name is totally absent from the product line, however. Barrymore actively promotes her Flower line of products in POP, through marketing, online, and on social media, just not on the product or packaging itself. Separating the celebrity name from the brand name, however, has proven somewhat elusive. Newman's Own still uses Paul Newman's image on the packaging. White Diamonds is still Elizabeth Taylor's White Diamonds. And so on. Both, however, have become true brands in their categories. The key learning? Your name is your brand, whether it be a corporate brand name or a celebrity name. It's challenging to create a new brand or a sub-brand through licensing, certainly in the short term, without resources, commitment, and a purpose (consider Coca-Cola's EKOCYCLE as one that has had some success, discussed in Chapter 2).

Tell a Story

Mere fame is not sufficient for turning a well-known personality into a brand. Instead, potential customers require a story that they understand and embrace consistently over a period of time (just like any good brand). In fact, this last requirement is why most celebrity licensing programs follow the retail exclusive model. Brands are not developed overnight. Even in our age of the Internet, true brands take time to be developed, nurtured, and marketed and to take hold in the minds of consumers. And that takes plenty of work. Celebrities, in general, already have a day job, so they are looking for a shortcut. Retail exclusives can provide that shortcut. The celebrity immediately has compelling floor space or online presence at a retailer, the product line is displayed in a comprehensive manner, it's marketed by the retailer, and it fills a consumer need. The retailer is hungry to generate foot traffic or page views and sales and to communicate an image that sets it apart from its competitors. And with that kind of retail commitment (whether it be brick and mortar or online retail or both), a story gets to be told. Their interests intersect. The model presents most of the same benefits and risks discussed in the preceding chapter on the retail exclusive model.

In examining the celebrity programs that have been announced and subsequently launched (or not), the vast majority do not survive for the long term. But that hasn't stopped the stampede, and retailers have taken the bait. Why? What drives success? Let's take a look.

Consider why consumers are interested in celebrity merchandise in the first place. It's all about aspiration and empowerment. The celebrity must evoke identifiable and aspirational brand-like equities in the minds of consumers. Consumers aspire to be like their favorite celebrities. They want to dress like them, look like them, smell like them, live like them. Purchasing products that are genuinely tied to the celebrity sprinkles consumers with some of that fairy dust while at the same time providing them with products to fit their needs and tastes (and price points). Kathy Ireland was a famous supermodel. Women wanted to be and look like her. It drove sales. And if the celebrity has a true story to tell, that story can also empower consumers to make certain purchase decisions. Consumers need motivation to buy, and the aspirational and empowering qualities of a celebrity might be the motivating factor. Kathy Ireland was always about the product and the consumer, not about her fame (although her fame is what got her started). And she had a story to tell. She wanted to provide cost-effective solutions for busy moms and women everywhere.

And women identified with this story. In today's 24/7 plugged-in world, consumers crave inside information and accessibility to their favorite personalities. Through the launch of relevant and compelling consumer products and services (and with a story to tell) licensing creates an organic, one-on-one experience between celebrity and fan/consumer. In many ways, the same can be said of existing consumer brands. Licensed products tell a story about the brand, they connect with consumers in different ways, and they allow consumers to further identify with the brand and invite the brand into their lives.

However, as is always true of licensing programs, this works only if authenticity exists to drive that first purchase. To retain the consumer, to get that consumer to buy again, the products must be well designed, priced correctly, and offered to the consumer where he or she shops. The consumer must believe that the celebrity's "signature" is on the product, that the celebrity has been deeply involved in the design and aesthetic of the product, and that the products reflect the celebrity's tastes, style, and confidence. All true for any brand engaged in licensing.

Drew Barrymore

Again, consider Flower Beauty (Drew Barrymore). She is a famous actor, author, producer, and model. We have watched her on screen in countless movies since she was six years old in *E.T. the Extra-Terrestrial* (1982), and fans have been following her public career ever since. She formed Flower Films in 1995, which has produced many motion pictures over the years. In 2013, she launched Flower Beauty[10] with a line of beauty products sold exclusively at Walmart. In 2017, Barrymore launched a lifestyle brand named Dear Drew on Amazon Fashion, which includes apparel, bags, jewelry, and

---

10. The Flower Beauty products are actually a hybrid license. Flower Beauty is a venture owned by Drew Barrymore and a company named Maesa. Barrymore owns the intellectual property and licenses it to Flower Beauty, which sells the product to Walmart through Maesa, which also pays a royalty to Barrymore. Other categories (e.g., eyewear) are straight licenses from Barrymore.

hair accessories (perhaps the first celebrity launch on Amazon Fashion). Prior to launching Flower Beauty, Barrymore served as the co-creative director for Cover Girl cosmetics for eight years. She was part of the brand's advertising and marketing campaigns, and she was involved in concept development and photography, in addition to having other responsibilities. In short, she received a real education in the beauty space and established herself as a credible authority to consumers—that in addition to the fact that she has been sitting in makeup chairs since she was six years old. Barrymore also believed that she had a positive message, a story, to communicate to women: that they could make themselves up (with makeup products) to be themselves and not to be someone else; that they deserved the best quality products at an affordable price—a message and story of empowerment and self-confidence.

Walmart viewed her beauty line as a natural transition from her role at Cover Girl and placed the product in the same aisle as Cover Girl products and other major brands in the category. Flower represents premium product at an affordable price at Walmart—what women deserve, according to Barrymore. There is a story and a vision attached to the brand. But it's also about fairy dust.

As is necessary for any retail exclusive program, Barrymore is actively engaged in all aspects of the Flower beauty line. She and her staff work closely with the product development company on all of the products and stays on top of trends in the category as well as innovations for new products. Thirty to 50 new products have been introduced almost every year. And she actively supports the line on her websites and social media, particularly Instagram, where she has over six million followers. In 2017, she launched an e-commerce site featuring text-based and video tutorials offering makeup tips. The product line has grown in each of the past five years and, in 2017, was expanded to Walmart Mexico. More Flower-branded products are expected. Moreover, her plan is to develop a group of global lifestyle brands at different tiers of distribution, all "powered by" Barrymore (such as Dear Drew, mentioned earlier). All of these efforts lend an air of authenticity to this celebrity licensing program and are examples of how a brand licensing program can and should be supported.

Assessing Celebrity and Retailer Motivation: Why They Do It?

The best licensee and licensor relationships are reciprocal. When both parties realize desired benefits, the relationship flourishes and the licensing program is usually successful. This dynamic, however, is complex. What each party gets out of the relationship must involve more than money. Understanding the motivations of celebrity and retailer—the licensing dynamic of these two parties—can provide insight for any brand owner seeking to enter and maintain the necessary outcome that both licensor and licensee seeks.

Let's Start with Celebrity Motivation

Why are celebrities interested in licensing? They make a great deal of money, for example, acting, performing, and endorsing products. Is it just ego? Remaining "top of mind" over the long term, particularly if their career as an artist is fading? A passion for a particular product category? A message they want to communicate? Or is it the hypercompetitive reflex of "if that guy can do it, then so can I"? Perhaps there's some truth to all of those sentiments.

Many times, however, licensing is the first step to building a personal brand—a goal for many celebrities. Consider the Kathy Ireland story. She started as a celebrity, but over a period of time, with a full commitment, a vision, a story to tell and a passion for product, she made the transition to a brand. Perhaps Drew Barrymore will also make this transition. Licensing gives the celebrity a way to interact with fans through channels outside of entertainment, turning them into consumers. And licensed products allow celebrities to transcend "flash-in-the-pan" type popularity gained through endorsements, creating a much more sustainable, long-term presence. It also represents a career path with long-term potential (Kathy Ireland's modeling career ended

25 years ago). Here are three of the more salient reasons celebrities try to pursue a consumer products path (all apply to consumer brands as well):

1. **Increase consumer touchpoints.** Sound familiar? Licensing allows celebrities to engage and grow their fan base. Celebrities today are able to diversify between appearing on television or motion picture screens or the concert stage, on social media and on mobile devices. This omnipresence facilitates creation of an engaged base of people who are excited about products the celebrity is licensing. Consumers have increased access to the celebrity through the licensed products, increasing consumer engagement with and awareness of the celebrity. And, of course, as celebrities age and see their fame or the activity that made them famous fading, a successful consumer products plan can become a key ingredient of their future career. Indeed, it can become their entire career (again, see Kathy Ireland). Consider all of the legs of Drew Barrymore's career—actor, producer, author, director, model, consumer products. As some of these activities become less important in her career, consumer products can become an even more important focus. Others have made the leap as well, such as Jaclyn Smith, Martha Stewart, and Daisy Fuentes (at Kohl's), or are getting there, such as Jennifer Lopez and Gwen Stefani.

2. **Become an authority.** When celebrities enter into licensing because they are passionate about a certain product category, they want to position themselves as an authority the consumer can trust. The celebrity has something to say, a story to tell, about a product category. This is particularly true of digital celebrities, discussed later in this chapter. Again, it sounds brand-like to me. But celebrities (and any licensor) need to remember that product development is a "hands on" process. Clout, trust, and fame are not

a replacement for quality product. And given that the celebrity is the connection to the consumer, the celebrity needs to be front and center communicating the value and vision of the product. Celebrities who ignore this are at great risk of failure. Drew Barrymore is passionate about the beauty category, she is educated in the category, she has a story to tell, she is authentic in the category, and she works hard at it—she's committed. Ditto Kathy Ireland. Her company has its own design studio where she and her designers meet regularly with its partners and set the design tone and inspiration as well as the color palettes for multiple product lines. Brand owners need to be prepared to make the same kind of commitments.

3. **Drive revenue.** If the product line is successful, the royalties can generate a powerful revenue stream over a long period of time. In particular, this represents a great opportunity for celebrities whose careers have peaked. With CD sales disappearing and the rise of iTunes, musicians have had to rely mostly on concert tours for revenue. Licensing has helped musicians not only to generate revenue for themselves but also to remain relevant between album launches and concert tours and, in a way, to reinvent themselves—a new way to burnish their reputations. Sean John (a.k.a., Diddy) is a good example of a musician who has developed a genuine fashion apparel brand that has lasted for many years.

And why are retailers so interested in celebrity licensing programs when many of them (actually, most of them) fail (if they even get off the ground)? Consider the following three reasons (which also generally apply to brand owners):

1. **Engaging fan base (loyalists).** Retailers benefit from the celebrity's fan base that wants to interact with the celebrity in new ways, through licensed product. Drew Barrymore's fans trust her credibility in the category.

2. **Attracting new consumers.** Celebrities can deliver a fresh audience to a retailer. This will only happen, however, when a celebrity resonates with the retailer's core customer. In the case of Drew Barrymore, Walmart's core customer wants a premium-like product she can afford. Flower delivers on that consumer need. Famous designers won't sell their apparel to mass merchants, so celebrity lines take the place of designers at an affordable price. That's the white space Jaclyn Smith filled at Kmart so many years ago. Always look for white space.

3. **Remaining relevant (retention).** Staying relevant to consumers is a major retailer concern, and associations with celebrities help them demonstrate relevancy. Celebrities allow retailers to connect with a wider array of consumers who the retailer may not have been able to reach through its traditional product and service offerings. This is particularly true with younger demographics and digital celebrities. But even more importantly, *relevance* encapsulates the entirety of the program, including selecting the right product category for the right consumer audience at the right price point at the right retailer. Every part must work together to ensure success. Flower competes with many major brands with substantial advertising campaigns. It is able to compete without those kinds of resources because of its relevancy to consumers that is communicated by Barrymore. Social media has enabled new brands to emerge without the massive resources required by traditional advertising (see Chapter 12).

Of course, retailers need to be mindful about the possibility of negative publicity with celebrities, much more so than with consumer brands. One media scandal can send sales of an otherwise successful product plummeting. Consider what happened with Paula Dean, whose racist comments got her kicked off The Food Network and sales of her licensed products collapsed.

After some initial setbacks, Martha Stewart ultimately survived going to jail in 2004. Kathy Lee Gifford lost her apparel collection at Walmart (over $700 million in sales) in 2000 because it was revealed that sweatshops in Central America were used to manufacture her licensed apparel products. And with digital celebrities largely unscripted, this is an even bigger risk. Negative publicity will always be a risk working with celebrities, particularly in the early years.

With so many failures over the years,[11] what's the secret sauce that allows one celebrity to succeed and causes so many others to fail? Obviously, poor quality or ill-conceived products will fail no matter what celebrity (or brand) is attached to them. Beyond that, however, following are five factors that are necessary for celebrity success (and that although less exaggerated, more or less generally apply to any brand):

1. **Vision:** The celebrity must have a strong product and/or aesthetic vision for a product category, whether it be fashion, accessories, home products, health and beauty products, food, or some other category where there are volume opportunities. Drew Barrymore has a strong vision for beauty products as well as the business acumen to understand Walmart's consumer and drive sales. Kathy Ireland had a strong vision when she started her home product line in 2003, and that vision remained constant even as she became a brand.

2. **White space:** Retailers don't need more of what they already have. The celebrity needs to be filling a gap in the retailer's product assortment. There must be a need. For example, Mary-Kate and Ashley Olsen were very successful at Walmart for ten years with their *marykatean-*

---

11. A quick Google search reveals scores of celebrities announcing licensing programs that never got off the ground or managed to make it to a retail shelf for only a short period of time. I'll save them the embarrassment and not list them here. But there are many of them.

dashley line of fashions because Walmart was weak in offering fashion apparel and accessories for tween girls. The *marykateandashley* line filled the gap. (See the case study below.) Kathy Ireland uses her brand on products for everyday use by everyday consumers. Jennifer Lopez at Kohl's and Sofia Vergara at Kmart satisfy the underserved Hispanic market.

3. **Time commitment:** A celebrity needs to put in the time and be involved in all aspects of planning, product development, design, approvals, and then marketing. She needs to promote the line of products. When I meet with celebrities, I try to scare them off with the work that will be required. If they survive the scare tactics, at least I know they are serious. Many celebrities are simply not prepared for the demands a licensing program will place on them. If they don't make that commitment, the products will likely lack authenticity and the consumer will "smell" it. Drew Barrymore, Jaclyn Smith, Kathy Ireland, Mary-Kate and Ashley Olsen, among others, all have devoted significant and meaningful time to their consumer products programs. Licensors need to be operationally ready, whether they are celebrities or consumer products companies.

4. **Staying power:** The celebrity must be able to sustain his or her fame long enough for products to be developed, reach the shelves, and sell through. Waning fame or a public relations misstep can take its toll before product is even in the market. Certain types of celebrities clearly pose risky strategies (e.g., the "now" celebrity). Trying to ride the wave of recent exposure or semi-celebrity status is a short-term tactic (that might generate some revenue). That's why so many gold medal Olympians, with high expectations of developing product lines, never get that far. Their fame dissipates quickly. Consider Gabby Douglas, gold medal winner at the 2012 London Games, or Michael Phelps, all-time Gold medal swimmer. In both

instances, their fame faded before product could be developed and launched. Also falling into this category are the 15-minutes-of-fame television reality stars. Consider the failed licensing program of Snooki Polizzi, star of the relatively short-lived series *Jersey Shore*. Indeed, the only star of Bravo's *Housewives* series to seriously succeed with product has been Bethenny Frankel with her Skinnygirl low-cal margarita mix (other Skinnygirl products, however, largely faded from the market). The same is generally true of influencers (see Chapter 12). With few exceptions, they haven't demonstrated (yet) the staying power necessary to launch a consumer products program that lasts. Equity takes time to build, and flash in the pans are not in the public consciousness for a sufficient period of time. Public figures can also be risky given the potential for controversy. Donald Trump's licensing program is a perfect example. When controversy struck during his 2016 Presidential campaign, retailers abandoned him (e.g., Macy's). On the other hand, once launched, a successful licensing program can create staying power for the celebrity, reviving his or her celebrity status in brand form. Consider Jaclyn Smith who launched her program at Kmart in 1983 at the height of her fame as a television star on *Charlie's Angels* but who is now "famous" for her line of apparel at Kmart. Ditto Kathy Ireland who is now "famous" for her consumer products and not as a *Sports Illustrated* cover swimsuit model. Both have transitioned from "celebrity" to "brand."

5. **Credibility:** The celebrity must have credibility with the right consumers. People in the target demographic must believe in what the celebrity is selling. It's not enough for a given Hollywood star to like fashionable clothing; she must at least seem like a fashion authority. Think about Sarah Jessica Parker's role on *Sex and the City*. That role made Sarah Jessica Parker appear to be a fashion author-

ity (unfortunately she chose to work with a retailer, Steve & Barry's, that went bankrupt). Or consider Drew Barrymore's credibility in the beauty space. Celebrities as well as consumer products brands can easily misfire in the wrong category where they do not have credibility.

The *marykateandashly* Program

Let's take a look at a licensed celebrity retail exclusive that hit all of the right buttons, ran its course, but lasted almost a decade. The *marykateandashley* program, exclusively at Walmart, serves as a good example of what any brand owner can accomplish with a retail partner if the brand owner and the retailer are committed to the program.

In 1987, when they were only nine months old, Mary-Kate and Ashley Olsen were part of the ensemble cast on the ABC sitcom *Full House.* The show was an instant success, and the girls grew from tots to school age right before the viewing audience. Young girls grew up with Mary-Kate and Ashley on *Full House* and their second television series, *Two of a Kind* (which premiered in 1998).

The girls always seemed to be wearing trendy outfits in their videos, and moms started contacting the girls' company, Dualstar Entertainment, asking where they could purchase the fashions for their own young daughters, fans of Mary-Kate and Ashley. The idea of a line of fashion apparel began to take shape. There was virtually no well-known fashionable clothing for tween girls (approximately ages 5–12) at the mass market channel of distribution. The strategy became clear—offer the Mary-Kate and Ashley fashion line to a single retailer that would commit to sufficient floor space to display the full range, make a fashion statement at the store, and support the line with marketing. The brand found a champion at Walmart. Dualstar licensed companies recommended by Walmart to manufacture the goods and sell them solely to Walmart. Dualstar demanded very aggressive contract terms from its licensees, including industry-high royalty rates and expense reimbursements (which would later come back to hurt Dualstar). It was the year

2000, and license agreements were signed for apparel, handbags, hats, sleepwear, footwear, eyewear, and hair accessories. Dualstar Central Design was created as an in-house studio that designed the fashions and stayed current with the trends. The company also designed the logo and brand architecture for the *marykateandashley* program at Walmart. Dualstar created the photography for hang tags and packaging that licensees were required to use and provided the photography to Walmart for all of its in-store signage and rack displays.

Before the launch, Walmart supported the introduction of the program with internal stakeholders. This included educating store managers with "kits" about the line as well as an appearance by the girls and a presentation of the program and some of the products to approximately 300 senior executives of Walmart at its Bentonville, Arkansas, headquarters, a meeting run by Lee Scott, CEO of Walmart at the time.[12]

The *marykateandashley* line launched at Walmart in Spring 2001. Sales were explosive and sell-through of the products beat expectations. The program tapped into the aspirations of young girls and filled a white space in the mass market channel of distribution. Many stores could not get the merchandise from the warehouse to the selling floor fast enough. The program continued to grow over the years, and more than 20 new categories were added to the mix, including cosmetics, fragrance, intimates, jeans, outerwear, socks, watches, and a home collection that included furniture, rugs, and lamps. The cosmetics and fragrance were also sold outside of Walmart, and the home collection was sold entirely outside of Walmart.

---

12. It was a regular meeting held every Saturday morning, called the Saturday Morning Meeting, and executives were told in advance that they could bring their children to meet Mary-Kate and Ashley and get signed photos. Over 2,000 children showed up at 7:30 a.m., lined up inside and outside the building. That outpouring of fans (only for internal stakeholders with no publicity) became very persuasive for those executives who were, up to that morning, lukewarm about the program at Walmart.

However, due to the success of the program, Dualstar (and Walmart) began to stretch too far with products and introduced some head-scratchers—toothpaste, boom boxes and CD players, and camping chairs, to name a few (all of them failed). Success emboldened Dualstar to become even more demanding of its licensees. Walmart complained that the extreme financial demands being placed on the licensees was resulting in higher retail prices. Friction developed (which soured some senior executives at Walmart) but was overshadowed by the program's continued success. Walmart relied on *marykateandashley* to be the store's stylish, hip, fashion-forward, fun, and sassy collection for tween girls. It was on its way to becoming a brand.

Dualstar supported the brand with marketing both inside and outside of Walmart, as did the retailer. The company worked with Walmart to create and support what Walmart called "retailtainment" events in the stores to drive customers to the stores. The brand was featured prominently in Walmart circulars, received at the time by almost 100 million households. Walmart experimented by opening several shops within its stores dedicated solely to the brand. CEO Lee Scott spoke of the success of the brand at the 2002 Annual Shareholders Meeting and introduced the girls onstage (that year Walmart became the #1 company in the United States). In addition, the brand was prominently displayed at semi-annual meetings for employees.

Dualstar was very aggressive garnering publicity for the girls and engaged in online marketing (fairly rudimentary back then compared to today) and print advertising. Barely a week went by when they were not featured on the cover of a pop culture magazine or in an article or photos. Press included lifestyle stories about the girls as well as product placement in magazines and newspapers.[13]

---

13. It was estimated by Dualstar that during the years 2001 to 2009, Mary-Kate and Ashley made more than 100 talk show appearances around the world, were featured on over 50 magazine covers, were mentioned in hundreds of articles, and were the first child celebrities to appear on the front page of *The Wall Street Journal*.

A similar strategy was implemented in 10 countries around the world, always with an exclusive retail partner. International programs were more challenging for Dualstar given the girls' inconsistent fame in various countries. Some territories were successful (e.g., the United Kingdom and Australia); others were not (Japan and Germany, for example).

The brand survived one very bad episode. During the summer of 2004, photos of an exceptionally thin Mary-Kate started appearing in the press with rumors of anorexia and, even worse, drug abuse (which turned out not to be true). And in July, Mary-Kate entered rehab for an eating disorder. The press was all over the story, and, indeed, Mary-Kate was in and out of rehab several times that year. Dualstar was up front with its retail partners and stayed in front of the story. Retailers did not abandon the program, and moms across the country empathized with Mary-Kate. The storm passed largely because the brand owner was transparent with its retailers.

By 2008, the girls had become interested in fashion design and were growing weary of their work to support a tween mass fashion brand. They were too old at that point to wear the product, and without their support, the Walmart program faded away. Today the girls have abandoned their careers as entertainers and are accepted as fashion designers with successful brands under the Dualstar roof, such as The Row, sold at upscale department stores and manufactured and distributed by Dualstar, and Elizabeth and James (named after their siblings) initally licensed to a third party in 2007 but taken in-house by Dualstar in 2016 and for department store distribution.

What can brand owners (and, of course, other celebrities) learn from the *marykateandashley* program? What did they do right, and what did they do wrong?

Right

1. **Vision:** The girls, supported by their Design Studio, understood fashion trends and how to apply them to the

tween girl market. And Dualstar had the business acumen to develop and execute a strategy to implement that vision—a vision aligned with the product. Dualstar created great product design that addressed a consumer need.

2. **White Space:** Dualstar and Walmart both recognized weakness in trendy fashion apparel and accessories for tween girls at the mass retail level. This was a case of retailers not addressing a need.

3. **Time Commitment and Control:** Dualstar executives and the girls devoted time and resources to ensuring that the program would be successful. And Dualstar worked hard to control as much of the process as possible (not an easy task given Walmart's dominance). The company developed designs and guidelines that it compelled licensees to use to project a consistent image for the brand. And Dualstar's agency employed two full-time executives located in Bentonville, Arkansas, to help manage the program (including data collection).

4. **Credibility and Fan Base:** This was a strength of Mary-Kate and Ashley. They were young girls when the program started, admired by a large fan base of tween girls for the trendy, fashionable way they dressed. The target demographic believed in the authenticity of the product that was offered for sale.

5. **New Consumers and Relevance:** Neither Walmart nor any of its major competitors were adequately serving the tween girl market with fashion product. This program not only served the existing consumer but also drove new consumers to the store. And let's not forget that the actual consumer for this product was the mom. Driving the mom into the store meant that Walmart could pick up sales in other aisles. Further, many of Walmart's customers would shop for their groceries at Walmart but not cross the aisle into the other part of the store. This program motivated moms of tween girls to make that short journey from groceries to

apparel (a similar goal of Walmart with *The Better Homes & Gardens* program, as mentioned in Chapter 7).

6. **Consumer Touchpoints:** Mary-Kate and Ashley already touched the lives of young girls with their television programs, videos, and books. Developing the Walmart program and its extensions allowed the girls to expand those touchpoints. Their audience was now able to bring the lifestyle of the girls into their own homes, bedrooms, and closets.

7. **Becoming an Authority:** Although the girls were well known at a very young age for wearing fashionable clothing, it was their deep involvement in the Walmart program, which was often mentioned by the media, that established them as authorities in fashion design—so much so that by the time they disengaged from the *marykateandashley* program, they were able to jump-start an entirely new and successful career as authentic designers of owned and licensed fashion brands. Licensing can create an authoritative voice for a brand in a new category.

8. **Revenue:** This will appear in both the "Right" and "Wrong" sections. Suffice it to say that Dualstar made a great deal of money from the royalties paid by licensees.

9. **The Right Retailer:** Walmart was the right choice as a retailer; it reached the core customer (tween girls and their moms) for the licensed products. The chain was nationwide and easily accessible by virtually the entire U.S. population. And there was an initial senior executive at Walmart who championed the concept.[14] Although weak in fashion apparel for tween girls, Walmart had a strong presence in clothing for the target age group with a fair amount of floor space devoted to this customer. And given

---

14. The brand champion who initially embraced this program was Lori Meyer, then the Divisional Merchandise Manager for Department 33, Girls apparel. As other buyers became associated with the program, many of them became supporters as well.

the size of Walmart's floor footprint, the retailer was able to present the brand in a cohesive way in diverse areas of the store with floor space, coordinated signage on the shelves, and racks, hang tags, and in-store marketing.

10. **Marketing:** The marketing of the program undertaken by both Dualstar and Walmart, to consumers, the media, and internal stakeholders, was robust, comprehensive, and continuous. It included cross-marketing among different categories of the brand across the store (e.g., hang tags promoted not only the particular product but also other products offered by the brand in the store).

11. **On-Floor Competition:** For any brand to stand out and succeed in a retail exclusive program, the brand must be differentiated from other similarly situated brands also being offered by that retailer. Walmart and Dualstar agreed early on that the *marykateandashley* brand would be the most fashion-forward brand for tween girls at the store. Walmart had other brands, both third-party and private-label brands, that could have competed with *marykateandashley,* but Dualstar and Walmart worked closely during every season's new product development to create distinctions among the brands and avoid overlap. This required a good deal of collaboration and advance planning. And Dualstar had to advocate with Walmart executives to sustain this strategy and ensure that the best trends were utilized for their brand.

12. **Data:** Dualstar was data-driven. The company was on top of orders placed by Walmart; manufacturing, shipping, and delivery timelines to ensure that nothing arrived in Walmart's warehouses late; daily sales data from Walmart's internal systems in order to analyze what was and was not selling well; and approval tracking. Dualstar held regular meetings with buying teams at Walmart and presented what was and was not selling as well and how to correct errors and take advantage of opportunities. Collecting and

understanding the available data was very important to the success of the program, as is true of any retail exclusive program (and today, just ten years later, data collection is exponentially more sophisticated and comprehensive).

Wrong

1. **Staying Power:** Dualstar was convinced that the success of the *marykateandashley* program would create a brand that would allow the program to continue as the girls aged and moved on with their careers. Mary-Kate and Ashley were immensely popular with their target audience. And as their original audience aged, new girls entered the age group and became fans of Mary-Kate and Ashley and the program at Walmart. What Dualstar didn't account for was Mary-Kate and Ashley's personal ambitions and desires to move on with their careers. As they disengaged, the program stumbled. Celebrity programs always run this risk of disengagement, which was magnified in this instance by the girls growing up. If *marykateandashley* had truly become a brand, it might have survived. No brand owner can ever take the success of its licensing program for granted.

2. **Revenue:** Yes, Dualstar made a great deal of money. But at what cost? From inception, the company was extremely aggressive leveraging the fame of the girls as well as the power of Walmart's commitment to the program by insisting on demanding and one-sided provisions in the agreements with licensees. In particular, this included exceptionally high royalty rates to cover use of the brand, marketing, and design costs as well as requirements that the licensees reimburse the company for certain expenses, such as fashion shows and travel, particularly to Walmart's headquarters in Arkansas. As the program succeeded, these tactics became even more aggressive. Licensees complained to Walmart that then, in turn, complained

to Dualstar. It caused friction and resentment, which did not benefit the program or the girls' reputations within Walmart (although they clearly were not on the front lines of the business dealings). Don't chase the money!

3. **Commitment:** There was no contract between Dualstar and Walmart. In fact, Walmart made it clear to Dualstar that the products could expand beyond the walls of the retailer. Despite that freedom, Dualstar was extremely selective when it came to allowing products to be sold outside of Walmart, limiting it to the health and beauty products that were licensed to a category leader, Coty, and the home products, such as furniture, which were not a strength of Walmart. But the absence of a contract also meant that there was no formal commitment by the retailer for a minimum buy of product or a commitment to floor space or marketing. The program had to continue to deliver strong sales, season by season, to deserve the retailer's commitment. And Dualstar always had to be a strong advocate of the product line with Walmart executives. Any brand is on shaky ground without a contractual commitment as part of a retail exclusive.

The *marykateandashley* program was groundbreaking in many ways—and it got more things right than wrong—but its real value is as a case history that can teach us a great deal about brand licensing and retail exclusives. Although it obviously is relevant for celebrities and retailers considering a celebrity licensing program, it is just as valuable for brand owners considering any type of licensing strategy, particularly those contemplating a single retailer approach. Importantly, the *marykateandashley* example highlights that the dynamics of working with a single retailer are different from working in a broad licensed product distribution strategy. The celebrity or brand owner in a retail exclusive relationship must oversee all of the moving parts from design to manufacture to shipment and delivery to on-floor or online presence and marketing. But in the end, "all of your eggs in one basket" can be a highly successful partnership if you meet the challenge of maintaining commitment, relevance, and sustainability.

YouTubers, Bloggers, Vloggers, and Influencers

Over the past several years, new online personas have emerged with large and engaged followings.[15] Although some are "vloggers," others are "bloggers." But the predominant term for these personas who have gained large followings on social media is now *influencer*. Precise definitions are elusive and constantly in flux depending on who you are talking to, but I'll give it a try.

"Vloggers" are personalities who have developed a strong following by making videos on a regular basis. "YouTuber" is a term often used interchangeably with "vlogger" since YouTube has become the predominant and most accessible platform for distributing videos. A few other platforms are or have been available for vloggers to distribute their videos (such as Vimeo and Vine). However, Vine was discontinued in October 2016. Vimeo, on the other hand, has increasingly been positioned as a platform for high-quality videos—in other words, it lacks the same homemade, amateur appeal of YouTube. Therefore, because YouTube is so accessible and facilitates conversation with its "comment" and "sharing" functions, "YouTuber" has become synonymous with "vlogger". One interesting thing to note is how well YouTube

---

15. It is reported that some influencers have millions, even tens of millions, of followers. On the day I submitted my manuscript to the publisher, an exposé in *The New York Times* detailed a shadowy industry where personal identities on social media platforms are stolen by companies, then often slightly modified to impersonate the real user and sold to people or organizations seeking to boost their number of followers, not knowing that they are purchasing fake followers (called "bots") or likes or shares. The purchasers are distorting their own base of authentic followers, but unbeknownst to them, the followers aren't even real people. The sale of bots necessarily leads to some ambiguity about the accuracy of reported numbers of influencer followers. What's real and what's not? Who's purchasing bots and who's not? I'm sure there will be more to come on this subject. "Buying Online Influence From a Shadowy Market," *The New York Times*, January 28, 2018, page 1. For suggestions on what brand owners can do to combat this practice, see the discussion in Chapter 12.

continues as the primary platform for vloggers, especially with the rise of video offerings by other social media channels, such as Snapchat, Instagram, and the more recent Facebook Live.

Vloggers make videos about everything. They create videos about their lives, video games, PhotoShop hacks, and even their cat playing the piano. Examples include Jake Paul (who vlogs about anything that comes to his mind, the zanier the better) and Dude Perfect, which is a group of three "best buddies" doing sports tricks and pulling pranks. As vloggers gain strong followings, they become characterized as "influencers" because of the ways they can influence thoughts and attitudes or, ideally, consumer behavior.

Bloggers are using social media platforms or other websites to write about subjects that interest them and, presumably, where they have expertise. There is no video. When I start updating this book on the website identified in the Afterword, I will be a blogger and what I write will be a blog. Some people might also consider online magazine-style sites such as Refinery29 and Brit + Co also to be bloggers, but in today's world of heightened connectivity though social media, these bloggers have a much stronger voice than ever before. Because of this, I prefer to call them Digitally Native Brands (DNBs) because they have evolved past bloggers and transitioned into meaningful brands that are native to the digital space. They create and distribute content across multiple online channels such as their website and social media. However, some might even distinguish between sites like Refinery29 and Brit + Co. Brit + Co was started by a person, Brit Morin, an influencer who became a media brand. The fact that she is still involved means that she is doing her "influencing" through Brit + Co. Refinery29, on the other hand, does not have a single personality associated with the brand. So to some, Brit + Co. could be considered an influencer and Refinery29 a digital magazine. To make this even more confusing, a Digitally Native Brand is to be distinguished from a Digitally Native Vertical Brand (DNVB), which is discussed in detail in Chapter 12. (In brief, DNVBs sell their own branded product and control manufacturing, retailing, and distribution.) DNBs can also achieve a sufficient level of fame to become licensable properties in their own right (the same can be said of DNVBs).

"Influencers" is a bit of a catch-all name, perhaps just a rebranding of bloggers and vloggers. The term is a relatively new creation that applies to bloggers and vloggers who have built their fame from the Internet up; who produce original content; and, more importantly, who influence their large and dedicated followings.[16] As more social media platforms become popular, such as Instagram, the definition of influencers has widened beyond vloggers and bloggers. For example, "instagrammers" are considered influencers but may not produce videos or write lengthy blogs. It is solely because of the original content they produce and loyal following they have.

I am most interested in influencers who are focused on a product category, influencing the purchasing decision. They are much less about "selling" and more about creating content, telling a story, sharing their "expertise," speaking about the equity of a brand's products. This is because influencers have usually started speaking about their favorite products or brands long before paid posts and sponsored videos were even on their radar screen. Think about it this way—YouTube started in 2005 as a platform for anyone to create videos and connect with people around the world with common interests. In the early days of YouTube, YouTubers were the enthusiasts—the PhotoShop geeks, gamers looking for cheat codes, and makeup fanatics. For example, beauty influencers have been posting about their favorite makeup brands for years, not because they were paid to do so, but because they were so passionate about a product they felt compelled to speak about it in a video. These influencers are truly authentic because they have

---

16. Some of these influencers, particularly the ones simply portraying their lifestyle and sharing observations, aren't as original as their fans may be led to believe. Some are acting and not really exposing their true (less exaggerated) personalities; some use editorial teams or advisors to help craft themes and posts that appear, to their fans, to be spontaneous.

always considered their beauty vlogging hobby as simply that—a hobby. But for some, that changes.

Influencers bring a level of storytelling to product categories and brands that brands struggle to do on their own. They encourage their audience to "participate" with a brand. It's a high-energy, engaging, conversational interaction for the audience. And importantly to brand owners, they "influence" consumers' product category decisions. Then in addition to influencing the purchase of product (sometimes paid by the company, sometimes not), some of these influencers become so famous that they venture into licensing on their own, either through limited collections of branded product or through retail or brand collaborations. There will definitely be more to come.

All of these categories of personalities fall into a bucket we can call "digital celebrities," provided that they attain a certain level of fame. For those digital celebrities who do achieve that level of fame, it often is all about moving from content to commerce. For the purpose of evaluating digital celebrities in a brand licensing context, I look more to the influencers who have gained an audience due to their expertise in a particular product category rather than those celebrity influencers who become famous for posting about virtually anything that comes to their mind.

Although a traditional celebrity, the arc of Gwyneth Paltrow and her blog *Goop* is useful to examine. She started with an online blog named *Goop* in 2008, so she technically became a blogger. *Goop* then rose to the level of Digitally Native Brand because it started creating video content on its website, providing advice about all sorts of lifestyle categories from food to fashion and gained a large and devoted following across multiple platforms such as Instagram (although because Paltrow is still the driving force, one could argue that *Goop* is a DNB *and* an influencer). Paltrow is technically blogger, turned vlogger, turned influencer, while having created a DNB along the way. Now she is not only curating product but also selling *Goop*-branded product on the site. She made the final transition from content to commerce and successfully made *Goop* a DNVB. As noted at the beginning of this section, definitions in the digital space are somewhat confusing because the space is constantly being redefined. The introduction of new social media platforms could redefine the entire space tomorrow. The good news is that in this fluidity, there is much more opportunity to evolve and develop a brand, whatever it's called, as demonstrated by Gwyneth Paltrow's *Goop*.

With key demographic groups such as Millennials and Gen Zers, these "digital celebrities" can be equally or even more popular and influential than traditional celebrities.[17] However, although select traditional celebrities have demonstrated the staying power to inspire licensing programs and attract retailers for the long term, digital celebrities have not yet arrived at that juncture. Nevertheless, some of them are beginning to be accepted by retailers as they attempt licensing programs.

Digital celebrities interact with their audience on a more relatable, less scripted level, and they can shape trends and culture. But they need to maintain these attributes in order to sustain their audience. They are vulnerable to stumbles precisely because they communicate without filters, and those that make a great deal of money promoting particular brands can be perceived as sellouts, losing the trust and respect of their fans and, as a result, likely their "licensability." Consider one of the top YouTube vloggers, PewDiePie, who, in 2017 (with 60 million subscribers!), fell out of favor with brands because of his anti-Semitic and anti-black comments.

So how do some digital celebrities, particularly influencers who focus on a product category, do with regard to satisfying the five metrics for celebrity licensing success identified earlier in this chapter? Clearly influencers have *Vision*. They identify themselves with a single product category or groups of categories. Their

---

17. Compared to traditional celebrities, YouTube influencer collaborations have proven four times more effective at driving brand familiarity and two times more effective at driving brand affinity. Nielsen/Carat/Google YouTube Branded Video Study, May 2017.

fame is actually based on this association (and, naturally, their personalities). Should they choose to attempt consumer products through licensing, they are able to fill *White Space* with products that are aligned with that vision and are often priced very competitively. Whether they are prepared to devote the *Time Commitment* it takes to develop and nurture a licensing program and licensed products remains to be seen. A few will probably be able to accomplish this, and we are seeing the early signs of success among some digital celebrity influencers. *Staying Power*, among the most important metrics to retailers, is the big unknown. We don't yet know if a digital celebrity can sustain his popularity over the long term. And, finally, *Credibility* is complicated. Yes, influencers have credibility because they are unscripted and "experts" in a category (or more), but they can easily lose that credibility as they embrace commerce by accepting compensation from companies to endorse their products or, dare I say, licensing their name for products. Their fame is based not on their talent (as is true of traditional celebrities), but on their objectivity about products.

But just because they have launched their own line of products or actively promote a brand of products doesn't necessarily mean they have lost their credibility as an influencer. Here are some questions to ask: Is the percentage of "sponsored" posts higher than organic posts? Has the audience stopped believing what the influencer is saying? Has the influencer become associated with a brand that doesn't seem natural to who he or she is? Has the influencer been seen using competitive product? Has the influencer done something, even innocently, that has backfired for another brand? It's a difficult balancing act.

Nevertheless, signs of the increasing popularity of influencers is the increasing rate at which they are licensing their names for a line of products. Following is a short list of ten influencers who have ventured into licensing their own brand names either solo or through collaborations. There are, of course, many more; however, these ten are representative of different product categories.

1. **Michelle Phan**, one of the early YouTubers, built her fan base with tutorials on fashion and beauty. In 2013, she collaborated with L'Oréal for a line of makeup and other beauty products named Em Cosmetics (which at its height had over 300 SKUs). The product line was not well received and disappointed L'Oréal. Fans apparently complained that it was priced too high, and she was subjected to accusations of "sellout." L'Oréal sold the brand in 2015 to Ipsy, a subscription box service co-founded by Ms. Phan (valued at $500 million in 2015), and in 2017, Michelle Phan purchased the brand from Ipsy and relaunched it online through her own company with new formulations and packaging (presumably with a stronger focus on her "community"). In 2016, Michelle Phan, certainly one of the most successful YouTubers, took a hiatus from posting.

2. **Nash Grier**, named one of *Time* magazine's 30 Most Influential People on the Internet in 2015, developed a line with fashion retailer Aeropostale but faced backlash due to homophobic comments.

3. **Bethany Mota**, on the other hand, a fashion and beauty trendsetter, reported $80 million in retail sales of licensed product in 2014 (mostly through her partnership with Aeropostale).

4. **Gabi Gregg**, a plus-size influencer, has licensed a line of plus-size lingerie in the United Kingdom.

5. **Lauren Rihimaki**, known as LaurDIY, has licensed a full range of DIY crafting kits and products as well as a very successful line of sleepwear.

6. **Zoe "Zoella" Sugg**, a leading beauty influencer, has a full line of licensed candles, lotions, and other beauty accessories.

7. **Cassey Ho**, a Pilates instructor who set up her YouTube channel in 2009, now has fitness DVDs and books as well as a line of workout apparel and accessories under her brand POPFLEX.

8. **Chiara Ferragni** launched her fashion blog, The Blonde Salad, way back in the pre-Instagram days of 2009 and now has a line of apparel and accessories under her own name at department stores.

9. **Coco-Cozy**, a home influencer who chooses to remain anonymous (she's a television executive by day), has a comprehensive line of textiles and home furnishings.

10. And finally there's **Grumpy Cat**, who first appeared in 2012 and has a host of licensed products including T-shirts, stuffed toys, pet toys, and a comic book.

The licensing power of influencers was further on display at Target during Fall 2017 when six influencers inspired a collection of children's apparel and played a role in the marketing of the line by using Instagram to talk directly to their audience (well over 10 million followers among them) about the collection and how much fun they had working on it. Indeed, to help communicate with consumers and drive purchases, other brands and retailers are now beginning to develop longer-term collaborations with influencers instead of transactional ones. Nordstrom has been building a relationship with fashion influencer Arielle Charnas for several years as part of the retailer's effort to reach younger consumers. For Fall 2017, the store offered a capsule collection named "Treasure & Bond x Something Navy" (*Something Navy* is the name of Charnas' blog), which reached $1 million in sales in 24 hours. In 2018 Nordstrom is expanding the association with an exclusive women's apparel collection named "Something Navy." As is true of traditional celebrities, retailers will be attracted to digital celebrities for retail exclusive programs, with both risks and benefits.

These digital celebrities break onto the scene very quickly but can lose their audience just as quickly. For example, JoJo Siwa is, at the time of this writing, a 14-year-old YouTuber (five million YouTube subscribers, six million Instagram followers) who promotes not only her life but also her oversized hair bow (the JoJo Bow) as a symbol for anti-bullying. Nickelodeon partnered with her and has launched a full-scale licensing program. But will she have staying power as she grows up? Brands need to be cautious about using influencers as licensing or communication tools. Retailers are still largely taking a wait-and-see attitude (or using influencers for intentionally short-term promotional programs) given the risks (as there have always been about the risks of celebrity licensing). But licensing programs developed by digital celebrities are already here, and they are in our future. The successful ones will earn the trust of consumers, and once that trust is combined with a high level of fame, consumers will want products these digital celebrities endorse by simply speaking well of a product or by attaching their ame to the product through a mechanism such as licensing. With traditional celebrity licensing, consumers aspire to "be like" the celebrity. With these digital celebrities, it is less about aspiration and more about trust in their opinion. They are and will continue to transition from "advisor" and "curator" to "licensed brand."

As you may recall, celebrity licensing may have begun with the Teddy Roosevelt teddy bears but has since evolved from Charlie Chaplin dolls to Shirley Temple dresses and then made an even bigger leap to Cheryl Tiegs apparel, Jessica Simpson footwear, Donald Trump steaks, Bethany Mota apparel, and Snoop Dogg cannabis (more on cannabis in Chapter 12). Celebrity licensing will continue to evolve and grow as consumers aspire to live like their favorite celebrities, feel empowered by those celebrities, and trust those celebrities, and retailers look for differentiation. A few of those celebrities will actually become brands, largely through their licensing activities. Brand owners can learn much from their successes and failures.

CHAPTER 9

Dead or Alive? Bringing Brands Back to Life

We can all remember brands we loved (or not) that have disappeared. Frequently they are household name brands to which we became emotionally attached—brands to which we were loyal and for which we still have positive associations, brands we trusted. Most importantly, these brands often retain significant equity. Equity that is difficult to measure and value.

Under the right circumstances, licensing can resurrect these brands. With a well-conceived strategy, licensing can capitalize on their hard-won equity and overcome whatever challenges destroyed the brand. And as was true of celebrity licensing, we can learn a great deal about brand licensing as we examine successes and failures experienced in bringing brands back.

Brands can easily be taken off the market, but not so easily erased from our memories. There are many possible reasons for a brand's demise, decline, and disappearance from the marketplace, but poor brand management usually is one of them. Bad management decisions and the inability to keep up with changes in the marketplace can cause an iconic brand to falter. Here are some other reasons (but not all of the reasons) iconic brands disappear:

1. The parent company stops investing in the brand's marketing, innovation, and product development in favor of investment in other owned brands of a similar character. Example: Brim coffee ("Fill it to the rim with Brim") ended up at Altria (the reconstituted General Foods), which also owned Maxwell House, which discontinued Brim. As companies continue to merge, brands we love may fall away as part of a large multinational's brand portfolio.

2. Challenges in the larger economic environment limit consumers' continued participation with the brand. Example: *Gourmet* magazine, founded in 1941, beloved by foodies, couldn't survive in a marketplace with declining magazine sales and was shuttered in 2009 to give Condé Nast's other food magazine, *Bon Appétit,* a better chance of survival in a challenging magazine market.

3. Strong new competitors steal share. Example: Linens 'n Things lost out to Bed Bath & Beyond.

4. Inability to keep up with trends and changing market conditions. Example: Kodak. Although not dead, certainly comatose (Kodak has licensed its name for digital cameras and 3D printers, for example). Kodak kept manufacturing film as the market turned to digital cameras and then smartphones.

5. Changes in consumer behavior, which, over time, erode the brand's relevance. Example: Netflix saw the future, but Blockbuster didn't. Internet services and on-demand cable services changed consumers' behavior for accessing movies. When Netflix started sending movies to consumers, Blockbuster kept building stores. Demographic shifts in the U.S. population can also impact relevancy as immigrants and their U.S.-born children fail to develop emotional attachment to brands. Example: Hostess (maker of

Twinkies and other packaged desserts) disappeared and was revived. But by the time of revival, the U.S.-born Hispanic population had grown considerably. They are more attached to the Mexican snack brand Bimbo than they are to Hostess, to which neither they nor their parents may have any attachment.[1]

6. Financial challenges. Brands that have had great success and are beloved are not exempt from extinction. Example: Pan Am, a famous international airline carrier, fell due to financial challenges.

Consider some other recent examples of brands that disappeared:

Nokia, once the world's #1 mobile phone, was acquired by Microsoft, which had partnered with Nokia on the co-branded Lumia phone. Microsoft phased out the Nokia brand (an almost 150-year-old Finnish brand name) to focus on Lumia, which failed. Microsoft then sold Nokia, and a newly established Finnish company was granted a license by the brand owner to reintroduce Nokia phones. This brand may yet have a second life.

Hess gas stations are gone as the parent company focuses on oil.

The Amoco brand disappeared when it merged with British Petroleum, and the Amoco gas stations, a mainstay of America, were rebranded BP.

Oldsmobile, founded in 1897, an iconic automobile brand name in America, found its sales slipping when it couldn't compete with smaller, more efficient cars, including those of its parent company General Motors. The brand closed its doors in 2004.

And who can forget Woolworth's (well Millennials probably never knew it)? Founded in 1879, it was the leading discount retailer in the United States and changed consumer shopping

---

1. For more on the effects of demographics on brand memory, see "Build the Brand. Protect the Brand," www.rrpartnersblog.com/2015/05/07/is-your-brand-on-the-path-to-irrelevancy.

behavior. It paved the way for other mass merchants that followed its model. Losses mounted and the parent company closed the last stores in 1986.

Even famous Internet brand names have disappeared. Gone are Netscape, Ask Jeeves, Hotmail, and Excite. Following the Verizon acquisition in 2017, Yahoo and AOL are struggling to become Oath.

But some dormant brands make a comeback and are revived, often through licensing as well as other models. Examples include Puma, the VW Beetle, White Cloud, Polaroid, the Cleveland Browns, Ovaltine, and Breck Shampoo.

The brands that vanished all left behind strong equities and imprints on our memories. Often, these memories are strengthened by famous taglines such as "Fill it to the rim with Brim" or "Show us your Underalls" or "We Have to Earn Our Wings Everyday" (Eastern Airlines) or "Not Your Father's Oldsmobile." The loyalty and trust engendered by those brands doesn't disappear quickly. In fact, companies with a fresh or altered approach can often capitalize on existing equities, overcoming past challenges with greater flexibility, or a fresh strategy, a new consumer target, different product or retail distribution, a brand repositioning, or a modernized version.

And sometimes it's not just how we remember the brands, but *how we think* we remember the brands. River West Brands was a company established to acquire the names of dead brands. Paul Earle, one of the founders, says that brand revival can take place based not only on what we remember but also "misremember" about brands. Brim was a decaffeinated coffee (that's why you could "Fill it to the rim"), but do people really remember that or do they just remember that Brim was a coffee? River West brought it back as a full-flavored coffee, not limited to decaf. Earle believes that you can take the original value proposal of a brand and convert it into something related but different. He believes that people remember the essence of the brand but not the product specifics. This is consistent with The Sharper Image example below. And in a way, it's the secret sauce to bringing a brand back from the dead through licensing.

Private equity firms, entrepreneurs, and other marketing companies are constantly perusing the marketplace (and old magazines) looking for distressed or dead brands. Occasionally, a firm that owns a bunch of dead brands holds an auction. There's a market out there, and purchasing the intellectual property (legal rights to brand names) is generally not particularly expensive. In many instances, poor or out-of-date business models sunk these brands. Instead of going back to a failed model, the licensing model can be a cost-effective way to bring dead brands back to life, sometimes more than once. Remember, however, that all that glitters is not gold. Many entrepreneurs have purchased famous intellectual property assuming that these left-for-dead brand names can be brought back to life easily—that a new strategy will ignite consumers' attachment to the brand and convert this attachment into sales.

But it's easier said than done. Let's examine some case studies and determine what it takes to revive a dead brand or wake up one that's on the verge of dying. I'll examine two brands that succeeded at revival and one that did not.

The Sharper Image

Following the 2008 recession, rapidly changing consumer buying habits due to online shopping hit brick-and-mortar retail brands hard (see Chapter 11). Consider famous retail brands that shuttered during this short period: Linens 'n Things, Borders, Circuit City, Blockbuster, Fortunoff, Bonwit Teller, Bombay Company, Wilson's Leather, Sports Authority, The Limited, B. Dalton Bookseller, Tower Records, FAO Schwarz, The Sharper Image, and the list goes on. However, in most of these cases, someone believed that consumers would still be loyal to the brand, purchased the IP, and developed a licensing strategy. And a handful of those strategies actually made it to execution, that is, to distribution of products successfully offered to consumers at retail. Many of the failures are due to a lack of understanding about how to make licensing work in brand revival. Acutally, The Sharper Image is the only one of the above list of retailers to have succeeded in repositioning itself and taking advantage of the licensing model to tap into consumers' trust, loyalty, "memories," and affection and come back to life (although some of the others have developed small online presences). The verdict, as of this writing, is still out on two recently relaunched retail brands: FAO Schwarz, which relaunched at select Bon-Ton department stores for the 2017 holiday season and has announced the opening of a new flagship store in New York City as well as airport shops, and The Limited, which relaunched online in 2017 and announced a partnership with the Belk department stores in late 2017. How did The Sharper Image use licensing to come back?

In 1978, Richard Thalheimer named his small mail-order business The Sharper Image and launched his first mail-order catalog featuring all sorts of devices. The company grew throughout the 1980s, and the catalogs featured an array of products, some utilitarian and others somewhat peculiar but always interesting and fun to look at and sometimes purchase. The early, fairly affordable, exotic products satisfied the extreme consumerism of the times. Products included man-sized dolls as a defense against crime ($500), the Sit 'N Sip seat cushion in which you could store three quarts of your favorite beverage dispensed through a spout placed between your legs (perfect for attending sporting events) ($39), an automatic VHS tape rewinder in the shape of a car ($35), a cell phone antenna for your car to make you look like you had one of those new, expensive cell phones ($19), a talking scale ($99), the TSX1 in-home workout machine ($159), as well as other gizmos and gadgets.

By the mid-1980s, The Sharper Image surpassed $50 million in sales and published over 40 million catalogs annually. When catalog sales started to slow down, the company reinvented its strategy and opened its first stores in 1985. The Sharper Image went public in 1987 and by the end of the year was operating 42 stores across the country. The new store openings likely masked a sales decline that was probably attributable to increased retail competition and rising costs for its products. The brand became largely known, at this time, for very expensive luxury products and gadgets, such as a nostalgic Coca-Cola vending machine priced at $7,700. Consumers enjoyed looking at these products, but they didn't like them enough to buy them. So in the late 1980s, the company decided to offer more practical and less expensive items, but still gadgets that could be promoted as unique (e.g., for $39, a fog-free shaving mirror to be used in the shower [over 70,000 were sold]).

Up until this time, The Sharper Image's sales were driven by what was then called "the Yuppie Generation," young people who were avid consumers. However, by the end of the 1980s, the consumerism of this generation was in decline and the company turned to new markets, including toys for children and home furnishings for customers over the age of 50. The company continued to experience declines, and costs were cut, including reducing the number and quality of the catalogs. The company turned around in the early 1990s by establishing Sharper Image locations at department stores such as Bloomingdale's and Dillard's as well as offering products on QVC. In 1998, the company developed an online version of its catalog, and two years later online sales topped $60 million. But rising costs continued to plague the company.

In the early 2000s, most of the company's sales were generated by its own manufactured items (e.g., the $700 massage chair; the Ionic Breeze air purifiers, which sold for between $200 and $500; and the portable Personal Entertainment Center that included a DVD player, TV, and radio). By the mid-2000s, The Sharper Image had become an iconic American brand with almost 200 stores in 38 states as well as locations in 600 Circuit City stores, all selling many cool products.

Yet sales continued to slide; competition, particularly big-box retailers, increased (think Best Buy and Walmart); the company couldn't keep up with the fast pace at which new gadgets were

being introduced; and sales of the best-seller Ionic Breeze air purifiers plummeted due to lawsuits related to health concerns about
the product, as reported in *Consumer Reports* in 2005. The company fell victim to changing retail trends and financial and legal
challenges. In 2008, The Sharper Image filed for bankruptcy protection, and later that year a group of private investors purchased
The Sharper Image for $49 million at a bankruptcy auction. They
announced that all of the stores would be closed and the inventory liquidated.

No more stand-alone stores in malls with quirky products to
try out. No more catalogs. But the brand was relaunched at shar-
perimage.com where consumers could still find nose hair trim-
mers, handheld back massagers, and air purifiers. Consumers
could also find videos demonstrating the products. The company
licensed its name and logo to a host of companies to manufacture affordable Sharper Image–branded and packaged products
for general retail distribution at specialty stores such as Bed Bath
& Beyond and Best Buy. One of the first licensees was a company
named HoMedics, which manufactures health and grooming
products, and a luggage maker EnE. Since being acquired at the
2008 bankruptcy auction, the company has changed hands twice.
It was purchased in 2011 by Iconix Brand Group for $68 million
and is now owned by one of its major licensees, ThreeSixty, which
purchased it from Iconix at the end of 2016 for $100 million.

Today well over 500 licensed Sharper Image products are featured on its website and online catalog. Many of those products
are sold at retail, both brick-and-mortar retailers as well as online
retailers such as Amazon. And the products represent a very wide
price range from, for example, the Circulation Enhancing Ther-
mal Slippers for $59.99 to the Heated Shaving Cream Dispenser
for $39.99 to the Self-Balancing Scooter Bike for $1,599.00 and the
Human Touch Zero-Gravity Massage Chair for $2,999.00. And
interestingly, most of the products are branded "Sharper Image"
and are packaged in Sharper Image–branded boxes. That largely
wasn't true of the original Sharper Image products, which were

generally just cool products curated by The Sharper Image and all brought together in one retail location and catalog. Moreover, the products generally seem to be products that are available elsewhere under different brand names or, in many instances, no brand name. Today for this brand, it's less about the newest thing, the newest innovation, and more about quirky gizmos and gadgets but with a brand name attached, a brand that consumers remember as cool products. Although it's not the brand of yesteryear, it's a brand that has been snatched from the graveyard with a licensing strategy and updated for today's marketplace.

Lessons Learned
When evaluating a dead or dying brand to determine whether it can be brought back to life, we must understand what brought it down. It can't be brought back to life if the same mistakes are made—if, for example, companies fail to address changing retail and consumer dynamics. What brought The Sharper Image brand to its knees? Consider the following:

1. Trends changed. "Cool" products could be found everywhere, at other retailers and online. The Sharper Image lost its unique selling proposition (USP). It tried to pay attention to the warning signs, but failed to pivot successfully.
2. Catalog sales in general were and are a declining business model, and The Sharper Image failed to adapt quickly enough. E-commerce changed consumers' shopping behavior.
3. Technology changes every six months and with it the products using that technology. For these kinds of products, e-commerce is the perfect selling space.
4. Competition became fiercer. The same or similar products were introduced at lower prices, and in turn, these "innovative" products became commodities.

5. The company struggled to find its footing, changing pricing strategy and changing its target consumer, but in the end, the merchandising strategy was unfocused.

6. Ultimately, the "experience" the stores offered was overwhelmed by the "experience" offered by others, such as the Apple Store, and the ease of surfing the Internet for similar products.

The reinvented Sharper Image has done well not to repeat these errors and to take advantage of the new retail landscape and consumer shopping behaviors with products that benefit from the iconic brand name through licensing. The new owners are capitalizing on the memories of consumers, with some modifications. Time will tell whether the brand has been revived for the long term, but it looks promising.

What are the key learnings from the Sharper Image comeback? What can others who want to rescue a dormant brand learn from the Sharper Image story? Consider the following five things the brand did right:

1. Despite bad management decisions and some bad luck, the brand survived until it was purchased at a bankruptcy auction. It was gone for a very short time. In other words, consumers weren't given time to have the brand fade from their memories. Indeed, many consumers probably didn't even realize that the brand had disappeared for a while.

2. The new owners made some smart decisions, such as closing all of the offline stores and focusing on a more cost-effective strategy using the licensing model, requiring minimal investment and risk.

3. The brand jumped back into "cool gadgets and gizmos," the product space in which it had been famous. A wide breadth of products was and still is aligned with the Sharper Image brand. That was an advantage.

4. The catalog and website were redeveloped in a style that was consistent with how consumers remember the brand. In other words, the brand reignited consumer memory. (The print catalog looks just like the one of yesteryear.)

5. The brand owner stepped away from the original brand strategy of offering products of other brands (or non-branded products) and focused on branding virtually all of the products (and packaging) with the Sharper Image brand. It was simply a different way of offering brand-aligned products. This had the effect of further embedding the brand in the consciousness of the consumer.

6. Finally, in a very competitive landscape in its category, The Sharper Image was able to take advantage of its unique brand history and selling proposition to differentiate the brand from other similarly situated brands in the category.

Polaroid

This iconic brand, too, came back from the dead and attempted to reinvent itself. Let's take a look at Polaroid's demise and how its revival has fared. After over 60 years as a leader in innovation and technology, Polaroid entered a period of cyclical dormancy and revival.

The company was founded in 1937 by Edwin Land (starting out in his garage), who ran the company as CEO for over 40 years. In many respects, Polaroid was the Apple of its time and Land the Steve Jobs, always leading in technologically advanced, innovative product development. Polaroid's first product was polarized sunglasses (Land had patented polarizing polymer in 1929). But Land is best known as the father of instant photography. The world-famous Polaroid Instant Camera, which delivered a printed photo almost immediately, was launched in the mid-1940s, and many other product iterations and innovations followed. In 1963, Polaroid launched the first instant color film, Polacolor. In 1972, the company introduced the first automatic, motorized, and folding camera with instant color prints, the

SX-70 Land camera, a technological breakthrough. By 1978, Polaroid employed 21,000 people. In 1991, Polaroid generated $3 billion in sales, its best year ever.

But by the mid to late 1990s, Polaroid began to struggle against new technology and competition. The company did not anticipate the impact of one-hour film processing, single-use cameras, video camcorders, and digital cameras. Polaroid tried to compete by manufacturing digital cameras and scanners, but it couldn't achieve competitive market share.

Polaroid filed for its first bankruptcy in 2001 and a second bankruptcy in 2008. By 2009, the company was no longer making things. Instead, it was licensing the brand onto products it considered innovative and logically associated with the Polaroid name and logo. No more manufacturing, warehousing, inventory, or distribution. Low costs and high margins (licensing royalties). There had been a prior attempt at licensing by the owner following the first bankruptcy, but the products were generally considered poor quality and did not fare well. That and the arrest and conviction of the CEO (Tom Petters) of the Polaroid holding company (Petters Group Worldwide) in 2010 for running a Ponzi scheme caused what some thought was irreparable reputational damage to the brand. But the acquisition by Hilco Consumer Products and Gordon Brothers Group in 2009 at a bankruptcy auction was the beginning of a turnaround.

The most recent attempt to breathe new life into Polaroid began with the licensing of digital cameras; digital video cameras; digital photo frames; and in 2011, under the sub-brand PoGo, other mobile products and an instant photo printer. In 2012, the Polaroid brand was licensed for a smartphone powered by Google Android. And in 2014, the Polaroid Cube, a single-button action camera that can record up to 90 minutes of video and is about the size of pool cube chalk, shock-proof, and mountable, was launched under license. By 2015, Polaroid was solely an intellectual property company that licensed its name and logo for a variety of products that stand for "instant, sharing, ease of use, simplicity, fun, affordable and innovative." Other licensed products include the Polaroid Zip, an instant wallet-sized photograph printer that uses Bluetooth technology, TVs, tablets, and smartphones. Many of these products are designed to appeal to a younger generation that has grown up with digital technology, and they are selling well and reestablishing Polaroid as a "cool" brand, in keeping with its legacy. The company is now being careful to license only those products that are consistent with its equities and history. Products that print out a photo, in particular, are in alignment with that strategy. For example, the Polaroid Socialmatic combines instant printing of smudge-proof, water-resistant prints with Bluetooth uploading to social media. The Polaroid digital camera does what most digital cameras do but also can print the photo. And the licensing program is a global program with products selling well in, for example, the United Kingdom and France. Although privately held with no public financial information available, Polaroid reports that retail sales of licensed product reached $600 million in 2016.[2]

Polaroid fell victim to extreme changes in the market in which it had once flourished, failing to adapt fast enough to those changes, increased competition, and innovation, as well as poor management decisions. However, the current licensing strategy has enabled the brand to thrive again with a different brand product portfolio.

Let's consider what Polaroid did right as the brand owner continues to work on reviving this once dormant brand.

1. To start, despite being absent from the marketplace for quite some time, the brand had enough residual awareness, equity, and positive consumer "memory" to make it a candidate for a brand revival. This was an iconic brand, after all.

---

2. Polaroid is ranked #67 in "Top 150 Global Licensors." *Id.*

2. Polaroid had a rich history, a strong brand story, and authenticity, and the new owners endeavored to maintain the relevancy of the story.
3. The brand owner didn't just repeat the product offering of the dead brand (indeed, how could it given how irrelevant the instant camera that made the brand famous had become in the age of smartphones), but stretched the brand to new groups of products that were generally aligned with the equities of the original brand offering.
4. Polaroid has an elemental and unique selling proposition, differentiating it from other brands in the same or similar categories.
5. To succeed in competitive landscapes, Polaroid reshaped its product offering and brand messaging to be more competitive.
6. Polaroid (and The Sharper Image) managed to have success without a hefty marketing budget, relying instead on fame, emotional attachment, social media, and distinctive products in a crowded category. Both Polaroid and The Sharper Image have strong processes and resources in place to manage their licensing programs.

Nuprin

Many attempts at brand revival do not succeed or even get to market. But one that seemed to have a good chance at revival and then fell flat is Nuprin. Nuprin is the brand name for a drug that contains ibuprofen; it was used for pain and inflammation and to reduce fever. Ibuprofen was developed by Boots Laboratories, a U.K. drug manufacturer and retailer, with the goal of finding a drug that would be more powerful and tolerable than aspirin. Boots began selling the drug as a prescription medication in the United Kingdom in 1964. The Upjohn Company began marketing Motrin, the first ibuprofen in the United States, in 1974 under a nonexclusive license from Boots. In 1984, the FDA approved lower-dose ibuprofen for over-the-counter sales in the United

States, and other drug companies jumped in. Whitehall Laboratories launched Advil, which was followed by Nuprin, manufactured by Upjohn and marketed by Bristol-Meyers; both companies were licensed by Boots. The Boots patent for ibuprofen expired in 1985, and shortly thereafter, other drug companies introduced their own brands of ibuprofen. Bristol-Myers marketed Nuprin aggressively.

By 2004, however, Nuprin was off the market—the victim of greatly increased competition, financial challenges at Bristol-Myers Squibb, and perhaps faulty brand management. The trademark was acquired by River West Brands, which then sold it to CVS for use as a private-label brand. This was a seemingly strong strategy given CVS's leading position in the drugstore channel. But "brand memory" can sometimes run out, even with famous brands. CVS, relying on brand "memory," launched a full product assortment under the Nuprin brand name, a broader assortment than had been marketed by Bristol-Myers Squibb. Perhaps this was more about "misremembering" a brand. Yet the brand didn't perform to CVS's expectations, the company sold it for $180,000 in 2010, and it was pulled from retail shelves in 2012.

What went wrong with this brand revival? CVS seemingly had a good idea in trying to stretch the brand beyond its original single product. However, in this instance, heavy category competition, limited marketing in a heavily marketed category, and weak brand memory killed the revival. Brand memory is a tricky thing. The consumer not only must have a "memory" but also must care about engaging or reengaging with the memory and the brand. And, sometimes, counting on consumers being emotionally attached yet "misremembering" the brand results in a stretch too far. The current owner announced a relaunch in 2015, but as of late 2017, the official website advises, "Please check back this Fall for a list of retailers." Perhaps Nuprin will have a third life yet.

What a Brand Needs to Come Back from the Dead

Some brand revivals last for a short term (several years perhaps, such as Nuprin) and then die again for a variety of reasons, some limp along, and there are some that last for the long term. But in each case, the IP owner can reap a nice return on investment if the licensing model is used. With no manufacturing and very small marketing investment, the cost of entry is small. Even if the brands don't last long, consider the financial rewards already reaped by the owners of The Sharper Image and Polaroid trademarks. To be successful for the long-term, revival of a not-long-for-this-world or already dead brand needs to address the following factors:

Determine If a Significant Amount of Awareness Still Exists
Brand memory fades with time, so you must determine whether sufficient awareness still exists and whether this awareness is positive (versus the negative memory of a brand that failed in some way). The brand must have been successful in its time, iconic in its category. If the brand has suffered a scandal or reputational damage, it will be hard to bring back. Enron, a dead brand, is too often associated with fraud to be revived. The longer a famous brand has been off the shelves, the harder it will be to bring it back to life. Revival is often about nostalgia. We live in complicated times, and some brands remind us of simpler times (or at least that's the way we recall it). But it's anybody's guess as to how long too long is. Remember Metrecal, one of the best-selling brands of diet food in the early 1960s? Following concerns about FDA evaluations of ingredients, the brand died in the late 1970s. It was brought back in 2005 and lasted about four years, then died again. Or what about Ipana toothpaste? Founded in 1901, it was a leading Bristol-Meyers Company brand in the 1950s but lost its way due to heavy competition from companies such as Colgate and P&G, television advertising, and a corporate change of strategy. Date of death: 1979. Both were famous, iconic brands of their time. But their fame has faded, and despite some short-term success with Metrecal, they will forever remain buried.[3] Watch the landscape to find brands in trouble

---

3. Ipana was reintroduced as a gel toothpaste brand in Turkey in 1986 and as a "retro-brand" for the professional market (i.e., dentist offices) in Canada in 2011.

that, if they go out of business, could be brought back with a different strategy through the licensing model. Examples include Sears, Claire's (which filed for bankruptcy in March 2018), and Crocs, each struggling and anchored to its exisiting business model.

Consider Whether Emotional Attachment and Authenticity Exist

A large enough group of consumers must have an emotional attachment to the brand. It must represent something to them and strike an emotional nerve. If that's the case, the brand's equity can be harnessed again. In laymen's terms, fond memories must exist. Brain science research confirms why we care about the brands of yesteryear.[4] Many brands with emotional resonance and authenticity were used by baby boomers when they were coming of age; some, of more recent vintage, by Gen X. But for revival to succeed, the brands must not only create emotional attachment among older people but also appeal to younger ones—individuals who didn't use or buy the brand when it was around the first time but still know the brand and, importantly, the brand story. Indeed, these younger generations are seeking "authenticity" and "trust." Dormant brands provide that to them through their fame, with real history and story and with the built-in brand equities. That's what younger generations crave. Authenticity helps the brand stand out, it helps the brand with younger consumers (who were never emotionally attached to the brand), and it helps the brand compete with brands already in the market. Polaroid is a good example of this.

A wonderful success story of a dormant brand to which there was and is great emotional attachment and memory is the VW Beetle (also known as the Bug). Although the licensing model was

---

4. If you want to read more about brand memory and emotional attachment consider the following: "Teaching Old Brands New Tricks: Retro Branding and the Revival of Brand Meaning," by Stephen Brown, Robert V. Kozinets, and John F. Sherry, Jr., *Journal of Marketing*, July 2003, Vol. 67, No. 3; and "Sell Me the Old, Old Story: Retromarketing Management and the Art of Brand Revival," by Stephen Brown, Robert V. Kozinets, and John F. Sherry, Jr., *Journal of Customer Behavior*, June 2003.

not used in this instance, the example is still illustrative. The car was designed to be as mechanically simple as possible, distinctively with the engine in the back, and economical. The Beetle became an extremely popular cult brand in the 1950s through the early 1970s. In many respects, it was the "flower child" automobile of the 1960s, a symbol of an era. However, it began declining in the late 1960s and early 1970s as the brand faced stiffer competition from Japanese automakers such as Datsun, Toyota, and Honda (the three would soon dominate compact car sales in the United States) as well as Ford, Fiat, and Renault. VW tried to stem the tide with mechanical changes and the launch of the New Beetle in 1997, but sales never reached the levels of the original Beetle and production ceased in 2011. The brand was now dormant. However, over 21 million Beetles had been produced—many fond memories and an iconic automobile design.

In 2015, VW brought back the classic model, realizing that there remained a great deal of equity in the original brand, a great deal of emotional attachment. But bringing back a dormant brand doesn't mean bringing it back exactly as it once was. It needs to be modernized and meet the needs of today's consumers. Although the 2015 introduction looked much like the classic Beetle, it also had features the original Beetle couldn't have, such as a GPS navigation system, FM radio, and an engine that would go faster than 82 mph. VW modernized the product and relied on a brand story, a story of a simpler bygone past.

Fill a Gap with a Unique Selling Proposition
The brand must serve a need, fill a white space or a gap—and not necessarily the gap it may have once filled. The new IP owner may need to update the brand beyond what was once its core product (or service) to make it relevant again. A dormant brand is not encumbered by existing business; the new owner can make it something different. The new owner must be able to evaluate a potential clean slate of products. The brand should not be so associated with a single product that it can't be extended to

new products. Consider Polaroid, for example. There's no point bringing back the original, iconic instant camera, not in the age of smartphones. But the equities of the Polaroid name can be extended to other, more contemporary products, and that's what the brand owner is doing. But Polaroid has always been a photography-focused brand. Can it extend beyond that boundary? Should it even try to extend beyond that boundary? Does the Polaroid name make sense on televisions, 3D printers, drones, Bluetooth speakers, or headphones? Polaroid has done many things right in its successful revival, but some of these products may be a stretch too far. Time will tell. It all depends on what the brand means today, and Polaroid is working hard at building and extending its brand meaning.

The dormant brand should have a unique selling proposition. Otherwise what's the point? There should be something elemental about the brand. Sometimes, however, what's elemental about the brand compels you to conclude that it can't be revived. Apple's Newton was a failure in the tech community, so there was no path forward.

Owners trying to revive a dormant brand need to be very careful that revenue generation doesn't become the main objective (assuming that their goals are long-term brand revival). That will cause brand dilution (by driving product choices that are not necessarily aligned with the brand equity) and, ultimately, inauthenticity (the opposite of what a dormant brand has to offer). For revived brands to survive for the long term, they must remain close to their core equity. Otherwise, they run the risk of brand dilution and quality challenges that come with a diverse group of licensees simply jumping on the brand bandwagon seeking an easy "win."

Tell a Story
One of the strengths of a good dormant brand is that it tells a story. When a new brand is introduced, telling its story requires many resources and marketing costs. But a dormant brand already has the story built in. It certainly has the story of "a better time."

Today we are all subjected to constant marketing—in every media and on every device and screen we have and use. Often, we want to "turn it off." Dormant brands remind us of a time when this wasn't so (although that's not entirely true, it's what we believe). When reviving a brand, the IP owner must not only update the product's portfolio and its performance but also, importantly, maintain "the story." That can't be lost, or all is probably lost. The new brand owner must focus on retelling the brand's story so that it once again touches that nerve with consumers. And "retelling" doesn't mean telling exactly the same story as before. As mentioned earlier, it's not just about reviving what the brand once was but reviving what we think we remember it was. So The Sharper Image really isn't telling the same story as it did in its heyday. But it's close enough to that story—a retelling of the story of cool gizmos and gadgets. On the other hand, no one much cared about a Nuprin "story."

Consider the Competition

The competition (likely different when the brand was once successful) must not now be so challenging that there simply isn't a way for the brand to compete. For example, launching a new toothpaste in the United States would be extremely difficult given the strength of the competition (consider Ipana trying to make a comeback against Crest, Colgate, and Aqua Fresh, for example). But a dormant brand can be reshaped to make it more competitive. Every brand has a power that can be unleashed. The owner must find the USP that will provide the path against the competition. For example, Bold laundry detergent was brought back and positioned as a detergent for guys (which was not its positioning in its heyday). But licensing a brand doesn't insulate it from competition (as is true in any brand licensing). Polaroid, for example, is, with some of its photography-focused licensed products, trying to compete in a category that has experienced a great deal of consolidation—a category in which fierce competitors in the smartphone category have crippled famous brands such as Nokia,

BlackBerry, and Motorola. Polaroid is doing it with some products that have special features and technological innovation. And to whatever products the Polaroid brand is extended, those products must perform, and the owner has processes in place to ensure that quality. The Polaroid brand is authentic and trustworthy due to its history (its story). It is now focused on not losing that trust with poor-quality products, which is what happened to Polaroid during its first revival.

Provide Brand Management and Marketing Support
This is a recurring theme in all brand licensing programs: the need for strong brand management support and marketing support. When an IP owner licenses a dormant brand to a manufacturer, the owner is asking someone, a third party, to rebuild the entirety of the brand (by definition, other than memory, the brand has disappeared from the market). The IP owner and the licensee(s) control the entire brand positioning and can do with it whatever the market will bear. There are no restrictions, as there may be when licensing a famous brand that is successfully in market with its core products. In other words, there is no fear that the licensing program can cause damage to the core products because there are none. In fact, the IP owner can offer a total brand exclusive to a retailer or potential licensee in all categories or, importantly, in what is considered the core category. This can be very appealing. That's not the case in other licensing areas. But there needs to be strong brand management and there must be marketing support in order to compete. Seems like a no-brainer, right? Yet many of the short-term revivals have died a second death because they don't have the marketing support they need, particularly in product categories where brands are heavily marketed (such as health and beauty products, pharmaceuticals, and snack foods). Either the new brand owners don't believe they need marketing, that the fame of the brand will carry the brand to success, or they simply don't have the resources or budget for marketing. A potential way around this is to offer a retailer an exclusive. In effect, the brand

becomes that retailer's private-label brand. That's a common route with the revival of many dormant brands. However, as is true of any retail exclusive, the license lives or dies with that retailer and because the brand doesn't exist any longer outside of that retailer, it's pretty much do or die. Again, consider Nuprin. Nuprin had a chance at a comeback with CVS, the largest drugstore chain in the United States. But when sales didn't meet expectations, CVS dropped the brand, which meant that it once again disappeared from the marketplace. The competitor brands (e.g., Advil and Motrin) are heavily marketed by their owners. CVS is not particularly sophisticated at marketing its own brands, relying instead on brand owners doing the heavy lifting. Without robust marketing, the Nuprin brand couldn't survive in that competitive landscape.

A retail exclusive, dormant brand success story of sorts is White Cloud. P&G owned both White Cloud and Charmin. To focus on #1 Charmin, P&G discontinued White Cloud, which had a respectable 5 percent market share (in the $4 billion category), in 1993 and allowed the White Cloud brand to disappear from the marketplace and the trademark to expire. The trademarks were subsequently "acquired" (actually simply reregistered) by some entrepreneurs in 1996, who then licensed the brand as an exclusive to Walmart in 1999. Walmart then turned it into a store brand positioned as a premium product at a value price. In 2009, the owners sold the tissue rights (retaining other potential Walmart categories for future licensing). Walmart carried other White Cloud–licensed products over the years, including paper towels, cotton balls, and wipes. In 2013, *Consumer Reports* named White Cloud the top toilet paper in the United States (in terms of quality, not sales).[5] However, Walmart's strategy changed several years earlier, in 2009, when the retailer ended the White Cloud retail exclusive arrangement, largely to focus on private-label brands, and sales of White Cloud at Walmart declined from their peak.

---

5. "Attention Walmart Shoppers! White Cloud Toilet Paper Is Tops," *Consumer Reports News*, June 18, 2013. It also received top marks from *Consumer Reports* in 2014 and 2016.

Even with the strategy change, nevertheless, Walmart continues to this day to sell White Cloud toilet tissue (including a "green" version), cotton pads and cloths, wipes, facial tissue, and training pants for toddlers. The brand is also a national brand at Walgreens and is sold at various regional supermarkets. White Cloud is the story of a dormant brand that doesn't seem to die. Like Polaroid and The Sharper Image, the brand has been snatched from the dead and established and reestablished, surviving for a decade and still in the market.

Don't Forget the Law

There are always legal restrictions to consider. Sometimes the trademark is totally out of use for the requisite period of years and is, therefore, considered legally abandoned. A new owner can then use and register the name, as was the case with White Cloud. If that's not the case—that is, if the trademark is really out of the market but being maintained with the legally required nominal use—then an interested party can offer to purchase the trademark from the brand owner. Another option is that it can be licensed from the brand owner for particular categories with the intent to market the products or sublicense the rights to yet another party. Generally, a trademark owner will be a willing seller or licensor as a means to generate revenue or to maintain the trademark registration's validity—unless, of course, the owner has another competing brand and is not interested in fighting its "dormant" brand in the marketplace.

Feel the Power

Finally, each case is different. To assess the potential of reviving a brand through licensing, apply each of the previous eight metrics to the brand and see if it meets the stated criteria. Sometimes, nevertheless, it helps to use instinct and common sense as part of your assessment. In other words, "you'll know it (a brand with good revival potential) when you see it." The brand worked before, so reimagine how it can work again. Sadly for football fans in Cleveland,

Ohio, the Cleveland Browns moved to Baltimore in 1995 and were renamed the Baltimore Ravens. In 1998, Cleveland was awarded a new NFL franchise. What to name it? The Cleveland Browns! Can you feel the power of that brand name in Cleveland? Perhaps the same will happen in Montreal someday, and we will be watching the Montreal Expos competing again in Major League Baseball.

I'll conclude this chapter on reviving dormant brands with a cautionary note. As you are probably aware from the discussion of revivals that failed, this can be a challenging landscape. Nonetheless, we recall brands in their heydays and convince ourselves that many millions of people besides us have fond memories of these brands. Those memories, attachments, and loyalty, while necessary, aren't always enough for a successful revival, certainly for the long term. Brim and Nuprin, among other examples, survived for the short term, earned some revenue for the new owners, but basically disappeared again. Those brands that make it have special attributes that help them along, such as Polaroid, The Sharper Image, and White Cloud. Often, dormant brands exist in highly competitive categories where a great deal of money is being spent on marketing and advertising. Of course, the Internet provides a boost for these revived brands as social media can provide substantial exposure at very little cost. Still, you're up against some fairly stiff competition and some fairly big brand names in many of these categories. Something caused the brand's demise. Sometimes it's hard not to repeat the mistakes. Although consumers may have long memories and fond associations, it's also true that they have moved on and adopted new brands. And besides winning at least some of them back, you must win new consumers, younger consumers who may have never used the brand. In all likelihood, marketing has changed significantly since the brand was in its prime, particularly the use of social media and digital marketing. Developing an omnichannel strategy can be an opportunity but also a challenge. Successful brand revival, using the licensing model, takes time, resources, and commitment. All of these factors must be in place to prevent history from repeating itself.

Postscript: Toys"R"Us

As this book goes to press, the saga surrounding Toys"R"Us (TRU) is unfolding. TRU filed for liquidation on March 15, 2018, seeking to shutter its 735 stores and sell off its inventory. This followed the Chapter 11 bankruptcy in September 2017 when the retailer announced a turnaround plan. Alas, the iconic retailer just couldn't steady the ship in the rapidly changing retail waters while saddled with over $5 billion in debt incurred when the company was acquired in 2005 by KKR, Bain Capital and Vornado Realty Trust. Much more will be known about the fate of TRU by the time this book is published, but as the book goes to press, we are witnessing the death throes of an iconic brand. So, is this goodbye to Geoffrey the Giraffe, the TRU mascot? Are we never again to be serenaded by the jingle "I'm a Toys"R"Us Kid"? Let's examine this in the context of the discussion about dormant brands above.

What caused the decline of this iconic brand? First, TRU could not keep up with the changing retail landscape. Walmart and Target were able to offer toys at very low prices, perhaps even as loss leaders. Those retailers have many other products to sell to their customers when they are in the store. TRU only had toys. Plus, Amazon upped its game with regard to the toy category. Strong competitors stole share. Second, TRU never really mastered online sales. It desperately tried to partner with Amazon, but that only further diluted its own brick-and-mortar sales. It couldn't keep up with changing market conditions. Third, TRU used to be a store where children (and their parents) could have an experience. But the stores deteriorated due to the absence of investment and a "good experience" simply wasn't drawing consumers to the stores as it once did. TRU couldn't keep up with consumer behavior and expectations. And, fourth, financial challenges plagued the retailer since the acquisition in 2005 and the loading on of debt which diverted much needed investment cash to interest payments. It just wasn't able to invest and innovate. These are all common factors that often contribute to the extinction of iconic brands.

Now, as consumers rush to buy toys at deeply discounted prices at the dying TRU, what's the future for the retailer? There's a potential buyer for the Canadian operations (which might include some of the stores in the United States). And Isaac Larian, the CEO of MGA Entertainment, the company behind Bratz dolls and Little Tikes toys, has pledged $200 million and started a GoFundMe campaign to raise more in order to save about 400 stores (TRU represents about 20 percent of MGA's toy sales and it is the ninth largest creditor of TRU). And, perhaps others will step forward. But if all of this falls through, is that the end? TRU takes its place in the dustbin of failed and lost retailers? As discussed in this chapter, brands can die and live again, often through licensing. TRU has many of the necessary attributes of a successful brand revival, as discussed above.

First, there is a significant amount of brand awareness. The stores are closing in 2018. Awareness is strong.

Second, children and their parents have fond memories of TRU, there is strong emotional attachment and the brand has appealing authenticity. And these fond memories cut across generations—TRU has been around for 70 years. And there is no need to educate younger generations about the brand, they already know it.

Third, the demise of TRU creates a substantial gap that needs to be filled. TRU had a market share of about 19 percent in the toy category. Those sales and the consumers they represent have to go somewhere. Walmart and Target are already poised to pick up share. KB Toys, once the #2 toy retailer in the United States with 1,300 stores at its height, went out of business in 2009 and is already a dormant brand. But the owner of the IP, Strategic Marks, has announced 1,000 pop-ups for Black Friday and the Holiday season in 2018 in an attempt to pick up some of the sales left behind by TRU. TRU is creating its own gap to fill.

Fourth, TRU has a good story. It is (was) a brand that brought fun and delight to children and their parents. It has Geoffrey and the jingle. When it was running on all cylinders, it entertained its customers. Walmart and Target don't have that. Amazon doesn't either.

Fifth, the competition is, however, challenging and to succeed the new IP owner will have to invest in brand management and marketing support. A "new" TRU will not be able to compete without such an investment. It will die again.

This iconic brand has power. Can you feel it? If all else fails, someone will purchase the IP. Perhaps they will open fewer, smaller brick-and-mortar stores, perhaps there will be a better online presence for the brand, perhaps pop-ups or a flagship, or stores-within-a-store. This is a brand that will either be saved or, eventually, revived.

CHAPTER 10

Brand Licensing Outside the United States: It's a Big World Out There

Introduction: It's Different

Many brand owners look to extend their brands (sometimes to establish their brands) through licensing outside the United States. Some brand owners are more successful with licensing in other countries—different brand perceptions as well as cultural sensibilities dovetail with the brand message in a different ways than in the United States. Pantone is a good example of a product with more licensing breadth outside the United States than within. For example, the brand has been licensed in categories such as paint in Italy, Spain, France, Ireland, South Korea, Portugal, and the United Kingdom; apparel and apparel accessories in Asia, Switzerland, Italy, Germany, Australia, Monaco, and Japan; bedding in Italy, Greece, Japan, Chile, and Colombia; kitchen products in Italy, Asia, and Chile; home and home décor products in the United Kingdom, Denmark, and South Korea; luggage in South

Korea and Italy; paper and stationery products in Greece, Italy, France, Mexico, South Korea, Poland, Chile, and Turkey; and cosmetics and nail polish in the United Kingdom, South Korea, and Australia. That's a great deal more licensing outside the United States than this American brand does at home.

U.S. magazine titles offer excellent examples of frequently having more opportunities in licensing overseas than domestically (see *Esquire* and *Playboy* examples later in the chapter). Rodale's *Men's Health*, with over 100 editions around the world, mostly licensed editions,[1] is the biggest men's health magazine worldwide. Although the subject matter of *Men's Health* is on trend and universal—health and wellness—there is not a great deal of licensing activity in the United States. However, the brand is actively licensed for consumer products in the United Kingdom, its largest overseas market, for exercise equipment as a DTR with Argos as well as vitamins, beef 'n beans, healthy snacks, beef jerky (a healthy snack), "tools" for exercise, and natural foods in pouches offering on-the-go snacks.

Why should brand owners consider licensing their brand overseas? If the brand is already active in its core category in an overseas market, it receives many of the benefits enumerated in Chapter 3. Licensing overseas also creates a halo for the brand and a greater brand global presence and brand essence. Even if the brand is not active in its core category in a particular country, that doesn't mean it isn't well known. Licensing becomes a route to allow consumers to engage with the brand. *Playboy* is a good example of a brand that doesn't offer its core product in China (i.e., the magazine) but is very successful with licensing in categories such as apparel. By doing your homework and having clearly stated goals for licensing in any country, brands increase the odds for success. At the same time, those odds decrease if you are reactive—responding

---

1. Many U.S. magazine titles license the magazine overseas (or enter into joint ventures), allowing the foreign publisher licensee to take advantage of U.S.-developed content while also permitting the licensee to present content specific to local tastes and customs, thereby "localizing" the magazine in a particular country.

reflexively to local opportunities that are presented without being familiar with the market.

Be aware, too, that brand licensing outside the United States is inconsistent across territories (mature in some countries and embryonic in others). The practice is advanced in countries such as the United Kingdom and Australia where there is a long licensing history, an understanding of the value of intellectual property, and a well-oiled licensing infrastructure and community (and where retailers and consumers are most like those in the United States). On the other hand, brand licensing is barely developed in other areas of the world (e.g., Latin America, Russia, Japan, and the Middle East), where the concept is largely not understood by manufacturers, retailers, or consumers (although other areas of "brand-like" licensing is present, such as celebrity, fashion, and museum licensing). In these markets, consumers don't make the connection between the core brand product and the licensed product extension: Jim Beam is a bourbon; it's not chips. Corporate brand extensions that do succeed in Japan, for example, make a fashion statement, such as the candy Pez iconography on apparel.

Of course, entertainment licensing can be found virtually everywhere a vibrant consumer market exists. It has always been the entry point for licensed products in any country (see Chapter 2). Indeed, the history of licensing in any country reveals that Disney was generally the pioneer, followed by other entertainment brands. That's true in countries as diverse as Germany, Saudi Arabia, India, Mexico, and Brazil, for example. Sports licensing (such as the Olympics and FIFA World Cup) and fashion generally followed entertainment licensing in many of these countries. But with regard to licensing a corporate brand, key stakeholders in many countries (such as Latin America and Asia) or consumers (such as in Japan) demonstrate a lack of understanding or acceptance. Manufacturers don't understand that it's not, for example, Stanley Black & Decker asking them to manufacture a product that Stanley Black & Decker will then purchase from them and sell. But that's starting to change.

When seeking to expand a licensing program overseas, first consider a wide and general range of factors. Before plunging ahead, know the facts and statistics about the targeted country—size of population; language or languages spoken; category sector growth; political, economic, and cultural factors; market dynamics; tourism statistics; and even climate. These factors, both macroeconomic and specific to retailing, all affect your potential for success. Demographics, socioeconomic metrics, consumer attitudes and shopping behaviors, religion, education, geography, trends, tastes, relevant laws, and regulations, among other considerations, differ country by country, all affecting the ability of brand licensing to succeed in a particular market. The 2008 recession in Europe still affects consumer spending in countries such as Italy, Greece, Spain, and France. Some countries are so small (e.g., Denmark and New Zealand) that it will be virtually impossible to generate enough royalty revenue to make the effort worthwhile, if revenue is a goal. In the three countries making up Benelux—the Netherlands, Belgium, and Luxembourg—there are four official languages! The Nordic region is made up of five countries each with its own language and culture and with small populations. Then there is the Middle East and North Africa with a combined population of over 350 million, basically one language (Arabic), and over half of the population under the age of 16, but with other significant challenges to penetrating this vast market. In some countries, communication is frequently difficult between brand owner and licensee, as is getting the message across to consumers

Even within regions there are major differences. Greater Europe, for example, consists of over 40 countries [as of publication, 28 in the European Economic Community (EEC)]. There are substantial economic and cultural differences throughout those countries as well as languages. To a lesser extent, the same is true in Latin America (at least language is less of an issue). The political climate also has an impact on business in many countries and, in some regions, can change quickly depending on who is in power, making business planning difficult. An extreme example is Venezuela. The political situation today is so unstable, combined with high unemployment, a weak economy, and weak intellectual property laws, that it's an unfavorable market for any kind of serious licensing activity.

Therefore, it's important to become knowledgeable about the conditions in each country that are (or are not) amenable to brand licensing.

Ten Steps to Take Before Moving Forward

Although a chapter could be written on each country's licensing opportunities and challenges, I will not get into the details of every specific characteristic, nuance, retail environment, regulation, and idiosyncratic policy country by country or region by region.[2] Instead, I'll focus on major considerations that pertain to extending a brand through licensing in markets outside the United States. Examples will be provided of what has worked, what hasn't worked, where there are opportunities, and where there are challenges (in some cases, absolute roadblocks). Doing your homework and *being prepared* for addressing the many differences country by country should be any brand owner's approach. To put that into practice, in addition to understanding the facts and figures mentioned above, the following 10 considerations will help any brand owner develop a strategy for implementing a licensing program outside the United States.

1. Understand Your Brand's Fame, Meaning, and the Local Perception of the Brand

A brand's fame and perception may be different outside the United States, and brand owners must be receptive to those differences.

Don't be arrogant about your brand. Many brands are famous all over the world, such as Coca-Cola, Apple, Google, Harley-

---

2. For a country-by-country/region-by-region summary of licensing activity with chapters written by local experts (primarily in the entertainment arena), see "Basics of Licensing: International Edition," by Danny Simon and Gregory J. Battersby, Kent Press, 2014.

Davidson, and Pampers. But some brands have not achieved such global status, and fame varies by region. In some instances, a brand famous in one country is virtually unknown in another country. China was mostly an agricultural society when the Polaroid brand was in its heyday, so awareness today is very low and the path to market is difficult. Ford's Mustang brand, actively licensed in the United States, is virtually unknown in India.

Even where a brand might be famous, the local perception of that brand may be different than it is in the United States. Stanley is a U.S. brand that has been in the United Kingdom for over 100 years. Unlike in the United States, where it is known for all sorts of hand tools, in the United Kingdom, its real fame is as a utility knife. In fact, Brits call utility knives a "Stanley" and generally think it's a British brand.

Jaguar is another good example. Although a global brand, it's known as a British brand (albeit owned by an Indian company, Tata Motors Limited). In the United Kingdom, the brand has lost some of its premium cache. But that's not true outside the United Kingdom, where the premium equity is still strong. Developing a line of licensed small leather goods to compete with other premium brands in the United Kingdom was not successful. In the United States, a line of high-end Jaguar small leather goods has no place in department stores (where the brand owner wanted to be) given the competition of fashion designers and premium brands already in the category. But in China, the intersection of retail dynamics and brand perception worked in its favor. Its high-end British heritage is an advantage; the brand is aspirational for the rising middle class; and due to high import duties, the price of the auto remains high. And in China, mono-branded stores (frequently licensed) have proven to be a successful retail strategy. Over 100 stand-alone licensed Jaguar small leather goods stores were opened across China.

Although *Esquire* is published in 27 countries around the world (mostly by licensees), the brand has licensed the opening of *Esquire* lounges in India, a country where the magazine is *not* published. Nonetheless, the brand has fame in India, representing "Man at his best." However, when it came to designing the lounges, what appealed to the brand owner, Hearst, was a clubby atmosphere that drew on the brand's 80-year-old heritage. But that design concept didn't appeal to the licensee, who wanted a more contemporary look for the local consumer. Hearst needed to filter the brand voice through the local brand perception and follow the licensee's guidance on what would appeal to local consumer tastes. Hearst moved forward with the contemporary designs.

Of course, the Internet has given consumers local access to brands sold in other countries and allows them to see how the brand is presented in those countries, complicating brand perception. For example, PVH's Arrow brand is sold at different price points in different parts of the world. It's a higher-priced brand in Europe and a lower-priced brand in the United States. Consumers can see those differences online, if they care to, affecting brand perception.

2. Adapt to Local Market Needs, Habits, and Customs

Be Flexible and Adapt

Do not assume that market needs, habits, and customs are the same around the world, despite globalization. Yes, the Internet has pushed us toward a global marketplace. But, no, consumers are not all the same. Every country is unique, and brand owners need to address strong local habits and customs. That doesn't mean that you must change your product or brand completely, but it does mean that you must be flexible, that you must adapt to local needs. Potential product categories as well as brand positioning also might be different. Take the local culture into account to avoid making incorrect assumptions about what consumers in any particular country want.

Products Are Used Differently in Different Parts of the World

Cleaning dishes may seem like a universal task, but significant variations exist. So when P&G contemplates licensing its Fairy brand (dishwashing liquid) for a basic product such as sponges in Europe, it must consider the various ways people clean in different countries in Europe. In the United States, the sponges that consumers want in California, Nebraska, and New Jersey are basically the same. Not so in various countries of Europe. In the United Kingdom, a large portion of the population use a washing up pan where they soak their dishes and use a sponge to wipe off the dish. In France, consumers put the dishwashing liquid on the sponge to clean. And in Spain, people clean, rinse, and drip dry on a pad. These unique cleaning habits require different kinds of sponges in each country. The same is true of brooms. In the United Kingdom, consumers sweep from front to back like we do in the United States. But in France, they push their brooms. Different products designed for local habits are required. Even entertainment licensors must address things such as different paper sizes for school supplies and different bedding measurements throughout Europe (there are over twenty different sheet sizes across the Continent).

These differences in the same products across a region such as Europe mean that you will probably not find one licensee that can address, for example, all of Europe (although you will hear companies claim that they can). You will need different licensees in different countries. Ideally, you will find a licensee that can service a group of countries but generally not a pan-region (or certainly global).

The Consumer's Needs for a Particular Product May Differ Around the World

Sometimes what you may consider a natural product extension or design doesn't make sense in a particular country. Stanley has a line of licensed ladders in the United States, but in China, where the Stanley brand is well known, consumers have little use for ladders. Most Chinese consumers live in cities, in apartment blocks, and in small apartments. Besides not needing ladders, they have no place to store them. The same is true of garden tools, a successful Stanley licensed product category in the United States and the United Kingdom but not appropriate in China. In many Asian countries, they don't use ovens, relying more on stove tops where they use woks and cook rice. Those countries don't present much of an opportunity for licensed bakeware, a popular licensing category in the United States and the United Kingdom. Less obviously, the nostalgic artwork for a brand that has strong connotations in the United States may have no meaning in other countries where the brand lacks the same history.

Be Aware of Cultural Customs That May Affect Product Choices or Designs and Processes

Brand names have different meanings in different parts of the world and, therefore, can be licensed for products in one country that will not necessarily work in other countries. Consider the famous lollipop brand Chupa Chups. In Germany, the brand is licensed for a range of beauty products for the body, face, lips, and nails; a collection of pop-designed furniture and accessories is licensed for distribution in various countries of Europe; and a collection of underwear, sleepwear, and other apparel is licensed with an Italian company. These products would be a challenge in the U.S. market. Consider some of the other examples from around the world described below.

Animals are very important in China (every year is the year of a specific animal). As such, Chinese consumers want animals incorporated as features on products. Izod in China is Izod with a "twist." The brand owner, PVH, requires the licensee to use Izod-provided designs for 20 percent of the line. The remaining 80 percent can be designed by the licensee. This common method allows fashion licensees to "localize" their product assortment. Izod is a preppy brand, but the Chinese don't understand "preppy." So the Chinese Izod licensee needs to adapt the brand to the culture. The licensee designed Izod shirts emblazoned with animals—big T-shirts featuring a bull dog wearing the Izod plaid and shirts and sweaters decorated with moose (moose stand for prosperity in China). Although the licensed Izod stores in China did a good job of accurately reflecting the brand as it's known in the United States, the animal prints were specific to Chinese tastes.

Licensees in emerging markets sometimes don't understand the licensing process in totality, and you need explain it to them at the beginning of the process as well as while it is ongoing. In the case of the Izod animal print apparel items, the Chinese licensee "neglected" to submit them to Izod for approval in advance of going to market, and the brand owner saw them for the first time when visiting the store in China.

And consider *Playboy*. The brand earns more revenue from licensing its brand worldwide than it does from publishing, and almost half of that licensing revenue comes from China. In China, *Playboy*, which has *no media presence*, has been a household brand representing fashion, aspiration, and luxury for over 20 years in a host of licensed product categories (e.g., apparel, accessories, footwear, and luggage) sold in over 3,000 retail locations. This iconic American brand is perceived differently in China than in the United States, resulting in a licensing program that is more successful in China. *Playboy* is also successful in Japan, where it is perceived yet another way. In Japan, it's a fun logo and a fashion brand for young girls licensed for products such as bicycles and backpacks.

The Japanese consumer, in general, is extremely sensitive to design aesthetics (i.e., what's pleasing to the Japanese eye), often placing more importance on the design of a product than the core values of a famous brand itself. Corporate brands that do succeed in Japan tend to make a fashion or design statement. Swimsuits adorned with the iconography of the Kellogg's Corn Flakes brand work in Japan. The Japanese consumer tends to resist true brand extensions and often is more open to fanciful licensing. To succeed in Japan, brands also need a strong history; European brands often do well because of their heritage and authenticity.

The experience of London's Victoria and Albert Museum (the V&A) in Japan is illustrative. The mission of the V&A is to promote an understanding of the designed world—in fashion, architecture, costumes, textiles, and industrial design. The V&A licensing program was launched in Japan in the 1990s with home décor products based on local interest following a major V&A exhibit of William Morris textile designs that traveled to Japan. With success in Japan, about 10 years later, the program was extended to England with affordable products to decorate the home. In addition to introducing more products in Japan, the program has since expanded in other Asian countries, including China and South Korea. And in late 2017, the V&A announced that it was partnering with Chinese companies for design exhibits at cultural institutions and malls as well as for the rollout of licensed offline stores and online presence on Alibaba, the leading e-commerce retailer in China.

As a licensing program that is focused on design, the V&A must take into account cultural differences among countries, including how designs are applied to product, the quality of the product, nuances in color trends, shapes, and sizes. In Japan and South Korea, for example, where women are more petite, the daintiness of the licensed jewelry wouldn't work in the United States or the United Kingdom. Homes are much smaller in Japan, so they don't want excessive decorative accessories such as throw pillows. They don't have wall space, and they don't have storage. Those conditions make Japanese consumers very careful about making purchasing decisions and have a significant impact on the categories the V&A can pursue in Japan versus the the United Kingdom, for example.

Famous brands may need to adapt to having their brand name on products that seem strange or "foreign." Women like to buy on-the-go facial masks in Korea—a product category largely unknown in the United States—and *Cosmo* (another Hearst magazine) is very successful with licensed facial masks in Korea. In China, when the brand's licensee submitted designs for its bedding collection, Hearst found the designs too childish and was concerned that a magazine targeting adult women would be influencing a young girl audience. As it turns out, adult women in China, particularly Millennials, are attracted to "childish" designs, and the submitted products were on target for the right age group. Baileys has licensed a line of canned cakes in Germany and panettones for Christmas in Italy. Guinness has a line of Christmas desserts in the United Kingdom. In addition, Chupa Chups has entered a number of categories, as mentioned above. In Japan, the bathroom is a more elevated space than in the United States and can feature branded toilets, toilet mats, and slippers.

3. Know the Local Competition

Understand the Identity of Local Brands, How Embedded in the Culture They Are, and How Successful They Are

Be aware of what brands are active in the categories and retail channels into which you want to extend your brand. Generally, in the United States, those brands in other categories will be familiar to you. Overseas it's a different matter. In addition to global brands, unfamiliar local brands may dominate. Sometimes they are brands that have been around a long time and for which consumers have an emotional (even a nationalistic) attachment. The French consumer, for example, is known to be extremely loyal to its local culture and French brands, particularly in the food and apparel categories. Powerful local electronics brands (of which you are no doubt aware) in Japan include Sony and Panasonic. Understanding the local competition is frequently not an easy evaluation, particularly if you are working long distance. But brand owners who don't take the local brands into account should be prepared for failure.

Although some local consumers may be particularly attracted to U.S. or European brands (such as aspirational consumers in the Middle East with fashion and food brands), many others are attracted to homegrown brands with which they have had a long-term relationship. Many of these local brands also have licensing programs in their home country as well as in neighboring countries. A brand such as lief! Lifestyle, a popular Dutch brand found in many homes, offers apparel and accessories, health and beauty products, and home décor products in the Benelux countries as well as the rest of Europe, with many licensees. Automobile brands have very successful licensing programs across Europe, but "local" global auto brands are the most successful country by country. For example, BMW, Volkswagen, and Mercedes-Benz all have global programs but are particularly successful in Germany. The same is true of Fiat and Ferrari in Italy.

If you're not German or haven't done much traveling in Germany, you probably have never heard of Käfer. Yet it is an extremely popular premium brand in Germany often ranking first in Germany in unaided awareness for gourmet foods; and it's a brand with a successful licensing program. Käfer, a family business founded in 1930 as a grocery store, operates numerous delicatessens, restaurants, and a catering business throughout Germany (and, in some instances, beyond Germany—the company has a franchise operation in Mitsukoshi department stores in Japan). Käfer has been successfully licensed in a host of categories in Germany—gourmet foods (packaged salmon and mustards); beverages (packaged coffee, wines, and spirits); frozen, fresh, and convenience products (chips, pastries, and bread); sweets (ice cream); and nonfood products (tableware and cooking tools). Any U.S. brand considering licensing into these categories in Germany would be smart to take notice of Käfer, the local competition.

The penetration of local competition combined with fewer retail choices can make licensing your brand in particular product categories in any overseas market challenging. You will undoubtedly need some local assistance to evaluate local competition (more about "feet on the ground" later in the chapter).

4. Understand the Consumer

Your Consumer in the United States May Not Be the Same Consumer in Another Country
Perhaps your brand is targeted at a mass market consumer in the United States, whereas overseas your brand is considered a premium brand and more appropriate for a higher distribution chan-

nel. The age of your consumer may differ country by country. Izod is not a "young" brand in the United States, but in China, the market is for those who are 18–23 years old, requiring a different strategy. Determining what demographic groups have spending power will also help guide you. In Spain, for example (and in many other countries as well), Millennials are gaining in spending power, resulting in the rise of fashion and sports licensing. Conversely, in Japan, the population is aging and birthrates are declining. In many countries such as Japan and the United States, Millennials and the emerging Gen Zers are less interested in many types of brands (but, of course, not entirely) (see Chapter 12).

Become Astute About Finding Your Consumer
Look for consumers where they live and where they travel. Although China is an important country to consider because of its growth, power, and size, brands also need to consider Southeast Asia in general (e.g., Singapore, Thailand, Malaysia, and the Philippines), where the Chinese go on holiday. Further, within China, the focus has traditionally been on what are called Tier 1 cities, but a growing middle class in the Tier 2 cities is spending money as well.

Airports around the world, too, are potentially strong locations for licensed (or franchised) stores. The Mac brand has a store at the Singapore airport that's 90 square feet and generated approximately $8 million in sales in 2016. As more people travel, including from emerging markets, airport stores are growing. Airports also are places to capitalize on different consumer motivations and shopping behaviors. Travelers are not there to shop, but they shop because they have time, because they need a last-minute gift, because they are attracted to the premium offerings and perceived duty-free savings.

Understand the Differences in Consumer Shopping Behavior Country by Country
Do your homework to take advantage of different shopping behaviors and motivations in countries around the world. This

requires some serious research, and you will find a great deal of literature on this subject that focuses on the societal forces affecting shopping motivations in different countries. The following is an excellent example of evaluating how to address shopping behavior in China: An emerging middle class exists in China where consumers care about their status. But they also care about economic issues. They are attracted to luxury brands (such as Jaguar) but also are aggressive about saving money. So how should brands address this seeming conflict in consumer behavior in China? Tom Doctoroff, in an article titled "Three Golden Rules of Brand-Building in China," provides some insights:[3]

First, maximize purchasing by offering consumers premium products that can be consumed and admired in public. He notes that Starbucks (where a cup of coffee costs 30 percent more than in the United States but the sandwiches are half the price) and Häagen-Dazs (with 600 stores in China and none in Japan and where a cone costs $6) have figured this out.

Second, externalize the payoff by offering products that deliver a means to an end. Although luxury brands are considered nonessential in the West, they are considered a sign of advancement in China. Johnny Walker's Blue Label has held whiskey summits that help professionals expand their networks. Cars such as Ford and VW demonstrate that the owner has achieved middle-class status.

Third, provide reassurance in a country where institutions don't provide much protection. Brands need to offer products that are value-added, reliable, readily available, and affordable. The e-commerce site Alibaba offers this reassurance. And Haier, China's largest appliance manufacturer, sells its products all over the world to burnish its reputation at home.

This analysis can be extrapolated for other countries and posits the following three questions: (1) What kinds of products, necessities, and nonnecessities does your target demographic want, need, or consider aspirational? (2) How can a particular

---

3. "Three Golden Rules of Brand-Building in China," *Ad Age*, June 20, 2017.

product category help consumers identify themselves? (3) What are the characteristics of the products desired by consumers that will satisfy them?

5. *Understand the Available Retail Channels*

Brands Can't Win in a Particular Country Without Fully Understanding the Retail Infrastructure.

Figuring out the network of retail distribution in any country is among the most challenging aspects of licensing overseas. Very few, if any, countries have the breadth of retail channels and stores as the United States. The choices are much more limited. Understanding local channels will also drive an understanding of how large the licensing program can be if it is successful (i.e., scale). China and India, with very large populations, have weak brick-and-mortar retail infrastructure. Japan has a large retail economy with strong channels across mass market, department stores, convenience stores, and fashion chains. And as we travel around the globe, we find different retail dynamics in virtually every major country. To understand channel and distribution opportunities, limitations, challenges, and (in some countries) obstacles, let's briefly examine some examples in various regions and countries.

Understand Channels and Leaders

Europe: In the United Kingdom, the population translates into potential program scale (a large enough segment of the population can purchase the products you intend to license). There are also strong retail channels such as Grocery (which sells more categories than in the United States) (e.g., Tesco and Sainsbury), High Street (e.g., Top Shop and Next), department stores (e.g., Harvey Nichols and Harrods), and Mass (e.g., Asda). In Germany, the largest economy in Europe, retail is more decentralized than in other European countries. The primary channel is Discount, such as Lidl and Aldi. Mass and mail order is also very strong (e.g., Otto Versand). In Spain, only two sizable retailers exist—El Corte

Inglés representing the department store channel and Carrefour representing the mass (hypermarket) channel. In Italy, channels are dominated by small specialty and mom-and-pop retailers—it's very difficult to reach critical mass there. France boasts several of the world's largest retail chains, such as Carrefour and Auchan. Other countries, particularly smaller countries, have even fewer retail choices.

Mexico: Due to socioeconomic conditions in Mexico (as well as other Latin American countries), most retail activity is in the mass market channel, including hypermarkets, warehouse clubs, and convenience stores as well as independent retailers and the "informal" market that includes street vendors. With retailers consolidating (resulting in fewer choices) and concentrated in the cities of Mexico, distribution nationwide can be challenging.

India: In India, despite its very large population, retail is disorganized and decentralized; distribution is challenging. Most consumers buy their products at mom-and-pop stores that sell everything from bubble bath to shirts to gum to hammers. Nevertheless, a small percentage of retail in India is very organized and, because of India's size, it's still a large population that is serviced by that small percentage of retail, which is concentrated in the five largest cities. A surprising number of brands are controlled, through licensing or franchising, by several major players such as Madora, Arund, Reliance, Al Tayor, and Alshaya. These large companies sell products through their own, often mono-branded (frequently licensed) stores as well as in department stores, which they also own. Al Tayor has over 200 stores and more than 35 brands, many of them licensed, including Gap, Harvey Nichols, Cosi, Coach, Kiehl's, and Bloomingdale's. Alshaya has over 3,500 stores and more than 80 brands, including Starbucks, American Eagle Outfitters, Boots, Pottery Barn, Bouchon Bakery, P.F. Chang's, and The Cheesecake Factory.

The Middle East: In the Middle East, retail infrastructure varies from nonexistent in some countries to top of the line in others. The largest mall in the world, featuring a plethora of

Western brands, is the Dubai Mall in the United Arab Emirates. The Middle East has also been a pioneer in taking licenses or, in some instances, franchises for Western brands for mono-branded stores. With fashion brands, the licensee is required to purchase a percentage of goods from the brand owner and can manufacture the rest on its own to appeal to local tastes. Five families basically control all organized retail in the Gulf states. Crate & Barrel, Gap, Magnolia Bakery, Macy's, and Bloomingdale's are all licensed store brands. And there are different financial models. Gap, for example, is a cost-plus model on the purchase of goods from the brand owner as well as a royalty on sales. The Bloomingdale's licensee pays a royalty on all retail and e-commerce sales.[4]

E-Commerce Must Be Considered and Likely Be Part of Any Licensing Strategy

E-commerce is upending retail channels in mature markets as well as many emerging markets where big brick-and-mortar retailers have had limited success outside the big cities. In India, the fastest-growing market in the world for e-commerce, Amazon, which already reaches hundreds of millions of consumers, is growing and betting that consumers will bypass brick-and-mortar retailers as they expand. In India, there are already 350 million Internet users (equal to the U.S. population) and another 900 million who don't yet use the Internet but will in the next five years. Online retailers such as Amazon and its local rival Flipkart[5]

---

4. The licensed mono-branded store concept, by the way, also works in China (as mentioned earlier in the Jaguar example). There are over 300 Stanley stores that sell and install Stanley-branded closet systems for the home. Similarly, there are Caterpillar-branded licensed stores selling everything from phones to boots, removable tatoos, diapers, watches, glassware, and more. These brands are also adapting to different brand perceptions in China. And the license/franchise model is also working in Western markets. In the United Kingdom, L Brands (formerly The Limited), an Ohio-based company, has granted rights for brands it owns such as Victoria's Secret, Bath & Body Works, and Henri Bendel.
5. In May 2018, the Directors of Flipkart voted to proceed with a sale of 75 percent of the company to Walmart, intensifying the overseas e-commerce battle between Walmart and Amazon, both of which lost out to Alibaba in China.

are bombarding consumers with reasons to shop online and competing to make it easier for them.[6]

And in China, e-commerce giants such as Amazon, Alibaba (the largest e-commerce platform in China and double the size of Amazon), and others are growing at warp speed, making China the largest e-commerce marketplace in the world. Despite a slowing economy, China, with its growth, power, and size, is poised to be the second-largest economy in the world by 2020 and is already the world's largest retail market and e-commerce market. The upper and middle classes are growing, incomes are rising, and the younger generation prefers to shop rather than save. E-commerce will continue to offer a greater range of product categories to a larger consumer population spread across a large geographic region that is difficult to reach through offline distribution. China has over 700 million online users, almost twice the U.S. population, who spend more money online than do U.S. consumers. Alibaba features over 70,000 brands; has over 500 million active monthly users for its shopping apps; attracts one in three Chinese consumers; and collects data about every consumer, including purchasing habits, preferences, media interests, and social networks. "Shopping Day" on Alibaba in 2017 generated $25 billion in sales in 24 hours! That was double Black Friday and Cyber Monday in the United States combined. The company has 8,000 consumer identifiers that help brands get to the right target consumers. The numbers are staggering. Brick and mortar is also growing, with 300 malls being built annually that are not only retail experiences but also social experiences in a country with little urban planning. Moreover, the intense rivalry between China's major e-commerce platforms Alibaba (#1) and JD.com (#2) is causing them to focus

---

6. Amazon is also forging relationships with Indian vendors by offering their products on Amazon.com in the United States. Over 25,000 Indian suppliers have signed up with the Amazon global seller program to sell their products on the site in the United States—from large Indian companies to boutique merchants. Amazon views India as a market to sell products as well as a source of cheap products for the U.S. market. "Amazon Woos India's Merchants," *The New York Times*, November 27, 2017, page B1.

on offline partnerships, delivery systems, physical locations, and online partnerships (for example, JD.com hosts Walmart.com in China). Not surprisingly, in many emerging markets, the challenge is not selling product online, but delivering the product in countries with bad roads and weak postal systems.

The truth is that in many emerging markets, e-commerce will lead the way to retail growth and offline retail will follow behind (Walmart, for example, is focusing on its e-commerce business in India before moving forward with brick-and-mortar stores and pulled out of physical locations to focus on e-commerce offering U.S. products in China).

Germany is #2 in e-commerce in Western Europe, following the United Kingdom, and accounts for 25 percent of e-commerce sales in Western Europe. Consumers in Germany are attracted to shopping online and on their phones, in part due to a long history of catalog shopping in that country. Consumers have a history of expecting their orders to be delivered to their homes and of being able to return items easily without going to a store.

The growth of e-commerce and the threat it poses to general brick-and-mortar retailing is not consistent across all countries. In France, for example, e-commerce is growing but is not challenging brick-and-mortar retailers the way it is in other European markets. France has a very robust online grocery business, but with regard to other categories such as apparel, online isn't as dominant as it is in other European countries. And in Japan, there's a "peace treaty" of sorts between e-commerce platforms and offline retailers. Japan is a crammed market with small roads and challenging delivery and distribution infrastructure, which is being strained by e-commerce platforms promising quicker and quicker delivery (it's even difficult to find enough delivery drivers). Amazon, for example, is seeking other methods of delivery in Japan. It partners with retailers where consumers can order on Amazon and pick up their order at the retailer. Nevertheless, the Internet is not a "typhoon" in Japan; it's more like "rainfall." The Japanese consumer enjoys experiences and likes going to stores. They often use the Internet simply for research and pricing and buy at offline retailers.

Brand owners engaged in licensing must understand the distribution options country by country as well as the ever-shifting dynamics of offline and online retailing and take advantage of those options that are aligned with their licensing strategy.

6. Choose the Right Partner and Build Trust and Personal Relationships Supported by Boots on the Ground

Choosing and vetting the right partner is always important, but overseas it is even more complicated due to distance, time zones, language, negotiating habits, fewer potential partners, and other unknowns about a particular market. Those complications make discernment critical.

Although Personal Relationships Are Important, Make Sure That Contractual Provisions Are Equally Important

Personal relationships and trust are very important, both in emerging markets such as China as well as sophisticated markets such as Japan. Greater loyalty often exists within companies overseas than in U.S. companies; be mindful of the expectations of local company management. In Mexico as well as throughout Latin America family-owned businesses are plentiful and contractual requirements are sometimes taken a bit less seriously than you would expect due to personal relationships. Contractual compliance is often more reactive than proactive among licensees. Therefore, establish clear requirements and remind licensees constantly of their obligations (such as submitting items for approval).

In many emerging markets, once you license your brand to a partner, they often act as though (or actually believe) they now own your brand. Make certain your prospective partner fully understands the relationship—you share responsibility, but your partner doesn't own the brand. Give the licensee all of the necessary tools to be successful and talk frequently about the road map from product development to product on the shelf or online. Many licensees don't understand (or simply ignore) the approval process (recall the earlier Izod example). Lay it out for them plainly and enforce it.

Feet on the Ground Is Essential to Doing Business in Markets Far Away

Local presence goes a long way in building this essential relationship in many countries. No brand can succeed in licensing outside the United States, in an emerging market, or in a mature market without some sort of local presence. That might mean a full-time employee in a given country or an agent or a consultant; it might also entail tapping into an already existing local office (which, by the way, should be vested in the licensing program as part of a brand owner's "operational readiness").

Whatever tactic you choose, know that you cannot build a long-distance relationship or manage a licensee in another country or, in some instances, region without someone local who is on the ground representing your interests. Issues relating to language, culture, approvals, packaging, contracts, laws, customs, habits, trends, distribution, and on and on, all need to be addressed locally. Retailers will also appreciate working with a local representative who understands their particular needs, seasonality of purchasing, product introduction details, and promotion/marketing opportunities. It's not uncommon for licensees who don't understand contracts written in English to sign them anyway—and then ignore their obligations. Boots on the ground can help avoid that pitfall. A local presence provides a brand owner with essential market and retail experience and perspective, necessities even when you are first evaluating a particular country or region.

7. Consider Different Partnership Structures

Creative Agreement Structures Are Frequently the Only Way to Move Forward

In most countries, you will find that you have fewer choices of partners and that you may need to consider alternative partnership structures such as distribution agreements, franchises, or joint ventures. PVH, for example, owner of brands such as Tommy Hilfiger, Calvin Klein, Arrow, Izod, and Van Heusen, is moving more toward joint ventures where it has more control. Joint ventures can also give brand owners a better opportunity to acquire their partner's rights in the future. In many countries, potential partners are afraid of not being treated properly by brand owners. For example, in Japan, multibillion-dollar trading company Mitsui, which heavily invested in and built the Burberry and Calvin Klein brands (prior to being owned by PVH), lost the license when the license term expired. No doubt, Mitsui will be more careful in the future about agreement structure.

Models vary widely in regions such as the Middle East and India, where brand owners and local partners are creatively looking for ways to extend brands in those territories. In the Middle East, virtually every type of partnership structure exists: the standard license agreement with a manufacturer (although there are virtually no manufacturers in the region), agreements with distributors, DTRs, retail agreements for mono-branded stores, location-based agreements (e.g., cafés and hotels), and agreements for theme parks and for live events. In Western countries, the standard license agreement is more prevalent and is generally accepted. In general, when working overseas be prepared to be flexible in terms of agreement structures while making certain the brand is fully protected.

8. Address Unexpected and Unusual Legal and Contractual Issues

Address Trademark Ownership
Be certain that you own your trademark not only in your core category but also in the categories you are targeting for licensing. One well-known automotive brand owned its trademark for automobiles in China, but when it came time to license the brand for apparel (with lucrative offers on the table), the brand owner discovered that someone else owned the intellectual property in

the apparel category. The entire licensing initiative in China was abandoned. Similar challenges exist in other countries as well, where famous brand names often have been registered by another party in important classifications of goods.

Understand Local Laws That May Affect Your Licensing Program

Many other legal issues arise, such as labeling requirements, repatriation of royalties, currency conversion and weak exchange rates, duty structures, complex tax laws including withholding taxes, and manufacturing origin of products. In addition, counterfeiting is a major challenge in countries such as China, Mexico, India, and Turkey. In China, a stunning majority of branded products are counterfeits. In Japan, on the other hand, counterfeiting is practically nonexistent. In some countries, direct promotions are forbidden. Restrictions on advertising to children varies country by country. The laws for licensing spirits brands in Europe, for example, are different by country from "dark" markets (highly restricted) to "semi-dark" (some restrictions) to open. A spirits brand owner could risk losing its right to sell its core product in a particular country if the licensed product violates the law. In some countries, particularly in the Middle East, laws prohibit designs that might be considered offensive to the Islamic religion (such as skulls and nudity).

In some areas of the world, there are import/export restrictions and trading blocs of countries. The EEC may be the most important. It's basically an open market, which means that products can move across borders, provided that the product is authorized for sale in a single EEC country or produced in the EEC. Limiting the contract to specific countries (or a language) remains a gray area as the brand owner must prove that the sale took place outside those defined countries because of open market rules.

Be Aware of Local Practices in the Areas of Human Rights, Environmental Standards, and Manufacturing Standards
Although not necessarily legal requirements, using the wrong partners can create negative publicity and consequences in the United States (remember the Kathy Lee Gifford example mentioned in Chapter 8). Brand owners who have specifications for how they want their partners to do business in these areas can have a very positive impact on local companies, making them better businesses. These areas should be addressed in the license agreement.

A U.S.-Centric License Agreement Often Contains Provisions That Are Not Workable in Certain Markets
Often, there are contractual provisions that are considered standard in the United States but are quite perplexing in other countries. Product liability insurance is one such provision. Consumers are not as litigious in many other countries as they are in the United States; therefore, insurance is less important, and the coverages are not as big. In some countries, consumers don't sue for product damage or injury at all (e.g., Brazil, China (where, for example, there is no such thing as workers' compensation), and France). Brands must accommodate these differences and accept insurance requirements that may seem inadequate from a U.S. perspective. In short, don't expect that the standard agreement provisions used in the United States will be applicable in other countries without requiring major modifications. Many brand owners have walked away from a potential relationship because the brand owner insists on contractual provisions that are outside the scope of the way business is conducted in a particular country.

9. Find Scale

Understand the Size of the Prize
As suggested, finding critical mass can often be a challenge. The countries with large populations (e.g., India and China) pose market penetration issues as well as other challenges that have

been mentioned; other countries with the right environment for licensed products might be too small to generate meaningful sales and royalties or to cover costs. Depending on a brand's objectives for extending the brand through licensing in a particular country or region, scale should be weighed before a decision is made. In general, take a country-by-country approach. You may be able to achieve scale in certain regions only by focusing on groups of countries. Will the United Kingdom alone achieve your goals, or do you need to focus on the European continent as well? Australia/New Zealand will always be small, but perhaps your brand needs a broader presence there. And so on.

It's often true that a U.S. brand or licensing success story doesn't translate overseas. Perhaps the brand is unknown in a particular country or the local competition is too stiff or local customs and habits are obstacles or any other number of issues become impediments to achieving scale. Nevertheless, sometimes the way to achieve scale outside the United States is to first develop a model in the United States and then seek to duplicate it in foreign markets. Calvin Klein underwear did it right. The brand opened one image store in the United States. From there, the brand owner achieved scale and was able to expand to over 3,000 Calvin Klein underwear stores outside the United States. A brand owner can also launch with a retail exclusive in the United States and then, once established, move to expand with retailers overseas that are impressed with the U.S. success story, as was done with the Mary-Kate and Ashley program discussed in Chapter 8.

10. Take the Long View

Licensing Overseas Is a Bespoke Business
Brand licensing overseas is a slow process, certainly to achieve any kind of critical mass. The brand owner must be prepared to invest and reinvest in time, resources, and marketing to support the effort. One policy generally will not work even across a region

such as Western Europe and, therefore, brand owners will likely need to pursue many small solutions. In Western Europe, you might find that the licensing "journey" progresses at about the same pace as in the United States, albeit with smaller country-by-country markets. So even in Western Europe, scale takes time. In Japan, what you might think is a "long time" to make decisions or get product to market is viewed by Japanese as a "short time." Agree on goals to avoid frustration on both sides.

Be Prepared to Explain the Licensing Process
In many emerging markets such as India and Latin America, manufacturers and retailers understand licensing in the entertainment, fashion, and beauty categories, where there has been some history. But with brands, markets generally must be created. Often, because brands are dealing with companies that are unfamiliar with licensing (not "the usual suspects," for example, as in entertainment licensing), the entire process needs to be articulated—repeatedly.

China Will Require the Longest View
Brand owners keep looking east to China because it is such a huge and rapidly growing marketplace. But the challenges can be overwhelming, and brand owners will always need to take the long view in China. Just consider the staggering statistics from a long-term perspective: In several years, China will be the second-largest economy in the world. Eighty percent of consumers are under 45-years-old, and they don't save. They are natural-born consumers. In 2015, China abandoned the one-child policy and now allows families to have two children. By 2030, there will likely be 85 million people between the ages of 10 and 14 and 82 million between the ages of 15 and 19.[7] Media consumption (including motion pictures, television, radio, and newspapers) is growing rapidly, and China now has the largest online community in the world. Social media is

---

7. "China in 2030: The Future Demographic," *Euromonitor International*, May 2010.

prevalent through popular domestic networks. QQ has double the user base of Facebook in the United States. Consider what these and many other statistics about China will mean for your brand and for licensing your brand in China in the years ahead. But the long view is required. Toymaker Mattel gets it. In 2017, Mattel expanded its partnership with Alibaba to develop, market, and sell playthings designed specifically for Chinese customers. The company recently entered into a joint venture with a Shanghai-based investment company to introduce learning and play clubs for children across China. Most recently in mid-2017, developed with online parenting portal Babytree, Mattel announced plans to open child-focused learning centers, using its Fisher-Price brand. Mattel understands the statistics and is taking the long view.

In Summary
1. Yes, it's a global marketplace, but brand owners cannot ignore local needs and requirements, laws, and regulations.
2. Opportunities must be approached country by country.
3. There must be local brand awareness and fame.
4. Local market execution is required, paying attention to local conditions; cultural, market, and retail dynamics; and consumer behavior, needs, and habits.
5. Brand owners must have a local employee or representative—boots on the ground.
6. It takes homework, strategy, and lots of patience.

CHAPTER 11

The Future of Licensing, Part I: The Shopping Battlefield

Introduction

Emerging trends can have a significant impact on brand licensing strategies. Like any product journey, licensing follows cultural movements and changes in consumer behavior. Brand owners considering licensing or already engaged in licensing must be part of the "shopping conversation." If they are engaged in this dialogue, they can optimize success and properly manage and support their licensing programs. This engagement translates into understanding how consumers are shopping today, where they are doing their shopping, and what the dynamics are of both online and offline retailing. If they fail to be part of the shopping conversation, they cannot develop the strategic plans necessary to drive a successful licensing program and will be leaving performance entirely in the hands of their licensees and the whims of the marketplace. That's the wrong approach. Although I cannot cover all of the trends that already or soon will affect retail (or even be certain which ones will develop and gain prominence in the coming years), I can focus on the rapidly changing retail landscape and shopping journey (this chapter) and the increasing number of paths used to communicate a brand message to consumers and the role of licensing (the next chapter).

Licensing succeeds or fails depending on how brand owners take advantage of the opportunities in this new retail environment and how they communicate their message. As time goes by, some of what is described in these two chapters will evolve and perhaps become outdated as new consumer behaviors, paths, and opportunities present themselves. What has been included here about these evolving trends is limited by space and time—an entire new book could be written on this topic, but before the book is printed, new trends will have emerged that will also be deserving of the attention of brand licensors.

As valuable as the observations in these final two chapters will be, you also should consider them as a guide for how to look at and what to look for in the marketplace in the years ahead; they can facilitate spotting movements and trends that will affect licensing programs. Take the time to look down the road; do the research; the clues are all there.

Retail Today

Consider the major trends unfolding today and how they might spin out in the future. We are in a period of retail innovation and transformation. Digital shopping, whether it be e-commerce, digitally native vertical brands, or other forms of shopping online, has turned the shopping journey on its head. It's now a "connected shopping journey." Technology has enabled this evolution in shopping behavior by lowering the barriers to access, providing transparency and information, and allowing brands to gain scale quickly while also maintaining a one-on-one connection with the consumer. Consumers can now shop wherever they are located at any time of the day or night. Shopping and commerce are happening everywhere. Brands and retailers possess the technological tools to find consumers and offer them the products they need or want, directly. Brand licensors and their licensees must, in this new environment, have a digital strategy for reaching consumers; otherwise, they will not be competitive. Even worse, they might find that their licensing programs (and perhaps their brands) are withering.

Another related and significant trend is the ability to collect data generated by purchasing behavior and the availability of data, providing insight into the shopping behaviors of consumers and different demographic groups. Brand owners need to use this data and to address each of those demographics separately and strategically given their differences. Strategic licensing plans should take advantage of available data. If a company doesn't already collect relevant data for the sale of its core products, it can tap into a great deal of data via online research.

Finally, winners and losers among traditional brick-and-mortar (offline) retailers are starting to materialize. Some are figuring it out and thriving; others are going bankrupt; and some are in the middle, surviving but closing store locations. The clear winners (such as Walmart and Dollar General) and the clear losers (such as RadioShack and Sears) are becoming obvious. But don't forget retailers in the middle, those that are, for better or worse, surviving largely due to the strength of their brand or the consumer need that they fulfill (such as Party City and Hallmark stores). Licensing strategies, to be successful, must take into account and recognize which retailers are likely not only to survive but also to thrive and how to blend an offline strategy with an online one. But here's a reassuring truth: We are not in a "retail apocalypse" as many would have us believe. It's actually a new retail age with all sorts of emerging opportunities.

The trends in this new retail age are having and will continue to have a substantial impact on brand licensing, and I will examine this impact through three lenses:

1. The Blurring of Online and Offline Commerce
2. The Evolving Shopping Journey
3. Digitally Native Vertical Brands (DNVBs)

Keep in mind that retail is generally healthy—sales are up; people are shopping. In 2017, more stores opened than closed, mostly off-price retailers, dollar stores, and convenience stores (although there were also a record number of closings in 2017, mostly in the specialty channel). It's just how and where consumers are doing the purchasing that's changing so quickly. Consumers are shopping differently—in different places and with different attitudes and expectations, impacting brands and licensing. That being said, consumers continue to want what they have always wanted—a fair price, ease in making purchasing decisions, information, trust, and great product. Now, however, added to those "wants," many consumers also want "discovery" and "experience." The mechanisms and processes for delivering on all of these requirements are changing quickly today. Which combination of these is more important at any one time will depend on the particular shopping and purchasing goal of the consumer. Two transformations must always be considered—brand value (however that is communicated) and consumer purchasing behavior (wherever it occurs). These are affecting and, for the foreseeable future, will continue to affect brands and drive brand licensing.

The shopping journey, regardless of the paths a consumer chooses, ends with a purchase. And that purchase must fulfill the brand promise and product expectations the consumer has for that brand and that product, which has been the case ever since there have been brands and consumers have been purchasing branded products. That applies to licensed product as well. Licensed products must deliver on that brand promise and that expectation. The changing retail landscape is the most important challenge and opportunity for brand licensing, and brand owners and their licensees must understand the shopping journey and where they can and must intersect with it. The shopping journey today is no longer the lineal journey it was not so long ago. It's unpredictable, inconsistent, and changing constantly. Sumaiya Balbale, Vice President, Mobile & Digital Marketing at Walmart, noted: "The amazing thing about the moment we are in in retail right now is that the future of shopping is just being written and there is no one technology, there's no one experience that is the dominant one. I think that we see a lot of opportunities to continue to innovate."[1]

The Blurring of Online and Offline Commerce

A broad, disruptive, and transformative restructuring of retailing has been going on for some time, and it's difficult for stakeholders (including licensors and licensees) to keep up with the unprecedented pace of change. Technology, of course, is the enabler that makes everything move faster, and digital commerce (which includes e-commerce) is largely responsible for what's happening. The online industry leader in the United States, Amazon, as well as other e-commerce retailers, have made shopping so easy and fast that brick-and-mortar retailers now struggle with how to take advantage of all of this connectivity—specifically with how to bring customers into their stores and then make purchases. Shopping malls are in decline (not so long ago major brands needed to be in every mall; not so anymore with the rise of e-commerce),[2] retailers are closing stores (e.g., Macy's, Sears, American Eagle, and Men's Warehouse) or going bankrupt (e.g., Aeropostale, Toys"R"Us, and RadioShack). Department stores are suffering because they are so predictable. The concept of a "flagship" store is in decline, being replaced by "showrooms." But, as mentioned earlier, there are also brick-and-mortar winners in this landscape and, as more offline

---

1. "Watch: Walmart's E-Commerce Game Is Off the Charts," AdAge.com, interview by Adrianne Pasquarelli, November 18, 2017.

2. That being said, it's been reported that between the months of November 2017 and February 2018 more than a third of all mall shoppers were Millennials. Several factors are the drivers of this statistic: malls are getting better at the experience and stores that they offer, Millennials (and most shoppers) still want to touch and feel the products, and Millennials, more than other groups, are social shoppers, although, in a seeming contradiction, Millennials are the driving force behind Amazon's success in the apparel category.

retailers understand what they must do to compete, there will be more winners, or at least survivors. For licensing, this means that traditional strategies targeting the "usual suspects" among brick-and-mortar retailers will no longer be adequate.

The best advice: Go beyond just traditional offline retailers and recognize that you cannot maximize success with the strategies that might have worked in the past. Do more research and thinking and become smarter about what's going on at retail. With this knowledge, you can develop a strategy that takes advantage of all of the new consumer touchpoints and occasions when consumers purchase product.

The book store channel was the first to go through the fire and come out transformed. Major chains disappeared, such as B. Dalton and Borders, while others survived, such as Barnes & Noble. Over half of the independent bookstores in the United States shuttered (but those that survived are figuring out how to continue surviving). And now, as consumers increasingly seek "experiences," independent bookstores are growing again. The experience of the winners and losers in the book channel, however, is a warning to other channels that are feeling the threat of digital shopping. Don't assume that any category is safe from this onslaught. Consider footwear and apparel. Not so long ago we thought that these categories were safe from the digital challenge. Consumers wanted to touch the merchandise, try it on—we thought. But we didn't anticipate the transformative effect of free return shipping or several sizes sent to a consumer to try on or, quite simply, the ease of buying online. In 2018, Amazon is expected to pass Macy's as the #1 apparel retailer in the United States. Even bars are threatened. In 2017, Amazon opened a pop-up bar in Tokyo to promote the sale of alcohol on Amazon.

But contrary to what you might be hearing, there remain significant opportunities to succeed in offline retail, and that's significant for licensing programs. Some retailers are actually putting it all together effectively and thriving. It's about survival of the smartest, and as offline retailers get smarter, the balance between online and offline retail will even out and blur. Brand owners engaging in licensing must take notice and advantage of the opportunities; they must understand how consumers are shopping and how retailers are selling in order to drive their licensing programs. They need to understand how consumers learn about their products; use the products; experience the brand; and, in the end, bond with the brand. Although the majority of sales still occur at brick-and-mortar stores (less than 15 percent of total retail sales in 2017 were done online, predicted to rise to about 20 percent by 2023), that doesn't mean devices are not part of the equation. And that's one part of the blending of online and offline. Consumers bring along their devices to the store to access more information about products before they make a purchase. Or they do the research online before going to the store. Or they go to the store to look at the products and then order online either when they go home or while still in the store using their smartphone. For brand licensors and licensees, this means that to drive the consumer to make the purchase, they need to have both an offline and online strategy and have mechanisms consumers can use to access licensed product information and to purchase easily either at brick-and-mortar retailers or online.

Those who question whether we really need brick-and-mortar retail any longer are in for a surprise. Yes, even the brick-and-mortar bookstore channel, with a frightening number of closings and dire predictions of the end of physical bookstores, is now starting a revival in this new environment. Store closings and declining sales at some leading retailers don't tell the full story. Brick-and-mortar stores, as already noted, still account for the vast majority of purchases today, and that's not expected to change much over the next several years (online retailers know this as well). That being said, most consumers (particularly the younger demographics) will be driven to the store or a product by going online or, as just mentioned, doing the research while still in the store. So if brick and mortar is to thrive, those retailers will have to figure out how to combine online with their physical locations. They need to consider themselves as places that create a brand experience that consumers will remember and as places where consumers convert what they learn online [what they come to desire (or are told they need) by going online] into purchases at the store. Some are already doing it well. Offline stores can offer a service experience (including touching the merchandise, which is still important) that online retailing can't offer, but they must work at it to stay successful and make consumers want to come into the store. The Apple Store is a good example of the "service experience," as are stores that are more showrooms than selling space, such as Restoration Hardware (now called RH). Nike has in-store soccer cages; Lululemon offers free in-store yoga classes; at Warby Parker, customers can sample products and then have them delivered via an online purchase. For offline success, it's about offering more than just shopping; it's about offering an experience (although soccer cages may not be the answer). (Stores as experiences are discussed further in Chapter 12.) Brick and mortar provides more opportunities for brand interaction (online is catching up, however). And after the initial shock of the digital challenge, brick-and-mortar retailers are beginning to figure out how to succeed online. It's not just about putting their goods on a website; it's about engaging with the consumer as if they were in the store and then engaging them when they are actually in the store. And, by the way, online retailers are figuring out how to succeed offline (more on that later in the chapter).

A comprehensive licensing program can help both offline and online retailers reach consumers in a more impactful way. Licensing programs deliver retailers a comprehensive assortment of different yet brand-aligned products that can be offered to consumers in their entirety (or at least in the appropriate categories), thereby offering more products with a trusted brand name and delivering a more powerful brand message. For example, the Black & Decker pages on Amazon seamlessly feature a mix of core and licensed products, a very impactful and comprehensive brand statement. Licensors and licensees can provide comprehensive information and transparency about licensed product that will appeal to consumers. In addition, brand licensors, their licensees, and selected retailers can work together to develop marketing initiatives, including experiences, that will drive consumers to the retailer and the product. There is power in numbers, and licensing programs offer the strength of multiple licensees producing a wide range of licensed product.

In the next several years, we will see fewer instances of online and offline retail fighting each other and more of online taking advantage of offline advantages and vice versa. Everything is being connected, and the demarcations between online and offline are disappearing. It's referred to as the consumer's "Connected Journey"—online and offline blurring into one consumer shopping experience. And it's not just about consumers using their devices before they go to the store or while they are in the store or going to the store and then using their devices to make a purchase. It's also about retailers themselves and the blurring of lines.

Amazon vs. Walmart

Consider the online leader Amazon and the offline leader Walmart. Both are smartly merging online and offline. Amazon, recognizing the importance of offline retailing, is opening brick-and-mortar bookstores (having put so many independent bookstores out of business). It is creating a seamless online/offline consumer experience, where the books offered for sale are driven by popularity data and usage information collected by Amazon. And it's why Amazon has purchased Whole Foods (because people generally don't want to buy their fresh groceries online and food is the largest share of a consumer's wallet). Amazon is using Whole Foods to sell fresh food (and to add other nonfresh product to the shopper's basket) and to compete with Walmart's grocery business (which represents over half of Walmart's total sales). Amazon is looking for more face-to-face interaction with customers.

In addition to bookstores and Whole Foods, Amazon is not sitting still. For Holiday 2017, Amazon teamed up with Calvin Klein to open pop-up retail stores where only Amazon customers could shop and offered a larger product assortment online at Amazon. The pop-up shops also offered other customer experiences, such as garment personalization, social media connectivity, and fitting rooms that contained Amazon Echo devices to answer questions about Calvin Klein apparel. In addition, in late 2017, Kohl's launched the "Amazon smart home experience" in ten of its stores (that could expand to all stores quickly and provide Amazon with over 1,000 "distribution centers"). In these stores, customers will be able to purchase Amazon devices in an Amazon zone staffed by Amazon employees who will be able to provide assistance. To round out the experience, customers can have an Amazon expert visit their home to evaluate the customers' needs and install products. Purchases made at the store as well as online at Amazon can be returned to Kohl's. This will be a partnership to watch over the next several years. Amazon and Sears have also partnered. Sears will sell Amazon Echo smart devices, and Amazon will sell Kenmore products. And in early 2018, Amazon opened its first Amazon Go store in Seattle where consumers can purchase on-the-go food items in a checkout-free experience (technology keeps track of what the consumers take and automatically charges their Amazon account). Online retailers recognize the power of offline retail and are making it part of their strategy to reach consumers along the shopping journey.

Conversely, Walmart is an example of a brick-and-mortar store reinventing itself to succeed in this new world order, and it is doing it quickly. (Walmart's online sales rose a whopping 50 percent in the United States during the third quarter of 2017—double Target and higher than Amazon.) Already, Walmart is not the store it was just a year or two ago. Walmart is acquiring businesses that not only build its expertise in e-commerce and technology but also allows it to pursue a coordinated online and offline strategy, often in smaller markets. Walmart's acquisitions inlcude the e-commerce upstart Jet.com, ModCloth (women's vintage apparel), Hayneedle (indoor and outdoor home furnishings and décor), Shoebuy (footwear), Moosejaw (outdoor retailer), and Bonobos (men's apparel). For example, Walmart is using digital brand Bonobos to reach a higher-end, technologically savvy apparel consumer to compete with Amazon. And each of these acquisitions appeals to important demographic groups, particularly Millennials. Walmart has also partnered with Google Express, Google's voice-activated virtual assistant, to offer a large assortment of products (hundreds of thousands of products actually) through voice shopping and to collect data (to be shared with Google) that will make repeat purchasing much easier. Unlike other Google Express partners (such as Target, Costco, and Walgreens), Walmart will do its own order delivery (including fresh groceries) through its 4,700 "warehouses" spread around the country (i.e., their stores). (Google Express doesn't carry inventory like Amazon does; instead, it uses third-party companies to fulfill orders.)

Walmart's push into e-commerce also allows it to collect a good deal of data about its customers. This has been one of Amazon's big advantages (knowing its customers). Retailers must accumulate data about their customers (by acquiring or investing in dot-coms or by using the data they have already collected) if they want to thrive in this new environment. Retailers who understand this will survive.

In New York City, Walmart is experimenting with same-day delivery service for online purchases (through its purchase of Parcel). It's easier to return products using the Walmart app. And just like Amazon, Walmart is starting to sell other retailers' products on its website, such as apparel from Lord & Taylor launching in 2018, which also supports Walmart's drive to have fashion credibility as Amazon gains fashion strength. And through its partnership with JD.com (the top competitor to Alibaba), Walmart is showing good results in China. Walmart is a formidable challenger to Amazon. Walmart will likely continue to move aggressively in the online world as Amazon moves aggressively to grow in the offline world—in both instances, often through acquisitions.

Accordingly, if you are a brand owner with a licensing strategy that includes retailers such as Amazon and Walmart, you and your licensees will benefit greatly if you grasp the retailer's competitive online/offline strategy. You will need to persuade the retailer that your licensing program not only fits but also supports that strategy. Be aggressive about ensuring that the retailer is giving the licensing program the attention it needs to succeed. Retailers will be subject to many "voices"; you just need to be one of the louder ones. Getting product on "shelf," although still a "win," is just the beginning of the journey.

Although the online/offline battle is often viewed as between two clear winners, Amazon and Walmart, there are other examples of the blending of offline and online and others who are figuring out how to win. Walmart is transforming itself; others are following. Target teamed up with Pinterest Lens for Holiday 2017. Consumers who used Lens via Target's app could take a photo of a product they wanted, and Target sent them potential purchases from Target.com. Online eyewear Warby Parker continues to open physical locations. And Casper is selling collateral product at Target and opened a stand-alone store in New York City in February 2018 (see discussion below of DNVBs). It's not just about brick-and-mortar retail figuring out how to go online (as Walmart has done), but also online retailers figuring out how to go offline (as Amazon and others have done). Expect to see more online going offline, that is, "clicks to bricks."[3] It's also about online *services* moving to providing products, thereby expanding their platform. Consider Spotify's 2017 expansion into beauty products. Users (meaning fans) can purchase makeup products on Spotify that are associated with the style and look of a particular musical artist (Instagram does some of the same thing). Social media is a place

---

3. I have already mentioned Casper and Warby Parker, and there are a host of other examples: Lingerie e-tailer, Adore Me, announced in March 2018 that it was opening 200 to 300 offline stores; other early 2018 announcements included men's e-tailers Indochine, Jack Erwin and Untuckit joining Bonobos and Everlane, which already have brick-and-mortar locations.

where brands and consumers can connect and have an experience. Increasingly, we will likely see social media platforms (e.g., Instagram and Spotify) connecting consumers with retail, with product offerings, and even with offline offerings. The next level is Amazon Spark, a shoppable social media platform. The app allows consumers to connect with each other, share stories about products, and then make a purchase. Converting user-generated content into easy and convenient retail sales is a space to watch.

Pickup, Return, and Advice—Consumers Care

How consumers get their purchases is another example of where online/offline blur. One of the advantages of brick-and-mortar retailers is that customers can walk away with their purchase. So Amazon introduced Amazon Prime's service that allows customers in some areas to receive their order in an hour. Then Target, already starting to win on its e-commerce site, purchased Grand Junction in 2017, a company that links retailers and distributors to ensure same-day delivery. At The Home Depot, almost 50 percent of its online orders are picked up at the store. Walmart has a pickup discount on certain items purchased on its website as well as drive-through grocery and pharmacy pickup at some of its stores. Walmart is also experimenting with perhaps an overly intrusive home delivery tactic. It delivers grocery orders, and the delivery person is able to enter the home and put the food in the customer's refrigerator (through a partnership with the smart lock company August Home). A final example is liquor, a category that up until recently has not been able to take full advantage of online shopping due to state laws and regulations restricting sales and distribution. Now online marketers (either third-party sites or the brands themselves) are providing consumers with many more product choices than a typical liquor store is able to offer, then taking orders and arranging delivery from a local liquor store that stocks the requested product. Making delivery easier, faster, and more convenient will continue to evolve and fuel the expectations of consumers across virtually all product categories.

Online versus offline retailing is also about consumer behavior; it's about where and how people shop and what drives them to shop. With so many choices and tools, constantly connected consumers are in control. Brand licensors, licensees, and retailers need to be where consumers are going. Indeed they need to stay ahead of where consumers are shopping; otherwise, they will lose them. Although some product categories are more appropriate for online shopping and others for offline shopping, consumers still look for what they have always looked for—convenience; information; price; and, of course, great product. For example, you might assume that online is more convenient, but that's not necessarily true. Consumers can get easily frustrated shopping online if it takes too much time or it's difficult to locate the items they want or they can't find everything they want in one place. Consumers often get frustrated with difficult return policies and processes offered by online retailers. It's about the user experience, and that experience can be bad. Online retailers should make sure that customers can get expert advice when making a decision (brand licensors can provide assistance in developing this, for example). E-commerce sites can provide help through guides and videos or online chat. Sales help can be good or bad in both online and offline retail. All of this affects consumer behavior and expectations. Make sure your licensees are not engaging in online retailing that hurts rather than helps the brand. Negative consumer experiences with licensed products have, to a greater or lesser extent, always hurt core brands, but more opportunities exist today for licensees to stumble. To avoid this possibility, be hands-on managers of your licensing programs and understand where, how, and when licensed products can be purchased.

China

No conversation about the evolution of online/offline retail and opportunities for brand licensing would be complete without focusing on China and, to a lesser extent, India. These are huge markets. Both are fast becoming fertile markets for brand licensing and should be addressed by any brand owners interested in establishing or strengthening their brand in those markets. Retail in Asia is not burdened with the big brick-and-mortar history and footprint that has evolved over the decades in the United States and most of Western Europe. As a result, retailers are more nimble in Asia, and retail innovation is moving at a different, faster speed. Meitu is a Chinese company that has developed a number of try-on apps for makeup, hair, and apparel. The apps have been installed on over one billion mobile devices, and the company is valued at $5 billion.[4] Alibaba provides insight into online/offline blending and is creating a seamless online/offline experience for consumers. Alibaba helps retailers know their customers so well that when customers are in the store, a smartphone app will recommend products on shelf, allowing order and delivery within 30 minutes. As of this writing, Alibaba has built 13 supermarkets named Hema Xiansheng where every product has been digitized. Customers can scan the barcodes with an app to get product information and to order and pay; the product will then be delivered to their home or another destination. Naturally, the app collects the data for subsequent purchase recommendations. Retail in Asia is a predictor of where U.S. retailers will be headed. (See Chapter 10 for more about China and India.)

How, Where, and to Whom to Sell

Brand owners engaging in licensing must consider where, how, and to whom their licensed products can be sold successfully—in the United States and overseas. The best licensors will help provide tools to retailers and licensees to help connect them to consumers. The smartest brands and retailers will be those that can serve the interests of consumers who want to shop online and those who want to shop offline or those who combine both. For the smartest marketers, the strategy is to pursue the best of

---

4. "Why Augmented Reality Will Be the Next Revolution in Retail," *Strategy + Business*, February 27, 2017, Summer 2017, Issue 87, page 7.

both worlds—accessibility and convenience as well as personalized service and "touch and feel."

Online and offline retailing will continue to blend and cross paths, all to the consumer's benefit. As a result, the consumer's shopping journey will continue to evolve, providing yet more opportunities for brand engagement and licensing. As mentioned earlier, it's not about "rounding up the usual suspects" when developing a channel strategy for a licensing program or when reviewing business plans by licensees or when managing a program. Instead, address how, where, and when consumers are shopping, including for licensed products. You possess your own comprehensive strategy for selling your core products to consumers, online and offline, wherever they shop. For example, it may include product transparency, product information, reviews, tutorials, videos, influencers, retail exclusives, cross-marketing and promotions, demographic targets, experiences, artificial intelligence, and augmented reality. Align the licensing strategy with the brand's retail strategy, in general as well as with specific retailers. Be prepared not only to encourage licensees to develop strategies that take advantage of both online and offline retailing but also to help with strategy development as well as implementation (and monitor implementation on a regular basis). The retail landscape is too complicated today and is changing too quickly to leave omnichannel strategy and execution in the hands of licensees. Leverage the shopping journey to connect the way consumers shop between physical stores and dotcoms. It will be well worth the effort to step back for a moment to make sure that an offline/online strategy is well articulated in any licensing plan, including how that strategy will be implemented and managed once licensees are on board.

The Evolving Shopping Journey

Brand licensors (and licensees) should be aware that the transformation of retail involves more than just a balancing act between e-commerce and brick and mortar. The shopping journey has clearly become increasingly complex. As such, licensing strategies must consider all of the ways that consumers purchase products and determine which are relevant for their particular licensing program, because where and how consumers shop is where licensed products can be offered for sale. Everything doesn't have to happen at once. A licensing program retail omnichannel and distribution strategy can be rolled out in phases over a period of time with one phase building on the last phase. Licensed products need to become established in the market; they need to have credibility with consumers. Where and how brands communicate with consumers about their licensing programs and how and where the licensed products are sold will unfold over time. The following trends are having a significant influence on retail; on the connected consumer journey; and, therefore, on licensing.

Mobile Use

Younger generations are spending 80 hours a month on their mobile devices. Most brands, licensees, and retailers are playing catch-up, but that will change. It's not about simply shrinking a desktop website to accommodate mobile. It's about an entirely new and different way to communicate and to offer purchasing opportunities. Some retailers (e.g., Target, The Home Depot, and Sephora) have invested heavily in providing consumers with a comprehensive experience on their mobile devices. Apps, if they are to be downloaded, must offer a strong brand message, engaging social content, and features that connect to offline shopping. An increasing number of users will access information on their phones before making a purchase. That makes mobile an important path in the shopping journey.

Brand licensing programs must provide licensed product information that is easily available via mobile devices, as well as licensed product purchasing opportunities. Creativity will be a big part of what is offered on mobile devices in the future (particularly as screens merge and we have fewer screens,not more). To take advantage of mobile opportunities, brand licensors are best advised to integrate their licensing programs with their core product mobile strategy, assuming there is one. Licensees in appropriate categories can develop their own apps that provide consumers with the opportunity to experience not just the licensed brand but also the licensed product. Licensors and licensees must work together closely to take advantage of the opportunities that mobile technology provides to connect with consumers both before and during a purchase.

Technological Connection

Technology drives data collection and continues to connect consumers, understand their wants and needs, give them information, and make the shopping experience easier in new ways. Collecting data is not limited to online retailers. Offline retailers are learning how to collect data to better lead their customers to make purchases when they are in the store—data that includes how customers walk the aisles, where they spend time, what kind of help they need, and what they are seeing but not buying. And offline retailers are using technology to make purchasing easier (such as reader-enabled bags that allow customers to avoid the check-out line; the abililty to preorder before getting to the store; brand-centric digital showrooms that save floor space; salespeople with tablets to use in checking inventory, reviews, customer data, and product information in real time; and in-store beacons that notify salespeople when a customer is on the floor, provide the customer with product information, and assist the customer in locating products of interest).

Personalization of service and products is getting more sophisticated both online with virtual assistants and offline with sales associates armed with technology (e.g., tablets) that give them access to data that will help the customer they are serving. Alibaba (in China) is among the most advanced in personalizing services (including product recommendations and reviews), as well as personalizing the sales experience both online and in stores that have access to its data. Hellmann's has a mobile app in Brazil that gives recipe advice based on a photo of what's in a person's refrigerator. To drive sales, retailers and brands will have to adapt and develop what works best for them, their licensing partners, and their consumers.

A strategic licensing program can address omnichannel retail innovations, data collection, and personalization among other technological advances across multiple categories and help strengthen the brand's relevance to key consumer targets. For instance, brand licensors should make sure that retailers have all of the licensed product information necessary to inform consumers. In some cases, the information itself can be a licensing opportunity. In the Hellmann's example above, the recipes can be a licensed recipe collection from a chef, a kitchen appliance brand, or a restaurant. Indeed, licensees, often more flexible than the brand owner, can lead the way by tapping into these trends and transformations ahead of what the brand is doing for itself and its core products.

AI, VR, and AR

Artificial intelligence (AI, computer systems able to perform tasks usually performed by human intelligence, such as speech recognition and decision making), virtual reality (VR, which takes you into a virtual experience, just like a video game), and augmented reality (AR, which augments what you are seeing in the real world) represent developments that make it easier to get information, see and experiment with products, and make purchasing decisions. VR has long received most of the publicity, but AR might be better suited to the shopping journey because it brings experiences to our real world instead of placing consumers in a fantasy world and also allows consumers to engage with a brand.

Some examples: Amazon's Alexa (AI) can give a consumer product information and make a purchase. P&G's Olay offers an online advisor (named the Olay Skin Care Advisor) that uses AI to provide personalized skin care analysis, advice, and product recommendations (after the user has submitted a selfie and answered some core questions). There's no reason such a service couldn't be a licensed service. On Google Home, Unilever has voice-activated tips for stain removal, and on Amazon's Alexa, P&G's Tide brand similarly provides tips on stain removal. In many categories, licensees (or groups of licensees or licensees in coordination with the brand owner) could develop the same type of programs that help support their licensed products. Walmart is working on an app that lets a consumer go to a lake to try out fishing gear. Augmented reality lets consumers create their own environment with products that can be licensed products as easily as core brand products. IKEA has an AR app, IKEA Place, that allows consumers to place IKEA products in their homes virtually, helping them better imagine what those products will look like there (you can also see where you should place your Christmas tree!). Similarly, Wayfair offers an AR app, WayfairView, that allows consumers to see virtual furniture at full scale in their homes. Luxury brand Swarovski has taken VR a step further with a VR experience in a high-end luxury home featuring its products that enables the consumer to purchase in real time. WebMD has AI programs with both Amazon Echo and Google Home. In Mead Johnson's partnership with Reckitt Benckiser, consumers can ask questions about ailments, with branded Mucinex responses provided on how to treat cough and congestion problems. And with the data available, AI devices can alert users to health concerns in their geographic area (in effect, answering questions before they are asked). Gap has an app (named the DressingRoom) that lets consumers try on clothes at home through AR.

All of these examples could easily be about licensed products or licensed AR apps. AR combines the digital with the physical, delivering a rich consumer experience that will be increasingly used to grow and support licensees and licensing programs. Understanding how to use these tools is important. Not long from now, we will have digital personal shoppers with so much data about our wants, needs, desires, and behaviors that it will be able to help us make purchasing decisions while online or in a store. And those purchasing decisions will include licensed products.

These and other AI-powered "personal assistants" (e.g., Google Now, Apple HomePod, and Facebook M) emesh brands with the consumer, providing information (sometimes before the consumer even knows she wants it), providing a direct connection between brands/products and consumers, and inspiring purchases (and even making the purchase for the consumer). In the not-too-distant future, all of our devices will merge and everything will be voice activated (some predict "eye activated" and then even "thought activiated"). Imagine the possibilities for brands with a family of core and licensed products to showcase through these mediums. Home décor brands such as Kathy Ireland and HGTV HOME can use AR to help you design and furnish any room of your home by placing products in various rooms. Brands such as Stanley, Black & Decker and Energizer can use AR to help you figure out what you need to organize your garage or answer questions through AI about what tools or equipment you need for a job or what kind of battery power you need for a certain activity. Frequently the products being promoted will be licensed products, often mixed with a brand's core products.

Rental Sites and Subscription Services
Online rental sites and subscription services give brands an opportunity to test products and get real-time feedback from consumers and, importantly, also makes consumer buying decisions easier. Rental sites such as Le Tote (women's apparel and accessories), Rent the Runway (designer apparel and accessories), and Gwynnie Bee (which is a rental site, a subscription box service, and a physical store in the plus-size fashion category), are providing a service to consumers as well as collecting useful data for the brands offering products. As of this writing, there are no licensed rental sites (or rental sites offering licensed products), but we will likely soon see brand owners in certain categories using licensing as a vehicle with respect to rental sites. Indeed, anywhere a product can be offered to consumers is an area ripe for licensing.

Subscription services operate across an ever-increasing number of categories and retailers, including apparel (the original is Stitch Fix) as well as baby clothes (Gap's Baby Outfit Box), children's clothing (Rockets of Awesome, Old Navy's Old Navy Superbox, and Target's Cat & Jack Outfit Box), women's professional attire (MM. LaFleur), contact lenses (Hubble), fashion rental (New York & Co.'s NY&C Closet and Ann Taylor's Infinite Style), big and tall customers (J.C. Penney), beauty (Walmart's Beauty Box), sportwear (Under Armour's Armour Box), and men's shaving (Dollar Shave Club). In general, a subscription box is a recurring delivery of curated specialized product. Subscription sites provide a service to busy consumers; curate products; offer direct-to-consumer delivery; operate at low costs, which enables them to offer low prices; and collect a good deal of useful data about their consumers. These sites are challenging traditional brands so much so that some are beginning to enter the space themselves, such as Nestlé's ReadyFresh, which allows consumers to create their own "box" of Nestlé beverages (e.g., water and tea) and the frequency of delivery (baby boomers might remember when milk was delivered in the 1950s and 1960s—"what's old is new again").

Licensed subscription boxes are already in the market, primarily in the entertainment and sports property categories. Hasbro offers a subscription box, named Hasbro Gaming Crate, that delivers a list of game titles. As early as 2012, Loot Crate started offering monthly subscription boxes of curated pop culture–licensed products, including those of Marvel, Disney, and DC Entertainment. It also offers more targeted licensed subscription boxes to the fans of WWE, Halo, and Sanrio (Hello Kitty). Dedicated fans of a brand enjoy the convenience of delivery and the curation of products that are often exclusive. Amazon is also getting in on the act with the launch of its STEM Club Toy Subscription in 2017, joining other educational subscription box services including Pley (a National Geographic box that includes products that teach about nature, geography, and animals), Groovy Lab in a Box (focusing on science topics in partnership with *Popular Mechanics*), and The Young Scientists Club (a license from Scholastic that delivers science-related products tied to Scholastic properties such as *The Magic School Bus* and *Clifford the Big Red Dog*). We will probably soon see subscription boxes offered by big brands such as Kimberly-Clark (perhaps a Huggies-branded monthly box for expectant and new moms). Branded boxes can be offered by the brand owner directly (and contain both core and licensed products), or the concept can be licensed entirely to a company that specializes in subscription boxes such as Loot Crate. It's another way to communicate with and deliver product to the consumer.

* * * * *

In many respects, the shopping journey, which includes purchasing, social media, and an experience, are all merging and is changing and offering many paths. This is good news for licensing programs because there are so many ways to offer information, advice, and licensed products to consumers. And given all of the ways we can collect data, there may soon be another benefit for brand licensors. Currently, unlike traditional advertising, there are no generally accepted tools available for measuring whether licensed products are lifting the sales of core products (always a goal of brand licensors) and, as a result, driving revenue and a return on the investment incurred from running a licensing program. It's mostly intuitive. However, some really sophisticated brands are starting to make this connection. By evaluating basket data, one major consumer products brand licensor was able to measure the bump in sales of its core product at a major retailer that also sold the brand's licensed product in a different aisle. In that instance, the brand licensor was able to confirm that the licensed products were driving sales of the core product. With all of the data that's now being collected, we will probably soon have generally accepted mechanisms to measure the extent to which licensed products are meeting the brand's objectives. It seems inevitable that data-focused technology will enable us to track the shopping journey, measuring whether the purchase of a licensed product also drives the consumer to the core product—during either the same shopping occasion or a subsequent shopping occasion. That's a development that those in the licensing field are anticipating eagerly.

Digitally Native Vertical Brands (DNVBs)

Sometimes called v-commerce, these brands are taking advantage of the rise of e-commerce but approaching retail in fresh ways and inspiring consumers with their brand messaging. DNVBs offer new ways for brands to be introduced to consumers and offer consumers a new way to access and purchase product and get product information prior to making the purchase. They are digital brands designed to sell their own branded product (see the Casper example below). We are in the early days of these brands, but they are exploding on the scene and are having an impact in many consumer product categories. DNVBs rely initially on social media and establish a one-on-one connection with their consumers, developing a community of brand loyalists. It's the intersection of brand-created content (including product information), user-created content, and commerce. They offer consumers not only products but also online brand experiences. DNVBs interact directly with and engage their consumers, control their brand message, control their distribution, and provide a high level of service. This allows consumers to "feel" their authenticity, and it generates trust. In addition, although born on the Internet and social media, once established, they embrace other more traditional forms of communication (such as advertising on buses) as well as offline brick and mortar either on their own or through partnerships, as noted earlier.

In this section, I am focusing on DNVBs, but let's not forget what are called digitally native media brands (or digitally native brands), mentioned in Chapter 8. These are "magazine" type websites, born on the Internet, that frequently sell product (generally branded and unbranded product from third parties rather than their own branded product). Examples (some already noted in

Chapter 8) include Refinery29, a lifestyle site focusing on entertainment, fashion, health, and more; PopSugar, which focuses on trends in entertainment, fashion, beauty, fitness, and food; and Brit + Co, an online media site that offers classes, DIY projects, and information and news about style, home décor, cooking, and more. Although not DNVBs (because they are not a vertical product company), these online media sites are also establishing their own level of fame. Just as traditional print magazines have been successful in brand licensing, we will likely see the same happen with online media brands, for the same reasons—their content makes them a credible authority across key product categories.

Similarly, as DNVB brands grow in importance they will, undoubtedly, extend their own brands through licensed product extensions. Indeed, we soon may see DNVBs created through licensing. New properties, including new brands developed by big consumer products companies, new brands created out of whole cloth, celebrity brands, and other types of "brand" owners, will choose the DNVB route to launch branded licensed product programs. It's very effective and not expensive. And why shouldn't the big consumer products companies choose this path to introduce a new brand? Small companies and individuals are doing it, and some break through the clutter, succeed, and start stealing market share.

Market leaders such as Tempurpedic and Serta Simmons, for example, got blindsided by a DNVB named Casper. Those two large companies certainly have the in-house creativity and resources to launch a brand this way. Casper is a very successful mattress-in-a-box DNVB founded in 2014. Mattresses are a boring category. But as a DNVB, Casper doesn't sell just product features; it also sells aspiration, values, and better, healthier living (more on having a purpose in the next chapter). And it does so through direct consumer communication using social media, contests, gifts to customers, experiences, and eventually more traditional advertising such as witty billboard advertising. Casper sells inexpensive, well-designed product with exceptional customer service and delivery—

all characteristics of this new model of a DNVB. And now Target (an investor following its failed $1 billion offer to acquire Casper) is selling Casper brand extension products such as pillows, sheets, and bed protectors and Casper is opening its own stores. Casper wants to be in other rooms of the home as well, and licensing could get it there. Bausch & Lomb faced the same challenge in the contact lens category when it got caught off guard by a DNVB named Hubble (which now advertises on television).

Big companies will probably be jumping into this space in the future, and they can do it through licensing, should they choose. Online media brands can also be created through licensing. That has occurred in the traditional print magazine space with magazines licensed by HGTV, The Food Network, Oprah, and Martha Stewart, among others. As proof of concept, a *Goop* magazine (on paper) launched in late 2017.

More than any other social media network, Facebook is the platform of choice for starting a DNVB, with Google not far behind. Placing an ad featuring a new brand and product is inexpensive and easy. Start-ups can rely on Facebook's artificial intelligence software to figure out what ads are most effective, then Facebook can help identify target consumers. In other words, Facebook can select the most effective ad for a new brand and find the right consumers for the product. "Anyone with a credit card can go online and test ads on Facebook's platform, one of the most sophisticated direct-marketing operations ever."[5] These start-up DNVBs are not limited to just Facebook, however. They also use other social media platforms to create buzz as well as other forms of advertising such as public relations and "influencer" campaigns. Although many (maybe most) of these companies will fail, some break through and are succeeding (Unilever acquired the Dollar Shave Club, a DNVB, in 2016 for a billion dollars). It's a wildly growing landscape of new brands and retail across many product

---

5. "The Ads That Know Everything" by Burt Helm, *The New York Times Magazine*, November 5, 2017, page 45.

categories. And, as stated above, why should big consumer brand companies limit themselves to waiting to determine who succeeds and then engaging in an acquisition? Why not create a brand and use their resources to launch their own DNVB? And it can be done through licensing, should they so choose.

Some of the top DNVBs include Away (luggage), Birchbox (health and beauty products), Bonobos (apparel and accessories), Casper (mattresses), Draper James (apparel created by Reese Witherspoon), Everlane (apparel), Harry's (shaving cream and accessories), MVMT (watches), Parachute (bedding), Perverse (sunglasses), Rockets of Awesome (subscription box of children's apparel), SAXX (underwear), Stance (socks), and Warby Parker (eyewear).[6] As mentioned earlier, DNVBs sell more than product; they sell purpose and mission. Consider Soma, a water filter company that says it wants to "hydrate the world," or Ritual, a multivitamin DNVB that promotes product transparency with clear pills and the tagline "The future of vitamins is clear."

Licensing, as noted, can play a dual role in this world. First, a DNVB can be launched by licensing the entire concept to a third party. Second, once a DNVB is successful, whether launched by the brand owner or through a licensing model, the brand can be extended to other categories through licensing, either online or offline. DNVBs will udoubtedly be an active area for licensing in the years ahead.

The Final Three Feet

The paths to what used to be called "the final three feet" (i.e., the purchase decision) have become more plentiful, complex, unpredictable, and sophisticated. And that makes opportunities for brands to reach consumers with licensed product more plentiful

---

6. The list comes from Pixlee's "The Top 25 Digitally Native Vertical Brands Report 2017." Pixlee is a San Francisco–based company that helps brands strengthen their marketing by offering consumer stories at the center of the brand experience.

as well. Every licensing strategy must address all of the options in order to maximize success. How?

First, include both online and offline strategies in your plans. Encourage licensees to have such a dual strategy and provide avenues and tools that will support such initiatives.

Second, be even more actively involved in the businesses of licensees—more creative about how to reach consumers and how to approach retail and retailers and to treat licensees as true partners—and do so comprehensively.

Third, address social media, transparency (the day will soon be upon us when supply chain and price transparency are contractual provisions in license agreements), purpose, mobile technology, and the DNVB path. Choosing from among the many available paths is more complicated today, but it also represents more opportunities for smart brands that are engaging in licensing.

Fourth, understand what retailers (drilling down to specific retailers) are doing to reach their consumers and know how your licensing program can fit into and, indeed, support those efforts, making them more successful.

Looking Back: A Nod to the Past

Finally, recognize the value of looking back. The early pages of this book emphasized placing things in an historical context. Let's not get arrogant about our particular times. True, it's a time of great and rapid cultural and market transformation in the ways we are offered products to purchase and how we buy goods. But there have been other transformational times throughout history when change has been dramatic and sellers of product have had to adapt. Here's an example from one period of time—the mid to late 1800s.

Consumers living outside of cities (that is, most consumers) purchased their goods by traveling, sometimes many miles, into town in horse-drawn wagons to make their purchases, mostly necessities, at the General Store, which had more or less a local retail monopoly and a limited supply of goods. Very inconvenient. Then the expansion of the railway system combined with the growing postal system in the United States created a revolution in retailing—the mail-order catalog. Consumers could now receive a catalog at home or at the local post office, peruse it at their leisure, place an order by mail and receive the product by mail several weeks or months later! Prices were lower, convenience was more than anyone thought possible, and the choices (way beyond the necessities) were exponentially expanded (sound familiar?).

The first "catalog" in the United States was Tiffany's *Blue Book* in 1845. Hammacher Schlemmer introduced its catalog in 1848 (the longest-running catalog in the United States today). Montgomery Ward published its first catalog in 1872, which grew from a single sheet of paper to over 540 pages in two decades featuring over 20,000 items. And in 1888, the Sears catalog, the "Bible," was launched and grew to 532 pages in seven years selling everything from sewing machines to, eventually, automobiles. The mail-order catalog changed retail forever, changed consumer behavior, and compelled brick-and-mortar retailers to adapt.

Amazon (actually a web-based mail-order catalog) is the successor to these early day mail-order catalogs. Just as those entrepreneurs took advantage of cultural and "technological" changes (the postal and railway systems), Jeff Bezos at Amazon (and others) has taken advantage of the Internet. Was the mail-order catalog more revolutionary than e-commerce? I will leave that debate to historians. However, what there cannot be any debate about is that the pace of change today is faster than at any other time in retailing history. And licensing is dependent on retail. You can do everything right; you can have quality licensed product offered at the right price. But to be successful, that product must sell. That means that licensing needs to be successful at reaching consumers where and how they shop and needs to be successful at retail and with retailers. If you and your licensees understand all of the dynamics of retail yesterday, today, and tomorrow, you increase your odds of being successful.

✳ ✳ ✳ ✳ ✳

The next chapter will finish up with a discussion of the new communication tools available to brands and their licensing programs. Every brand owner needs to figure out the most effective paths to get their message across: retail paths, new product categories, demographic strategies, or other types of brand messaging. Don't forget that consumers today jump around fast from brand to brand. In this environment, brands may struggle to determine the most effective ways to engage, communicate, and create a relationship with the consumer. Licensing is one of those ways. With an understanding of all the communication tools available, however, brand owners and their licensees can stay ahead of the consumer, keep the consumer engaged, and ensure that brands matter.

CHAPTER 12

The Future of Licensing, Part II: Delivering the Brand Message

Introduction

Although media spending is rising, brands are shifting their marketing dollars away from traditional advertising. That should not be surprising to anybody. A number of reasons exist for this change: Consumers are buying less in some categories, and companies need to cut costs; questions have arisen about the effectiveness and quality of digital advertising as well as television and print advertising; advertisers are turning toward YouTube stars and influencers to promote their brands (and in some instances, virtual reality and augmented reality).[1] There are many new paths for delivering a brand message to consumers, engaging and connecting with them, and brands are experimenting, and often struggling, to determine the best paths for their particular brand.

---

1. "Ad Industry Woes Deepen," *The Wall Street Journal*, August 24, 2017, page 1.

Brand messaging today is a stew of consumer experiences. A great deal of attention is being given to how to use marketing dollars effectively and how to best reach consumers with a brand message. James Quincey, CEO of The Coca-Cola Company, said "The way brands are getting created today is not just . . . making ads that people love. It's through interaction directly with customers without advertising at all."[2] Digital advertising revenues, which can be used to reach broad audiences, surpassed television advertising revenues in 2017. Large consumer goods companies such as P&G, Unilever, Kraft Heinz, and Nestlé, are reducing their overall ad spending, often by significant amounts. Is traditional advertising dead? Of course not. But marketers (both brands and their agencies) will continue to look for the most effective way to reach consumers with their messages and budgets.

There's a famous advertising saying: "Half my advertising is wasted. The trouble is, I don't know which half." Well, with so much data available today, that is no longer true. With data, marketers can target narrow slices of consumers (sometimes one-on-one), often directly, and can also reach broad audiences. They can offer branded content to consumers across multiple devices. They can use YouTubers and influencers to deliver a brand message—and much more.

Brand licensing fits perfectly into this new messaging and communications dynamic. As we have seen, licensing provides a vehicle for brand owners to achieve their communication goals and engage with consumers. It should be viewed in the context of all of the varying ways that brand owners can now communicate their brand message and brand promise to consumers. Considering it in this manner reveals how important licensing can be as tool to engage the consumer and create or strengthen brand connection.

With today's digitally savvy consumers (which are increasing as Gen Z comes of age), brand loyalty is more tenuous than ever before, particularly in our rapidly expanding information age.

---

2. *Id.*

Consumers in every product category are loyal within a range and, in some categories, often purchasing different brands of the same product. Retaining consumers as well as recruiting new ones has become increasingly challenging and will continue to require not only targeted marketing but also a broad reach. By broadening the reach of a brand with a more extensive family of products and delivering the brand message through those licensed products where and when consumers want to receive it and by fortifying brand connection and brand memory, licensing helps retain those who are already loyal to a brand (even light users of the brand) as well as recruit new users. In the case of licensing, the product is the message. Consumers are increasingly skeptical of direct marketing messages. That's why marketers are searching for more authentic ways to reach consumers. Licensing offers consumers the opportunity to bypass direct messaging and move directly to simply buying and trying out a product. But make no mistake about it, the licensed product *is* the message. The discussion below examines several of the most important communication paths for brands and their licensing programs.

Targeted Versus Broad Reach Marketing

Technology has made targeted marketing, slicing the marketplace into narrow consumer segments, much easier to do today. Segmentation is a strategy that all brands are and will continue to pursue (certainly when seeking to reach certain demographic groups). But the smaller your targeted consumer group is, the fewer consequences it will have for sales. Segmented targeting is still necessary because that's where a brand's consumers can be found, but it's not the end of the story. In Byron Sharp's book *How Brands Grow: What Marketers Don't Know,* the author argues that "[s]ales growth won't come from relentlessly targeting a particular segment of a brand's buyers." Sales growth will come from consumers who don't care much about your brand. Sales will grow by pounding your brand message into the minds of consumers with all sorts of cues, such as a logo and taglines. A broad reach, Sharp opines, is necessary to recruit buyers of your brand.[3] That broad reach can be achieved through several paths, such as television and digital advertising. Of course, a broad reach is not relevant in some categories. For example, luxury goods (such as apparel and jewelry) shouldn't reach broadly; rather, luxury goods should target that particular consumer. And although 2010, when Sharp's book was published, is not very long ago, a lot of technology has come along since then to make targeted marketing even more available and effective, despite Sharp's position.

There is a great deal of debate about Sharp's argument that targeted marketing is not effective marketing. But why can't both approaches be right? In fact, both approaches are being pursued by many multinational brands, such as Unilever and P&G. For example, Unilever continues to seek broad audiences with major brands such as Dove and Vaseline. But recently, it started developing smaller brands such as Love Beauty and Planet that target Millennials as well as an e-commerce only subscription skin care brand named Skinsei and an Indonesian hair care brand named Hijab, for Muslim women who wear head coverings. Nevertheless, contrary to some of the prevailing winds regarding digital reach, the biggest reach of all remains TV. Heavy buyers of a brand ("brand loyalists") must continue to be targeted (so that you don't lose them), but light buyers and new buyers also need to be targeted (so that the brand grows). Don't leave any group of consumers behind. If The Coca-Cola Company can get a light user to drink one more bottle a year or get a new consumer to buy a bottle, it has sales growth. You need to keep all of your consumer groups engaged and interacting with the brand. Licensing is a way to create more brand interaction.

Today more paths than ever before are available to reach and bond with consumers. This is why licensing is such a timely tool—it is a communications tool in and of itself (i.e., the licensed prod-

3. *How Brands Grow: What Marketers Don't Know*, by Byron Sharp, Oxford University Press, 2010.

uct), and the licensed products can also take advantage of many of the other communication paths available to reach consumers. A licensing strategy can focus on a targeted group of consumers (perhaps by age, ethnicity, or income level) or a broad group (e.g., homeowners) or both. For example, the goal of a brand's licensing program can be to reach Hispanics with a particular product offering, but that doesn't mean the product can't also appeal to a mainstream audience. Strategic licensing programs must delineate to whom the licensed product is targeted, and that should be aligned with to whom the brand wants to deliver its brand message. For licensing programs to be successful, the licensed products, the target consumer, and the manner in which the products are distributed (the paths chosen) must align with the brand's core product and messaging. That being said, licensing generally represents a broad reach.

"Entangling" with Consumers
In their book *Release the Power of Entangled Marketing*,[4] authors Stan Rapp and Sebastian Jespersen argue that brands today need to move beyond simply engaging with consumers and focus on "entangling" with them "in an enduring and supportive relationship"[5] (i.e., building a more solid and longer-term relationship with consumers). They believe that's what people want in this new digital world where they can easily communicate with each other about brands largely through social media. This is a world in which consumers want to be "entangled" and participate with the brand, as much as the other way around. Consider Amazon, Google, and Apple, the authors note as examples, as brands with which consumers want to be connected. Online engagement, they argue, is a short-lived attention grabber that really doesn't build a long-term brand/consumer relationship.

---

4. *Release the Power of Entangled Marketing: Moving Beyond Engagement*, by Stan Rapp and Sebastian Jespersen, The International Press, 2016.
5. *Id.*, 17.

The connection fades as quickly as it started. Brands need to forge deeper connections.

That's what marketers are trying to do with quality content marketing—"entangle" with the consumer, create a conversation. Done correctly, it spreads throughout and creates a user community. Consumers often see it for what it is—advertising. That doesn't mean they don't like good content marketing, but they often know it's advertising (indeed, sometimes it gives them useful information, such as how to maintain their car). The real goal, however, is what it's always been: to turn a consumer into a brand loyalist, one who keeps coming back to the brand and doesn't move from brand to brand. The authors opine that mass marketing and digital marketing are moving on to entangled marketing—where brand and consumer share a value-added connection.

Although Rapp and Jespersen's concepts make sense, they are neither new concepts nor a new day in marketing. Seeking to entangle consumers with brands, creating a long-term connection, is what brand licensing is all about—entangling (the authors' word, but a good one) the consumer with the brand. Consider how brand licensing entangles: It offers the consumer more product with which to engage or entangle (in different product categories and in varied retail locations) on brand message and through different communication pathways. The consumer *chooses* to purchase the licensed product and to participate with the brand and bring it into his or her life, using the product in different activities and different day parts and occasions. In short, it connects consumer and brand, embedding the brand into the consumer's life in fresh ways, strengthening brand memory, and turning the consumer into a loyalist (or sustaining loyalty). If you accept Rapp and Jespersen's thesis about where marketers need to go, then licensing should be in a brand's future.

Let's not forget about the importance of data as a way for brands and retailers to "entangle" with consumers and support licensed products. Data drives "entanglement." In fact, so much data is being collected now about our wants, needs, interests, purchasing history and behavior, social media interactions, and more that brand owners cannot get a handle on all of it without the help of artificial intelligence–powered analytics and machine learning algorithms. The data not only permits brand owners to target the right consumers but also helps them personalize communications with consumers with product suggestions even before consumers know that they want or need something. For example, based on customers' movements in the store and other information about them, brand messages can target consumers while they are in-store. Data can help retailers adjust pricing in real time, as well as inventory, to get product to where the customer is shopping. Consumers, particularly younger ones, expect brands to have information about them and understand what products they might want. They expect brands to deliver product information that is relevant to who they are based on the data collected.

But there's a dark side to all of this data collection (putting aside the important concerns about privacy invasion). Data can be converted automatically to target certain audiences with certain products or messages. But what about filters? "The same mechanism that decides that 30-something women who like yoga disproportionately buy Lululemon tights—and shows them ads for more yoga wear—would also show more junk food ads to impoverished populations rife with diabetes and obesity. . . . [Brands] will have to confront how to determine who is being nudged, and why, and whether that's benefiting the public or exacerbating societal ills."[6] There are ethical considerations to how all of this data is used. When used for what many might consider the support of societal ills, brands, their licensees, and retailers will take the fall (as well as the platform assembling the data).

Both online and offline retailers and the brands they offer must access the available data, but also need to ensure that it is used in an acceptable way—to use the data to offer consumers a positive brand experience that will increasingly focus on a direct-

---

6. *Id.* "The Ads That Know Everything," page 55.

to-consumer experience. Brand licensors and licensees will have to learn how to use the data available to understand what kinds of products consumers want or need and then deliver those products to them. The initial licensing plan developed for a brand should identify where useful data can be found or developed that will inform and support the strategy, including what categories are appropriate, for what demographic, in what retail channel, supported by what kind of communication, at what price, filling what white space or need and finding consumers where they shop. Data will inform and guide the strategy and optimize the opportunity for success. But data is just a guide. It's not the end of the analysis. Don't overly rely on data. Use it as a tool. But in the end, brand owners must ensure that the licensed product is on brand message, designed well, and priced right and that it delivers on the consumer's expectations of quality. The data alone will not get you there.

Different Generations, Different Strategies
Virtually every brand has, as part of its marketing strategy, a plan to reach a particular segment of consumers. Perhaps it's consumers with a certain household income level, a gender, an ethnicity, or other groups. There's usually an age target, whether it be an age group that is already a strong buyer of the brand or one the brand would like to capture. Accordingly, its important for licensing programs not only to align with this particular strategy but also to demonstrate an understanding of the characteristics of different age groups in order to target them effectively with licensed products.

Every generation has its own distinctive attitude toward brands and exhibits particular shopping behaviors and that drives how we deliver brand messages to different age groups. We know a great deal about those attitudes and behaviors due to data collection. Brand owners engaging in licensing must address these generational characteristics and use the available data to develop and implement licensing programs that reach these consumers in the ways they want to be reached.

For example, a majority of Millennials and, to a lesser extent, Gen Xers prefer to shop online rather than in-store for certain types of products. But they also like to hunt for products in brick and mortar. The numbers drop to less than half for Baby Boomers and Seniors (who actually care less about the "hunt" having grown up with brick-and-mortar retail), although Boomers value the ease and product assortment offered by online shopping. Millennials and Gen Xers spend much more time shopping online each week than do their elders (although, as noted earlier, Millennials also like going to malls). This makes sense. Gen Xers and, to an even greater extent, Millennials grew up with digital devices. Clearly, if you are trying to reach these generations, an online strategy for your licensing program is a must. Baby Boomers were raised with one screen and much fewer choices. They too, however, are a demographic not to be ignored. In general though, all age groups value the in-store *experience* (emphasis intended) equal to the digital experience. Don't forget, as mentioned earlier, most shopping is still done at brick and mortar, although there are often broad swings among product categories.

Millennials have perhaps been the most researched and coveted generation when it comes to consumer behavior, and marketers are still trying to figure out how to connect with them even as they begin turning to the next generation, Gen Z (born between 1998 and 2014). Millennials are no longer the "future" generation. They have come of age and are now a powerful force with regard to purchasing. Fifty-one percent of Millennials don't distinguish between national brands and private-label brands and have difficulty remaining loyal to a brand, according to a recent study by Cadent Consulting Group.[7] Millennials prefer to "discover" brands. They don't want to be sold products or brands by salespeople, they want advisors, curators. That's why Sephora

---

7. Study cited in "The Millennial Dilemma: The Generic Generation Doesn't Want Your Brands. What Are You Going to Do About It?," by Adrianne Pasquarelli, *Ad Age*, August 21, 2017.

is successful with this generation. It's a curator, not a seller (often described as the "Apple store" in the beauty category). Increasingly, we will see specialty retailers offering a curated experience, which is what department stores used to do. Millennials tend to seek experiences over straight product purchases (more on that later in the chapter). Unlike the generations before them, including Gen X, Millennials have grown up consuming media and product communication in a different way, which causes them to shop for products as consumers differently. Millennials also grew up during the time of the 2008 recession, when money was tight. They learned to shop carefully, with price as a major consideration. That's one of the reasons big retailers such as Target and Amazon are launching major private-label brands created in-house in multiple categories from apparel to home décor to food and drugs. It's also why discount grocers such as Aldi and Lidl are expanding in the U.S. Private labels (and "discounters") have been and will be a challenge for brands as they consume floor and screen space, generate high margins for the retailer, and provide the retailer with complete control.

Millennials, and to an even greater extent Gen Zers, use all sorts of media available to them to shop, including social media such as Instagram and Snapchat. Millennials in particular and to a lesser degree Gen Zers (probably because they are still so young) engage in research before buying; it's where the shopping journey begins. Sometimes they research offline and buy online; other times, vice versa. Brands need to communicate a good amount of product information about their core and licensed products to appeal to these generations. This includes transparency about pricing and, importantly, the supply chain. Consumers and retailers want to know where and how products and their components are manufactured. The younger generations care about issues such as sustainability and will make their brand decisions based on what they learn. You can easily capture and offer this information to consumers online as well as through codes on the packaging that can be scanned with a mobile device (blockchain technology will be in licensing's future). Unlike Baby Boomers, these younger generations have grown up and are comfortable with a lots of information and communication and they enjoy all of the options they have when shopping.

What does all of this mean for brand licensing? It means that Millennials care less and are skeptical about brands; they skip around without much loyalty. They care about price, brand story, authenticity, and discovery, and they care about products with a sense of purpose (see below). They will buy products that make them feel as though they are building a life with meaning. Smart licensing can address all of this and help drive or sustain brand loyalty (or at least brand affection) by offering, in different retail locations and purchasing occasions, consumers more brand-aligned products to purchase and use in their lives. Of course, missteps by licensees can have the opposite effect on a brand turning younger generations away.

But as much as marketers have been focused on Millennials in recent years, they are now, as noted earlier, turning their attention to Gen Zers—young people who are just getting to college and attaining consumer status. They make up 25 percent of the U.S. population and will be a bigger wave than both Millennials and Baby Boomers. They are already having an impact on purchasing. Gen Zers have been immersed in the digital age from the beginning of their lives. They are digital natives; they don't know a time before the Internet, smartphones, Google, Amazon, or Facebook. They have always had YouTube. Social media plays a large role in their purchasing and engagement behavior, more so than for Millennials and Gen Xers. They too want their "brands" to act more like advisors than salespeople, brands they can consider "real."

Because Gen Zers grew up (or, for the really young, is growing up) in the age of connectivity, they are familiar with and use multiple platforms and learned at a very young age how to research brands and products and use data and filters. They care about product performance but also about what a brand stands for. Gen Zers as well as Millennials rely increasingly on peer reviews and other social media content, causing brands and retailers to focus on user content that can be spread. Social activity leads to purchase activity. That's why Amazon launched Amazon Spark, which encourages users to post about products they like and offers the opportunity for others to comment. Instagram and Pinterest show images of products to inspire purchasing. And some brick-and-mortar retailers are tapping into social media interaction as part of their in-store experience, such as Nordstrom's featuring "top pinned" items from Pinterest in stores and evaluating the social media it generates to make merchandise planning decisions. It's also why brand licensors and their licensees who have Gen Z in their sights need to have a digital and social media strategy and must have policies about the transparency Gen Zers want with respect to the products they purchase.[8] Other than linking the websites of licensees to their own brand websites, no other brand licensor today has yet developed a sophisticated strategy in this regard, but they and their licensees must pay attention to it now and in the years ahead, particularly as it applies to Gen Z.

And don't ignore Baby Boomers. In size, they are equal to Millennials, but they have more time to shop and more disposable income. Although they are more likely to stay loyal to a brand than Millennials are, they too are willing to try new brands. They use smartphones, they engage in online shopping, and they appreciate the greater choices they have today than they did years ago. Brands need to reconnect with this demographic and keep them engaged.

Making matters even more complicated, *Ad Age* has identified a narrow group of consumers that it calls "Pivotals": "the sweet spot between Gen Z and Millennials."[9] Although the article is written from the perspective of the beauty category, it might apply to other categories as well. They seek products with "good vibes."

---

8. Sparks & Honey, an agency specializing in cultural insights and trends, published a valuable report in June 2014 (updated regularly) titled "Meet Generation Z: Forget Everything You Learned About Millennials."
9. "How Beauty Became a Cultural Movement for a New Generation," by Moj Mahdara, *Ad Age*, November 2, 2017.

This "demographic category" is mentioned only because it suggests the possibility of other overlaps; each age group does not fit neatly into its stereotypes, and yet brand licensors need to be aware of generational differences.

Recognize, too, that younger demographics want brands to stand for something, take a position, have a purpose. And that will filter down to licensed products as well. In the currently charged political environment, however, taking a position can be a challenge—every strong position can please some and offend others. Consider, for example, what happened to the Keurig company in November 2017. After *Fox News* host Sean Hannity seemed to downplay the sexual harassment claims made against Alabama Senate candidate Roy Moore, Keurig pulled its advertising from the program. Some consumers applauded the action; others not so much. Those who were offended and supported Hannity posted videos of themselves on social media destroying their Keurig coffeemakers and advocating a boycott. The videos went viral, and Keurig got caught in the crosshairs and had to contain the damage by apologizing for appearing to take sides. An even more recent example followed the mass shooting at Marjory Stoneman Douglas High School in Parkland, Florida, on February 14, 2018, when 16 companies discontinued their discounts for NRA members and asked to be removed from the NRA website, as well as several retailers who curtailed gun sales in their stores. Many consumers applauded their actions, but many were opposed and announced boycotts. In any event, whatever positions brands take, they should be consistent with the brand's business values. Often, brands will be called on to make difficult decisions.

Positions and purpose don't always have to be controversial, however. Everlane, a popular online DNVB fashion site, promotes transparency, acceptable working conditions, and sustainability by providing a great deal of information about how its products are manufactured and priced, the factories they use, and the conditions in those factories. In addition, the company encourages consumers to keep the garments for many years (instead of buying every season), thereby reducing textile industry waste. Younger consumers want to purchase products that have a story and a mission with which they can identify, such as Everlane. Consider how embedded the health and wellness movement has become in mainstream categories such as food, beverage, and beauty products. Unilever's Love Beauty and Planet is a new health and beauty brand targeted at Millennials that uses 100 percent recycled packaging, ethically sourced ingredients, and fast rinse conditioner to cut down on water usage. Further, the company is paying a voluntary tax to offset the brand's carbon footprint. Although you will probably find the brand at Walmart, you likely won't find it advertised on TV; rather, it will be marketed on social media where consumers can "discover" it.

Recently, licensing programs have become an extension of social controversy or change, and that will accelerate in the future as consumers are interested in knowing where brands stand on certain social and political issues. For example, in 2015, the Confederate flag was lowered from the South Carolina Capitol Building for the last time after years of controversy. The move was made even more poignant by the tragic shooting of nine African Americans in a South Carolina church by a white gunman whose clothing was adorned with patches of the flag. Many people noted that the flag was featured on all sorts of products. Retailers responded. Walmart, Amazon, eBay, and Etsy announced that they would no longer sell Confederate flags and flag-related merchandise, and Warner Bros. announced that it would no longer license the "General Lee," the famous *Dukes of Hazzard* Dodge Charger featuring an image of the Confederate flag.

When licensed merchandise becomes an extension of social controversy or change, retailers and brand owners must often think beyond profit and be responsive to social responsibility, perhaps alienating certain consumer groups in the process. Increasingly, consumers, across generations, will come to expect that. This comes into sharp focus for licensing programs tied to public personas who run afoul of public opinion and popular social movements.

Celebrity chef Paula Deen took a well-deserved hit after her racist remarks went public in 2013. Deen was dropped by The Food Network and many of her licensing partners. During Donald Trump's 2016 campaign, brands and licensees associated with him couldn't cut ties fast enough, particularly those that catered to the Hispanic community, following remarks he made about Mexicans. Macy's, Serta, PVH, and others dropped his license. And the Trump product and service brand (largely a licensed brand) has continued to suffer during Trump's presidency.

Fortunately, as noted earlier, brand reactions to social change will not always be seen in the context of negative trends (again, consider the Everlane and Unilever examples above). Although "purpose" is frequently about driving sales, sometimes it can also have an altruistic component (e.g., Walgreen's "Get a Shot, Give a Shot" program that administers flu shots to children around the world, promoting healthy living) and sometimes a societal component (e.g., Walmart providing products at low prices, enabling people to live better lives). Think of brands that promise not only good product at lower prices but also an identifiable charitable mission, such as Tom's of Maine. Smart brands are just as quick to respond to positive social movements. Sesame Workshop collaborates with the Partnership for a Healthier America to interest children in eating more fruits and vegetables. You may recall the (RED) logo that adorned products from Gap T-shirts to Apple iPods to Nike shoelaces in an effort to raise awareness and funding for the fight against AIDS in Africa. Brand owners must ensure that whatever they identify as a sense of purpose, it is consistent throughout their licensing program. Licensees will necessarily be connected to the brand owner's positions (as well as, sometimes, the other way around), for better or worse.

As brand owners and their licensees (and retailers) observe the political and social climate, increasingly, they can no longer remain on the sidelines, particularly if they want to reach younger generations. No large brand can truly be separated from the important transformations and conversations happening in society. The products that today's consumers, particularly younger consumers, buy are an extension of who they are as people and the causes with which they align. Licensing programs and brand owners can no longer turn a deaf ear.

In the years ahead, brand owners and licensees will have to work harder—with their brand message, on social media, with their storytelling, with the price/value relationship, with transparency—to reach the younger (as well as other) demographics and entice them to make a purchase. It won't be a one-size-fits-all strategy, and most brand owners would be wise to focus on each demographic separately. They don't have to choose one over the other. As has been true for a long time, licensing is but a tool in the toolbox to achieve those goals.

YouTubers, Bloggers, Vloggers, and Influencers: It's the Message

Chapter 8 provided a broader discussion of this topic and an overview of the emergence of digital celebrities, attempted some definitions, noted opportunities and risks, and focused on influencers who embark upon product licensing programs. Now let's look at these digital celebrities from a brand messaging perspective, starting with false reports of the death of "blogging." Just as the Internet is a changing landscape, so too is blogging. This is largely because channels of content distribution are constantly evolving and the current trend is about creating more digestible and short-form content. Today content must be dynamic and high-quality. Perhaps this is because content needs to compete in an age of information overload or because almost everyone today can be a creator, so the bar is set much higher than it was in the past. Photo and video editing tools are the norm among Millennials and Gen Zers, and social media platforms are constantly sparring in the battle for better in-app editing tools. The possibilities for content and, therefore, communication and messaging are much broader than before (e.g., video, infographics, podcasts, GIFs, and memes), so influencers are able to connect with consumers on many different levels. This is one of influencers' greatest strengths: They are high-touch. As mentioned in Chapter 8, digital celebrities are, for some demographic groups, becoming more popular than traditional celebrities. That doesn't mean that traditional celebrity endorsements and licensing are dead—they are as viable now as they were in the past. Keep in mind that to engage with fans, celebrities have the same resources as influencers. What matters is how they will adapt to this high-touch engagement that consumers and fans have come to expect because of the rise of influencers. Celebrities today have their best (and potentially most dangerous) brand-building tool in the palm of their hands: their smartphone. Although celebrities may not fade as influencers continue to rise, they may need to step up the ways in which they engage and interact with their fans.

Be aware, however, of what the digital celebrity trend means for your brand communications. You must factor this trend into your licensing strategy considerations in order to have a relationship with consumers. Unlike traditional celebrity endorsements, which are controlled and scripted, influencers are (supposedly) unscripted and brand owners, therefore, lose a level of control over the message. This "unscripted" nature of their presentation has been a problem for YouTubers and other platform celebrities who are more entertainers, such as PewDiPie and Logan Paul, than influencers who are or are perceived as experts in a product category. With influencers who are category experts and directly promote branded product, that's a risk that brand owners, licensors, and licensees are willing to take and can mitigate, at least to some extent, by capitalizing on increased consumer engagement—a key influencer benefit. Successful influencers build and strengthen consumer trust—trust that is built through their style, performance, functionality, quality, and the price/value relationship they create. They make the buying decision easier for the consumer. They are, in a way, a consumer's "personal shopper." Increasingly, brand owners are turning to these influencers to deliver their product message to the influencer's sizable fan base.

This strategy of communication should also be part of your licensing strategy. Getting licensed product into influencer's hands will drive sales and awareness.

Influencers will continue to be an important way for brands to provide a story, a message, and information. But be careful. Consumers are better at identifying who is authentic and trustworthy—who is reliable and who is simply being paid by a big consumer product company to influence their purchase.[10] Consumers no longer blindly rely on famous influencers, and sometimes these vloggers fall out of favor. Still, influencers are becoming increasingly critical to brand communication and messaging and are being relied upon by more brands than ever before. Remember, too, a major difference between traditional celebrity endorsements and digital celebrities: The former are often pushed at the consumer, while the consumer seeks out the latter, choosing to become a subscriber or fan of the site and possibly interacting with them easily and regularly.

Of course, there are risks when associating a brand with an influencer. Consider Logan Paul, a YouTuber with over 15 million subscribers. In early 2018, he posted a repulsive piece of video filming a dead body from suicide in a forest known for suicides in Japan. He was widely rebuked for the posting and tried to apologize. Imagine you had associated your brand or product with Logan Paul. Imagine the reputational damage. Using an influencer to communicate your brand or product message will take research and due diligence. Dig deep into past postings and, to the extent possible, understand the influencer's strategy and future plans. Contracts can help, including noncompete provisions and ways to terminate the relationship due to disagreeable content or violations of a morals provision. And what if the influencer is actually scripted or working with editors? That's not the authenticity expected by fans. Popularity can plummet quickly if that's the case.

---

10. In fact, under current Federal Trade Commision rules, bloggers using video must disclose whether they are being paid to endorse a product.

Also, as mentioned in Chapter 8, footnote 15, influencers can purchase followers ("bots") from companies engaged in the shady business of stealing profiles and selling them. Brand owners can't easily determine if an influencer is purchasing bots. I don't know if this is widespread, but there are some clues to look for during due diligence. Look for spikes in follower numbers over a short period of time. Randomly spot-check followers. Look at where the followers live (bots are often identified as living overseas). And, of course, brand owners can demand contractual representations about the authenticity of followers.

If due diligence turns up nothing to worry about, to a large extent, brand owners (licensors and licensees) still must trust their instincts when it comes to influencers. Nevertheless, they will continue to be an important and growing marketing and communications tool for brands.

Experiential Marketing

Experiential marketing, a way to pull consumers into a brand rather than pushing the brand at them, as a communication tool is not new, but its relevance has increased dramatically in physical locations or when combined with social media. As brands increasingly use the digital world to connect with consumers, they also realize that real, physical interaction cannot be left behind. Integration of the digital and physical environments must be seamless in the eyes of the consumer. It's what consumers want. The experience needs to be humanized. Not so long ago an experiential event could attract perhaps a thousand consumers. But now that those consumers can share the event on social media, it can go viral, allowing many more consumers to relate to the energy of the experience online. Unlike simply exposing a brand to consumers ("seeing" it), an experience lets the consumer participate in the brand ("feel" it), allowing the brand to interact with and have a "conversation" with the consumer, strengthening the bond between brand and consumer. No, it doesn't reach as many consumers as, for example, a television campaign, but it does reach consumers, many of them, at a much deeper level. The experience can be a virtual one, such as Mountain Dew's video featuring a human slingshot made of bungee cords (over two million YouTube views), or it can be a physical experience, such as Coty's New York City 2017 pop-up shop featuring a DIY nail bar, an AI mirror to use in trying on products without having to worry about samplers, a 3D portrait studio for selfies, and more, all directly engaging the consumer in new ways (and collecting useful data to share with retailers). "When people attend an event, they aren't just seeking to have [their] . . . needs met for the days—or sometimes just hours or minutes—the event is underway. They're building memories."[11] And those memories drive brand connection.

Consider, too, that a brand owner may not want to commit the time or resources to develop some sort of experiential event. That's where licensing comes in. Licensing third parties to develop a specific experience can be (and has been) an effective alternative to a brand owner investing in creating an event itself.

Licensed experiences are being pursued across a number of avenues. For example, although the themed restaurant has been around for some time (the Harley-Davidson Café, a licensed experience, opened in New York City in 1993), a new wave of branded, licensed cafés have been opening that immerse people in the brand experience. Examples include the Kola Café (licensed by Pepsi) in New York City, The Spotted Cheetah (licensed by Frito-Lay and based on its snack brand Cheetos), the Kellogg's cereal café, and the Nutella Café in Chicago (actually owned by Ferrero, owner of Nutella). These cafés not only immerse customers in the brand but also serve curated menus based on the core products (e.g., Cheetos-crusted fried pickles, Special K and Frosted Flakes with rum-roasted bananas and cashews, and fresh-roasted hazelnut and blueberry granola with yogurt and Nutella). These and other

---

11. This concept is noted in a white paper titled "Experiential EQ: Going Beyond Data to Understand the Power of Emotions in Experiential Marketing," GMR Marketing LLC, 2018, page 4.

types of experiences allow fans to be engaged with brands they enjoy and introduces brands to consumers who may not already be brand loyalists or users.

Pop-up stores (defined as temporary retail *experiences* open for periods ranging from one day to a couple of months), some licensed and some not, are rising throughout the retail landscape (the Coty pop-up was mentioned above). Birkenstock opened a pop-up in New York (part of a global pop-up strategy) as it seeks to communicate a new brand message and offer products that break away from its traditional image, such as beds and hand and foot creams. In addition, Birkenstock is touring a mobile retail store named the Birkenstock Box (a former freight container) that has already stopped in major cities around the world. Uniqlo opened a pop-up for one day in Vancouver and asked customers to leave with a free flannel shirt or to "gift" it to a newcomer. *Marie Claire* opened a pop-up with all sorts of technical innovations such as smart mirrors and payment options. Sections of the store were organized as the then-current issue of the magazine was organized, combining lifestyle and technology. Story is a firm that pioneered the pop-up shop in New York City around 2011 and in 2017 opened a temporary retail location for five weeks that serves as a "pop-up for hire" for brands that include American Express and Cover Girl. Recognizing the importance of this experiential concept, Macy's acquired Story in 2018.

Pop-ups also help brand owners understand other ways to merchandise and sell their products—knowledge they can pass on to their general retail partners. For instance, you might open a pop-up shop when you already have multiple retail locations or your products are sold at other retailers. Nestlé has opened pop-ups in Montreal and Toronto where customers can customize pizzas with Nestlé's cheeses or sample Häagen-Dazs ice cream.

Pop-ups are also a good tactic to use to revive dormant brands. The revived Sharper Image brand (see Chapter 9) opened a pop-up in Times Square for the 2017 holiday. Another revived brand, the Limited Too, which shut down in 2008, reappeared as a mobile pop-up for the 2017 back-to-school season. And even digital celebrities are getting in on the pop-up experience, blending their online presence with a physical retail experience. Influencer Jake Paul and his Team 10 (his team of other bloggers) opened a pop-up in Los Angeles in 2017 offering licensed merchandise (mostly T-shirts, sweatshirts, and hats). It was so overwhelmed with customers and fans that it had to close and seek a larger location. And rap singer Eminem opened a pop-up in Detroit featuring food and merchandise to promote his new album.

Although pop-up shops and some of the other branded experiences mentioned can be relatively inexpensive to execute, some very expensive branded experiences are also being pursued (consider the National Geographic example mentioned below). If a brand owner is considering this option, the brand owner must know that the project will require an experienced partner through some kind of joint venture arrangement or an outright license. As I noted earlier, branded restaurants already gravitate toward a licensing model. Pop-ups can as well.

Hotels as a way to extend a brand experience and immerse the consumer have been around for quite some time. Fashion footwear brand Ferragamo began opening hotels years ago. Indeed, many hotels of recent years have been opened by luxury fashion design houses such as Versace and Fendi. And several celebrity designers have taken to designing rooms at hotels. Now, however, we are witnessing the beginnings of more corporate-type brands getting into the hotel space to engage with their consumers and offer them an immersive, participatory experience. Among the first was Pantone, which opened a hotel in Brussels owned by Hotel Ascot. Ikea has a branded hotel in Sweden. Japanese retailer Muji is opening a hotel in Tokyo. Equinox and Shinola have also announced plans to open hotels. And as an example of the blending of online, offline, and experience, the bed and bath brand, Parachute, which started as an online business, has opened a brick-and-mortar store and a hotel above the store.

A final note about malls and the retailers in those malls. They are offering all sorts of experiences (that's one of their competitive advantages over online retailing), including spa services, tailoring, personal stylists, wine bars, pizzerias, and juice bars. They are seeking to provide their customers with activities they enjoy doing. Malls don't even want to be called "malls" anymore.

As this experiential marketing trend gains steam, brand owners will feel compelled to seek ways to engage with their target consumers and recruit new ones through brand immersive experiences. These include hotels, pop-up stores, cafés, themed events, theme parks (FC Barcelona has announced that it will open licensed leisure and entertainment complexes) and playgrounds (Playmobil plans a series of themed playgrounds in Spain), and exhibits (National Geographic Encounter: Ocean Odyssey in New York offers an interactive experience of life underwater). It's an active area for licensing given that partners need to be found to execute these experiences, particularly the more costly and complex experiences. The best "experiences" are about the seamless integration of the digital, the physical and the experience. Some executions will be well done, others not so much. But through trial and error, this is an area that will become increasingly sophisticated.

New and Reinvented Product Categories and Brands

Every era generates new or reinvented categories of brands and products as well as cultural trends through which brand owners can deliver their message and connect with their audience (the discussion about the emergence of influencers is a good illustration), often through licensing. For example, in the 1960s, the general population became acutely aware of environmental and safety dangers and the Green movement really took hold. The response (in the 1970s) was the birth of new brands such as Tom's of Maine and product categories such as granola which, although always a niche product, became mainstream. And "green" licensed products became a robust area of licensing. Sometimes old and tired categories or brands themselves are reinvented or take on new meaning due to cultural trends, such as "green products" or the Birkenstock example cited above. Nike reinvented the athletic shoe category in the 1960s. Much attention these days is being paid to products that allow Baby Boomers and Seniors to remain in their homes longer (such as grab bars, ramps, and special furniture), and we will likely see much more licensing activity in this category in the years ahead. Sometimes product categories that were once popular simply disappear (or largely disappear), such as portable CD players, typewriters, paper maps, Filofax, and men's dress hats, and they are replaced by new products. Sometimes entirely new categories appear in the marketplace, such as smartphones and accessories, wearable technology, hybrid cars, light beer, and wine coolers. And sometimes a brand is able to reinvent itself and become relevant again, such as KFC, or extend its brand meaning, such as Birkenstock.

These waves of new and reinvented product categories, properties, and brands will always drive licensing activity. Often, these will be true long-term trends and sometimes simply short-term fads. There's no way to predict; we must wait for the marketplace to speak. However, whether a long-term trend or a fad, they both have value to brands as they seek to communicate to and connect with consumers through licensing. Today some of those waves are technological (such as the connectivity offered by the Internet and social media), and some are cultural (such as a celebration of diversity, individualism, and gender neutrality). For example, the latter has given rise to a blossoming of the plus-size fashion category, where many choices are now available. No longer relegated to a handful of key players such as Lane Bryant, designers and private-label brands at retailers such as Target and JCPenney are adding sizes or complete collections for the full-figured woman. Both J. Crew and Madewell recently started offering larger sizes. Eloquii is a DNVB that caters exclusively to plus-size women. Gwynnie Bee, mentioned earlier, is a rental/subscription service specializing in large sizes for women. Some of these brands, as they become more mainstream, will undoubtedly extend into other product categories through licensing, further turning this once below-the-radar category into something more relevant and "real." There is no reason a popular plus-size fashion brand can't also offer footwear, small leather goods, and other fashion accessories, for example. There's even a movement underfoot to stop using "plus size" to describe the category. In addition, traditional celebrities such as Melissa McCarthy and digital celebrities such as Gabi Gregg have licensed their names for plus-size fashion. An increasing number of licensed apparel lines will likely include larger sizes. This is a tired category that has reinvented itself without apology, in response to cultural trends, and licensing has played and will continue to play a role.

The pet accessories category, with few recognizable manufacturer brands, has long been an active category for licensing as companies making pet accessories seek to differentiate their products with a well-known brand name. Generally, those licensors have been entertainment characters (such as Snoopy and Garfield) or celebrities (such as Martha Stewart and Ellen DeGeneres). But now the category is reinventing itself with more on-trend products and features, largely through licensing. Smart products connect collars and doors (licensed by Black & Decker), health and wellness pet products (licensed by the American Kennel Club), and pet products for travel (licensed by Goodyear).

There are many more examples of new brands, properties, product categories, and reinvented categories and brands arriving on the scene where licensing will play an important role. Among the many, here is an example of a new product category and a new property type that have recently emerged: Cannabis is an entirely new product industry entering the legitimate retail landscape;[12] and eSports is a new category of professional competitive sport that is already fertile ground for the emergence of new brands and licensing.

Cannabis

As cannabis becomes legal in more states (as of this writing, it is legal for recreational use in eight states and the District of Columbia),

---

12. We will have to wait and see how the announcement in early 2018 that the U.S. Department of Justice is encouraging federal prosecutors to pursue sellers of cannabis under federal law will affect the industry in states that have legalized marijuana under their state laws.

products once sold on the gray market out of back rooms (e.g., marijuana flowers, edibles, and concentrates) are now being marketed like any other consumer product. Companies are branding their product lines with witty names, sophisticated product development and design, and professional packaging. Licensing names for use on cannabis products has already started with celebrities leading the way. Licensed cannabis product lines include Leafs by Snoop (that is, Snoop Dogg), Willie's Reserve (that is, Willie Nelson), Marley Natural (that is, the estate of Bob Marley), Whoopie & Maya (that is, Whoopie Goldberg and medical marijuana grower Elisabeth Maya), and Chong's Choice (that is, Tommy Chong of Cheech & Chong fame). Products under these brands include marijuana flowers, edibles, concentrates, rubs, oils, lotions, tinctures, breath-infused THC strips, and ready rolls, as well as all sorts of accessories (e.g., grinders, pipes, and T-shirts). In August 2017, Netfllix partnered with a dispensary, Alternative Herbal Health Services, to distribute 12 strains of marijuana based on 10 of its shows in a pop-up shop in West Hollywood (working closely with the state of California on all of the legalities). Different strains of pot, with fanciful names, were paired with different shows, each trying to capture the feeling of the program. Vodkush was inspired by *Grace and Frankie*, and Riot was inspired by *Orange Is the New Black*.

As more states legalize recreational marijuana, the industry will evolve like any other industry (and let's not forget our neighbor to the north, Canada, where marijuana is scheduled to be legal for recreational use in 2018). Entrepreneurs and mainstream companies and brands will jump in to fill the niches that develop with products that need brand names. At least one app has been developed (named My Canary) to help users determine how impaired they are given that THC levels are different in different products. Wikileaf became the first cannabis app in the Apple Store to show prices. In 2017, *Time* magazine published a special edition titled *Marijuana Goes Main Street*. A company named Brewbudz has launched a line of coffees and teas containing cannabis flower in a single-serve Keurig-compatible pod. One of the first consumer products brands to enter the cannabis market is Scotts Miracle-Gro. CEO Jim Hagedorn calls the "pot market" the "biggest thing I've ever seen in lawn and garden."[13] Scott's has introduced products for gardens, soil, and retailers that target cannabis growers. In late 2017, Constellation Brands, marketer of Corona beer and Svedka vodka, announced an investment in a Canadian medical marijuana grower, Canopy Growth Corporation, with the goal of developing cannabis-infused beverages.

This is a new product category that will continue to emerge and, up until very recently, has been unbranded not only for the primary product (i.e., marijuana) but also for the associated products. For companies serious about creating profitable, long-term relationships with consumers, brand names and licensing will be needed—frequently a sine qua non for any new product category. Some brand names will be newly created to attract consumers, but in many other instances, companies will turn to licensing to ride the coattails of an existing brand's fame. Brand owners will likely be cautious given not only the newness of this category but also the legal complications as well as the fear of offending portions of the population. However, the category is here to stay.

eSports
Simply defined, eSports is organized multiplayer video game competition, increasingly between professional players and teams, for prize money. ESports has teams, leagues, championships, stars, and a great many fans. Hundreds of thousands of fans can watch online (a single event on eSports site Twitch, which in 2017 had over two million unique streamers per month, was viewed by over one million viewers), and thousands attend competitions in stadiums to watch their favorite players and teams competing in games such as *League of Legends* and *Call of Duty*. Blizzard Entertainment (a division of Activision Blizzard, publisher of game titles such as *Call*

---

13. "Cannabis Capitalist: Scotts Miracle-Gro CEO Bets Big on Pot Growers," *Forbes*, July 26, 2016.

of Duty and *StarCraft*) opened its own arena for players and fans for competitions, practice "rooms," and licensed merchandise sales. ESports, a new brand category, is already referred to as the next billion-dollar industry, and it's almost there. Revenue for global gaming will exceed $700 million in 2017. Newzoo provides data about eSports and estimates that the global viewing audience is 385 million. Events are run by many different organizations. These include game companies such as Activision Blizzard; Major League Gaming (now owned by Activision Blizzard); Riot (owned by Chinese Internet company Tencent), which runs the League of Legends Championship Series; and Germany-based Electronic Sports League (ESL) founded in 2000, which runs events around the world. And organizations own teams, such as Optic Gaming, which runs teams of professional players for games such as *Call of Duty*, *Halo*, and *Gears of War*.

Although this type of gaming competition has been around for some time (the conventional wisdom is that the specator sport had its beginnings in 2000 when a South Korean TV channel aired the video game *StarCraft* 24 hours a day for a week, and anyone could watch competitors playing the game), the industry is still in its infancy and disorganized. But that's changing. For example, the talent and event agency WME-IMG partnered with Turner Broadcasting in 2016 to run a league named ELEAGUE featuring games broadcast on TBS and online on Twitch. Twitch, which features competitions and also permits gamers to livestream themselves playing and chatting at the same time, was acquired by Amazon in 2014 for $970 million. ESL, which partnered with Intel in 2006 to create the Intel Extreme Masters, ran a 2017 event in Poland that drew a live audience of 173,000 and 46 million unique online viewers over two weekends. And recently, traditional sports leagues and associations have entered the space, generally through licensing. In 2017, the NBA partnered with Take-Two Interactive Software to debut in 2018 an eSports league for its *NBA 2K* video game. FIFA and Electronic Arts have partnered for the EA SPORTS FIFA 18 Global Series that will cap off with the FIFA eWorld Cup 2018. Electronic Arts has also partnered with the NFL for the Madden NFL Club Championship, which offers players the opportunity to compete from their homes.

Licensing has played a minor role so far (other than some licensing of the games by, for example, the sports leagues), with some team and game merchandise sold at venues as well as on e-commerce sites. But brands (and licensing) can't ignore the fan and media interest in this cultural phenomenon and the brand messaging paths it offers. Opportunities are emerging to build an authentic line of communication and connection between events and brands with a sizable audience of passionate and highly engaged gamers and communities (in particular, Millennial males). Brands can become sponsors of individual players, teams, or leagues. Red Bull, long a sponsor of professional players, has opened its own eSport training lab. Other brands that are attaching themselves to eSports include Arby's, The Coca-Cola Company, Buffalo Wild Wings, PepsiCo, Gillette, and Bud Light. Given the time fans spend accessing the sport, there are many opportunities for brands to communicate and engage with them, if done correctly (meaning communicating an understanding of the sport).

ESports athletes are also becoming celebrities in their own right. All of the top 30 players have earned over $1 million. With nicknames such as KuroKy (from Germany) who plays for Team Liquid, Miracle (Jordan) who plays for Team Liquid, UNiVeRsE (Wisconsin) who plays for Evil Geniuses, MinD (Bulgaria) who plays for Team Liquid, Matumbaman (France) who plays for Team Liquid, and ppd (Indiana) who plays for Evil Geniuses, these top players have lifetime earnings from $2 million to over $3 million. Brand endorsement deals are waiting!

Competitive gaming is also growing on college campuses (although loosely organized communities of gamers have been competing with each other for years across campuses), and many schools now offer eSports programs with coaches, staff, arenas, player recruiting, and even scholarships. The NCAA has yet to embrace the sport, uncertain whether eSports fits with its definition of "sports" or its other requirements. Although other organizations have tried to fill the void, no national organizing network like the NCAA exists for eSports, yet. Licensing will, of course, play an increasing role in promoting eSports on college campuses. The licensing of college and university names, logos, symbols, and slogans is a $5.26 billion business at retail,[14] and the addition of popular eSport teams will soon create licensable properties and collaboration opportunities.

Sparks & Honey notes that the eSports audience is growing at an unprecedented rate in the era of modern competitive sports, enabled by technology. The agency projects that "the eSports audience will continue to grow exponentially, driven by increased awareness of the industry, traditional TV broadcasts, larger events, more robust platforms and frequent eSports title releases." The fan experience, according to Sparks & Honey, is the next frontier for eSports.[15] Licensing will eventually be one piece of the brand strategy when it comes to eSports, which will include sponsorships, content, naming rights, experiential events, and player jersey branding as well as other marketing tools. Brands will begin using teams, leagues, events, and even players with which and with whom they are associated on licensed products targeted at these passionate consumers. Licensing will be one of the ways to connect with that fan experience.

✳ ✳ ✳ ✳ ✳

New product categories and new properties and brands generate more licensing activity and additional ways to connect and engage with consumers—more options for brands to "entangle" with consumers.

---

14. "LIMA Annual Global Licensing Industry Survey: 2017 Report, commissioned by LIMA and prepared by Brandar Consulting LLC, page 4.
15. Sparks & Honey Culture Forecast. The eSports User Manual: Connecting Brands with the Fastest Growing Sport in the World.

CHAPTER 13

A Concluding Perspective

The consumer's shopping journey has become a more complex and "connected journey." It's no longer just about pushing out a message as broadly as possible, providing a message to consumers, and relying on them to travel to a store to make a purchase. Technology now offers consumers the opportunity to participate with a brand and brand owners to communicate their brand message in a complex web of ways every hour of every day. Technology has also raised consumer expectations and put more pressure on "brand promise." The purchase decision can be made at many touchpoints. The complex marketing ecosystem presents challenges and opportunities for brands to remain relevant. The journey has many paths, and the number of those paths is increasing at an accelerated pace. No one can see around the bend in the road. The shopping journey of the future will be across devices and retail channels, relying on a number of merging interactions.

Therefore, it is incumbent on you—on every brand owner—to determine where and how you want your consumers to interact with your brand, what your consumers will value, and how you want to engage and build a bond with consumers. Bringing platforms, applications, and online and offline channels together is part of the equation. Using all of the online and offline options available to make the shopping journey informative, genuine, immersive, and easy is crucial. To achieve these goals, you will have the advantage of a treasure trove of data that will allow you to access various points in the shopping journey to provide a superior shopping experience for consumers and to meet their expectations.

Brands now have the opportunity to be regularly connected to consumers, make shopping easier and more convenient and deliver a personalized shopping experience both online and offline. In today's world, brands need multiple messaging strategies. Brand owners just need to choose among the touchpoints available to them and focus on those touchpoints that will accomplish their objectives. Brand licensing is one of the choices.

Although the availability and usefulness of data have been mentioned throughout this book, we must be careful not to rely on data too much. After all, purchasing products is, ultimately, about need or, at the very least, perceived or emotional need. You "need" that screwdriver or that red sweater or that frozen dessert. And brands are the point of entry for meeting those needs. Brands provide a bond with the consumer; they often connect emotionally with the consumer, and they certainly influence the purchasing decision (maybe brands are the original "influencers"). Licensed products broaden and strengthen all of those brand dynamics. And, importantly, licensed products help create a memory of the brand that will drive further purchses and perhaps loyalty. Brands presented through licensed products create a deeper and richer connection to the brand than many of the other marketing/communications tools discussed in this book.

Cultural trends often have internal conflict. Clearly, we are living during a time of great technological change and there is a trend supporting connectivity on multiple devices. But there is also a countervailing trend—consumers are also looking to get away from their devices, what Sparks & Honey calls "digital detox." That's why printed books are on the rise and e-books are in decline. It's why young people, who grew up with iTunes, are buying vinyl records. It's why Millennials worry about the effects of social media on their mental health and talk about reducing their interaction with social media. We are in the midst of a digital trend but also an analog trend.[1] Licensed products are versatile tools to use in reaching a broad group of consumers with the brand message—the brand promise—and engaging those consumers with the brand and its goals in a genuine way. Although technology, shopping, and licensing are all converging, recognize that licensing offers brands a low-tech (analog) strategy for communicating and "entangling" with consumers. Licensing can be complicated with many moving parts, but it doesn't demand that you struggle with high-tech messaging. Licensing is not overly reliant on data-driven marketing or segmentation (unless you want or need it to be); rather, as noted above, it relies on brand memory and emotion. It relies on the fame of a brand that makes the buying decision easier (the ultimate point of a brand). And licensing enables a brand to be present in more locations, in more aisles, and on more screen pages where consumers might see it—another way to expand reach.

The beginning chapter of this book broke down the elements of content marketing and argued that the same elements apply to brand licensing. Perhaps it's too much of a stretch to claim that licensing *is* content marketing. Although a consensus on the definition of content marketing is elusive (many are offered), it always seems to involve the communication of information in one form or another; it's not about just pushing out a brand message (like traditional advertising). Maybe a licensed product doesn't fall within any of the offered definitions, but it accomplishes many of the same goals that content marketing is designed to accomplish. The goal of content marketing is not merely to increase sales. The goals are also about telling a brand story, and it can be about sus-

---

1. "Our Love Affair with Digital Is Over," by David Sax, *The New York Times*, November 19, 2017.

taining or building loyalty, reaching new consumers in new ways, or achieving any other marketing objective (just like brand licensing). Product placement is content marketing. A brand-sponsored experiential event is content marketing. As marketing analyst Ryan Skinner has said, content marketing "becomes something the marketer has to define for themselves."[2]

Speaking at the Cannes Lions Awards in June 2015, Marc Pritchard, P&G Global Brand Officer, said that "content marketing is overused and under-defined." He continued that he preferred to call it advertising, based on the Latin root *advert*, which is to "turn people toward" your product.[3] It follows that if content marketing and its goals (a way to "entangle" consumers with a brand, a way to turn consumers toward your product) is on the rise, as it is, then so should brand licensing, for the same reasons. Licensing invites consumers to be more involved with a brand and motivates them to "turn toward" yet more products from the same brand by actually offering them something to purchase.

Licensing in all sectors—Entertainment, Sports, Character, Celebrity, Art, and Trademarks—will continue to grow and evolve, as it has for over 125 years. Brands will continue to stretch and harness their brand equity to reach more consumers. Some brands have more "stretch" than others. and some will be more successful than others. As has been true in the past, shifts in our culture, demographics, technology, buying habits, emerging licensable properties, new product categories, messaging, and things that we cannot even identify today will have an impact on licensing.

Above all else, keep in mind the two essential elements for a successful licensing program now and particularly in the future. First, you must have a brand that has a high enough level of fame and importance to appeal to a wide enough group of consumers. Second, that brand must have a path (or paths) to reach consumers

---

2. *Id.*, page 20.
3. *Ad Age*, "Is It Content or Is It Advertising?" by Jack Neff, October 12, 2015, page 18.

and satisfy their expectations in a way that drives them to make a purchase, online or offline. It's fairly simple: fame and distribution.

Be aware, too, that both of those "must haves" are evolving. Existing brands, faced with the possibility that they are losing their value, their relevance to consumers, need to reposition themselves and present themselves to consumers in new ways to remain relevant and desirable. As for new brands, they must establish and maintain relevancy. And retail (i.e., the way brands reach consumers for purchasing opportunities) is changing so quickly that many traditional retailers are finding it challenging to keep up and change fast enough, but more and more retailers are winning at this. Offering strategically aligned licensed products can help a brand owner as well as retailers meet these challenges.

Breakthrough technologies have paved the way for a radically changing retail landscape. In turn, this metamorphic landscape has shaped evolving consumer behavior across demographics. As a result, marketers are scrambling to communicate with their consumers effectively and efficiently, all of which makes brand licensing an exciting enterprise today and into the foreseeable future. Eroding brand loyalty is perhaps the biggest challenge facing brands and brand licensing. However, the paths are there for smart brands to overcome this challenge. There will be winners and losers.

If the product is wrong and the customer is dissatisfied, no amount of messaging or process can fix the disappointment. Communication and process are nothing without good product. One of the main purposes of a brand is to tell the consumer that the product is good, that the consumer can trust his or her decision to make the purchase and that the consumer will be satisfied. A promise has been made, and it must be kept. That's the "home" advantage that brands have, both existing and emerging brands. The ability of brands to influence purchasing decisions is what continues to make brands strong and desirable and what will drive licensing programs. The digital landscape, if used wisely, only makes brands stronger because they can be found and can tell their story more easily. Licensing makes brands stronger because they can be found more easily in more places on more product.

Smart brands—those that are demonstrating strength and integrity, adjusting to the complexities of the market, and meeting product expectations—are still winning. The only proviso is that brands must work at remaining true to what they are and what they mean in order to retain and recruit consumers. This is the goal of brand licensing: reinforcing the brand message, the brand meaning, the brand promise, and communicating that message through product extensions made available to all kinds of consumers where and when they shop, recruiting them and retaining them.

Licensing is an *authentic* way to reach consumers and engage them. After all, making a purchase is a voluntary exercise; the consumer has to want to participate and engage with the brand by buying something offered by the brand, in this case a licensed product (or service). Licensing is persuasion and connection through product. Some might argue that licensing is inauthentic because the product is not actually emanating from the brand itself, but rather from a third party (the licensee). Yes, it's true that a licensed product is being made and, generally, marketed by the licensee. But, no, that doesn't make it inauthentic. Done properly, that licensed product has been developed with much oversight and control by the brand owner. It starts with the brand owner's strategic licensing plan followed by the due diligence conducted before a license agreement is even signed followed by the rigorous approval process of designs, samples, and final product, ending with active management of the licensee's every activity in selling and marketing the product. The most valuable asset of any brand owner is its brand (what could be more valuable to The Coca-Cola Company than the name "Coca-Cola"?). Licensing requires brand owners to ensure that the licensed product, which utilizes its most valuable asset, will meet consumers' expectations of the brand and the brand's product qualities and that the brand's equities, mission, and values will be upheld by the licensed product. That's exactly what smart brand owners engaged in licensing do, as illustrated in many of the examples and case studies in this book.

Like other marketing/communication disciplines, licensing can be *disruptive*. Licensing can be used to redefine a brand message, how a brand is viewed by consumers. Of course, that's not really true for decorative licensing, which largely characterized corporate brand licensing for many years. But more recently, as licensing has been used to stretch a brand, to extend the brand to other close-to-core categories (categories that are strategically aligned with the brand and its objectives), we can easily see how licensing can help a brand change brand perception. It can be accomplished in subtle ways (such as Baileys chocolates) or in big, splashy ways (such as Black & Decker small kitchen appliances). But licensing can be used effectively to help redefine a brand and reach consumers in new ways and at new touchpoints.

Licensing is *agile*. It can be used to help support big, broad brand messages or smaller ones. It can be used to reach large swaths of consumers or targeted segments. It can be used for a broad retail distribution or be limited to a single retailer. It can be targeted at groups of consumers in different countries around the world. In short, it can be tailored to meet a brand owner's needs as well as a licensee's and retailer's needs.

Finally, licensing is *creative*. Indeed, it demands creativity. Understanding the true essence of brand equities and then imagining products to which the brand can be extended, designing those products, and understanding how those products (or services) can reach consumers takes creativity. Understanding that Kellogg's can open a licensed cereal café takes creativity. That *Better Homes & Gardens* can extend to home furnishings because it has content credibility takes creativity. That Stanley Black & Decker can offer all sorts of licensed products that help consumers build things and take care of their homes takes creativity. Look around at the many well-run brand extension licensing programs, and you will undoubtedly see a great deal of imagination, innovation, and creativity at work.

Authenticity, agility, disruption, and creativity are all hallmarks of smart brand licensing programs. Trademark licensing has become much more than decoration on product, much more than a financial or legal tactic. In an era of digital revolution and retail transformation, it is a powerful path to engaging with, "entangling" with, participating with, and bonding with consumers.

Afterword

I have spent over 30 years in the licensing business, in large part assisting brand owners in developing, implementing, and managing their licensing programs and have been involved with many groundbreaking licensing initiatives over this time, working with some incredibly talented professionals, experts in so many different fields. Yet writing this book has been a journey of discovery and learning for me. Among the many things that have struck me is the innovative thinking and creativity that is so frequently apparent in the licensing business, as well as the pace of change in how consumers purchase goods and how retailing is conducted. I see evidence of this almost every time I pick up a trade or consumer publication (take note of many of my footnotes). It only strengthens my belief that smart brands will continue to thrive in new ways and that licensing is a strong path to engaging consumers and to supporting a brand's promise. So many things going on today exemplify licensing at its best or demonstrate market dynamics affecting licensing that I have had great difficulty finally "putting my pencil down" and delivering my manuscript to the publisher.

So I have decided that I'm not going to "put my pencil down." I will continue to write about licensing activations that illustrate or expand on what I have written about in this book, and I will continue to write about the market, retail, and consumer dynamics that are affecting licensing, or will likely affect it in the future. If you are interested in continuing this journey with me, look for my blog titled *The Power of Licensing* at www.beanstalk.com/beantalk.

Acknowledgments

Many people helped me with this book along the way, some I have known for many of years and some whom I spoke to for the first time. I received a great deal of expert advice, research, and insights, as well as encouragement, from colleagues and friends. I want to thank every one of them for their generosity and hope I haven't left anyone out. The help came from people inside and outside the licensing industry and many of the incredible people at the agency that I cofounded and of which I now serve as Chairman, The Beanstalk Group.

First, many thanks to Bruce Wexler, who edited each chapter as I wrote it and frequently edited my rewrites. He pushed and prodded me and kept me on track. I am grateful for his insights and guidance. And to John Palmer, my editor at Ankerwycke, who read the outline for this book and recognized that it was a topic that deserved attention.

Next, I want to thank the many professionals, some in the licensing industry and some in related fields, who were kind enough to give me time to speak with and interview them. Their expertise was invaluable and, indeed, greatly enriched this journey for me. In alphabetical order they are Roger Berman, President,

ZenWorks Co., Ltd.; Marty Brochstein, SVP Industry Relations and Information, LIMA; Elise Contarsy, *Better Homes & Gardens*, Vice President, Meredith Brands; Rob Coolican, Director, Business Development, GMR; Paul Earle, Principal, Earle & Company and faculty member, Kellogg School of Management at Northwestern University; Jane Evans, Managing Director, JELC Ltd.; Dean Grande, Director, Global Licensing at Stanley Black & Decker; Scott Hardy, President & CEO, Polaroid; Bobbie Hunnicutt, Partner, Blue Trellis, LLC; Kathy Ireland, CEO, Kathy Ireland Worldwide; Kevin LaBonge, formerly Executive Director, Business Development and Global Licensing at *Mens' Health* (Rodale); Shane Meeker, Associate Director, Corporate Storyteller and Company Historian, P&G; John Merrick, President, Lemur Licensing, Inc.; Phil Mooney, formerly Director, Heritage Communications at The Coca-Cola Company (retired); Kristin Payne, Vice President, Time Inc.; Ron Potesky, formerly SVP & GM, Pantone; Steve Ross, Chief Brand Development Officer, Global Head of Licensing & Consumer Products, Hearst; Yehuda Schmidman, formerly CEO, Sequential Brands Group; Morty Singer, CEO, Marvin Traub Associates LLC; Lisa Singelyn, VP Influencer Marketing Operations, The Marketing Arm; Lauren Sizeland, Director of Business Development & Licensing, Victoria and Albert Museum; Ramez Toubassy, President, Brands Division at Gordon Brothers Group; Perry Wolfman, Chief Executive Officer, CAA-GBG; Kenneth L. Wyse, President Global Licensing and Public Relations, PVH Corp. and his colleagues Lynn Marshall Flynn, SVP Licensing, PVH Corp. and John W. Pawlik, Senior Vice President, Licensing and Divisional Accounting, PVH Corp.

I received so much enthusiastic help from my colleagues at Beanstalk. As many times as I kept going back to them for input, information, editorial assistance, fact checking, and general support, they never disappointed me, they never wavered. They were always gracious with their time, advice, and guidance. I could not have completed this book without them. I will be eternally grateful to every one of them. They are Allison Ames, CEO & President of

Beanstalk and my colleague and dear friend for more than 20 years. She edited many of my chapters, frequently shared relevant articles and her keen thinking with me, and let me have the time and space to focus on the book in the midst of the busy work of our agency; Lisa Reiner, Managing Director, Europe & Asia Pacific, for editing Chapter 10 on international licensing, providing her general input and expertise on licensing outside the United States, and keeping me accurate about all things P&G; Kim Krizelman and Helen Prial, also for their input on all things P&G; Caren Chacko, who replied to my e-mails and questions about Stanley Black & Decker and the U.S. Army, 24/7, and faster than a New York minute; Rachel Terrace, Senior Vice President, Brand Management, for editing the portions of the book focused on HGTV; Emmanuel Fordjour, Vice President, Finance, for his knowledge about royalty collection and reporting; Debra Restler, Vice President, New Business & Marketing, for answering so many questions, providing suggestions on relevant subjects, and always asking me one question herself: "Is it done yet?"; Oliver Herzfeld, Senior Vice President & Chief Legal Officer, for reviewing all matters pertaining to the law; Marc Schneider, COO & CFO, for his P&L support and all around good humor; Bryan Graham, Senior Vice President Audit Services, for his astute insights on auditing; Dan Amos, Associate Vice President, Brand Development, for sharing his knowledge about eSports; Elizabeth Rodriguez for her astute editing (in some instances, rewriting) of my sections on YouTubers, Bloggers, Vloggers, and Influencers, as well as her research on many of the areas covered in the book; Todd Kaufman, who also educated me about Influencers as well as what interests younger generations; and Aimee Pavone, who was tireless in answering my many research requests and for providing my often much needed technical assistance. I also want to thank Steve Simmons for all of his technical and IT assistance (he's a wizard!); also many thanks to Jasen Wright, Serena Sibbald, Linda Morgenstern, Nicole Desir, Frances Alvarez, and Sherikay Chaffee. A group of Beanstalkers helped this "old-ish" author better understand the Millennial and Gen X generations; in addition to some of those already acknowledged above, they are Hope Angowitz, Ivonne Feliciano, Maya Kobray, Lauren McDonald, Lauren Montemaro, Jacqueline Pasharikov, Ariel Romero, Andrew Schenkel, Shelby Toohey, and Damar Wibowo.

I also want to thank Stephen Paskoff, my dear friend for almost 50 years, for his regular tips on how to write a book and for his frequent encouragement. And my Santa Fe buddy, James MacCreight, for his caring support.

And last but certainly not least, I want to thank my family. First, my darling wife, Patricia Grodd. Two or three years ago she said, "Why don't you write a book?" Little did she know the time, attention, and focus it would take. She supported me throughout the process with her love and encouragement and gave me the precious time I needed to work on this project. Thank you for your elegant patience; now we can get on with the rest of our life together. My son, Nicholas, and his wife, Eleanor West, for their love and support. My father-in-law, Clifford Grodd, for telling me that everyone puts his pants on the same way, one leg at a time, and giving me the confidence I needed to write a book. My loving mother, Barbara Stone, who encouraged the project at the start, but is no longer with us to see the final product. And finally, my dad, Allan Stone, one of the pioneers in the field of licensing, having started his career in 1948 and who, as a partner in *The Howdy Doody Show*, developed perhaps the first comprehensive television-driven licensing program and went on to achieve many other groundbreaking licensing accomplishments. His career turned my attention to licensing in my mid-thirties, and for that I will always be grateful.

You all have my heartfelt thanks and gratitude.

Index

Jaclyn Smith Collection at, 29, 148
Kathy Ireland program at, 174
as single exclusive retailer, 147
Kodak, 21–22, 206
Kohl's, 147, 153, 270
Kraft Food Groups, 97n.6,

L

L Brands, 250n.4
Land, Edwin, 215
Language barriers, in international brand licensing, 236
Larian, Isaac, 230
LaurDIY, 202
LCA (Licensing Corporation of America), 27
Legal and regulatory history, of licensees, 106
Legal issues, in international brand licensing, 255–257
Levi Strauss & Co., 42
Levine, Adam, 147
License Global magazine, 13n.3
Licensed products
and core products sales, 283–284
core products vs., xi
failure of, 124–126
of licensees, 107
reporting about, 116
Licensees
aligning with brand equities to convince consumers, 55
international, 253–254
in product development approval process, 110–112
managing of, 99–120
sharing brand information with brand owners, 109–110

social media use by, 132
vetting of, 123
Licensing Corporation of America (LCA), 27
Licensing goals and objectives, 79–81
Licensing Position Statements, 82–84
Licensing process, 259
Licensing programs, managing and supporting, 99–120
brand immersion in, 108–110
business plans, 105–108
business reporting in, 115–119
developed by Coca-Cola, 37
introductory information provided in, 103–105
licensor support for, 112–115
managing retailers in, 119–120
preliminary information gathering, 100–103
product development in, 110–112
Licensing strategies
digital, 263
of licensees, 107
online and offline commerce as part of, 274–275
Licensor support, of licensing programs, 112–115
Lief! Lifestyle (brand), 244–245
Lifestyle (brand equity)
Coca-Cola, as, 32, 33, 36, 39, 40, 42
provided by Weight Watchers, 58–59
supported by licensing, 36, 39, 43
LIMA (licensing industry trade association), xivn.1, 19n.2